James Gray surrounded by colleagues in the
pressroom at the Winnipeg *Free Press*.

James Gray, one of western Canada's finest social historians, was
born in Whitemouth, Manitoba, in 1906. He worked for the
Winnipeg *Free Press* for many years and went on to edit several
other publications. In 1947, he relocated to Calgary where he
worked with the Home Oil Company for twenty years before retir-
ing to embark on a new career as a historian. He passed away on
12 November 1998, in Calgary, at the age of ninety-two.

During his life, Gray received numerous honours, including the
Alberta Order of Excellence in 1987, the Order of Canada in 1988,
and the 1995 Pierre Berton Award for "distinguished achievement
in popularizing Canadian history." He also penned a rich legacy of
award-winning and best-selling books including *The Boy from
Winnipeg, Men Against the Desert, The Roar of the Twenties, Booze,*
and *Red Lights on the Prairies.*

Relentless winds whipped up dust storms that robbed farmland of precious top-soil; when the top-soil was gone, farms were abandoned.
GLENBOW ARCHIVES NA-2496-1

The
Winter
Years

THE DEPRESSION ON
THE PRAIRIES

JAMES H. GRAY

FIFTH
HOUSE

Front cover photograph reproduced with permission from Agriculture and Agri-Food Canada
Back cover photograph / front cover background, Glenbow Archives ND-3-6742
Cover and interior design by John Luckhurst / GDL
Proofread by Meaghan Craven, Alex Rettie
Scans by St. Solo Computer Graphics

The publisher gratefully acknowledges the support of
The Canada Council for the Arts and the Department of Canadian Heritage.

The Canada Council | Le Conseil des Arts
for the arts | du Canada
since 1957 | depuis 1957

We acknowledge the financial support of the Government of Canada through the Book Publishing Industry Development Program (BPIDP) for our publishing activities.

Printed in Canada by Friesens

03 04 05 06 07 / 5 4 3 2 1

First published in the United States in 2004 by
Fitzhenry & Whiteside
121 Harvard Avenue, Suite 2
Allston, MA 02134

National Library of Canada Cataloguing in Publication Data

Gray, James H., 1906–1998
The winter years / by James H. Gray.

Includes index.
ISBN 1-894856-20-1

1. Depressions—1929—Canada. 2. Prairie
Provinces—History—1905–1945. 3. Prairie Provinces—Economic
conditions—1905–1945. I. Title.
FC3242.9.D35G72   2003 971.2'02   C2003-910437-0
F1060.9.G72 2003

Fifth House Ltd.
A Fitzhenry & Whiteside Company
1511, 1800-4 St. SW
Calgary, Alberta T2S 2S5

1-800-387-9776
www.fitzhenry.ca

CONTENTS

For Kay, who was so much part of the surviving

~

Oh Winter! ruler of the inverted year,
Thy scattered hair with sleet like ashes filled,
Thy breath congealed upon thy lips, thy cheeks
Fringed with a beard made white with other snows
Than those of age . . .

William Cowper, *The Winter Evening*

FOREWORD

It was his favourite book. His others might have been more critically acclaimed, but for James Gray, *The Winter Years* defined who he was and where he had come from. In fact, the publication of the manuscript, after languishing for two decades, served as a reminder of the bleak times he and his young family had lived through.

The year 1931 was the low point in James Gray's life. After what he half-jokingly described as a five-month "detour" through a tuberculosis sanitarium, the young man was living on relief in Winnipeg with his wife, Kay, and infant daughter, Patty, in a single room in a boarding house on Furby Street. It wasn't supposed to turn out this way. At sixteen, Gray started work as an office boy and later worked as a bookkeeper at the Winnipeg Grain Exchange. He then became a margin clerk for a stockbroker and seemed to have the future by the tail, especially during the boom years of the late 1920s. But then, the bottom fell out of the world economy, and like thousands of other Canadians, he lost his job to the Great Depression and any hope of working at anything he knew how to do.

Utterly destitute, Gray decided to become a writer. He came to this crazy idea after finding several boxes of back issues of the *American Mercury* magazine. He read every copy from cover to cover and kept a scribbler at hand to write down any words that were new to him and then looked up their meaning. He also began to hone his own writing skills and filled scribblers with stories. Gray sold his first article to the Winnipeg *Free Press* weekly magazine in 1933. Then, the *Canadian Forum* published several items. He eventually wrote his way into a reporter's job with the *Free Press* in January 1935. Six years later, he was writing editorials.

Gray's successful newspaper career ultimately took him to Ottawa, where he served as parliamentary correspondent during the last two years of the Second World War. These were heady days as the Canadian government began to prepare for the demobilization of thousands of soldiers. No one wanted a return to the soup kitchens, bread lines, and massive unemployment of the 1930s— the debate was over how to avoid it. Gray waded into the discussion with characteristic zest and quickly earned a reputation as an authority on the policy pitfalls of the Great Depression. His comments also attracted the attention of Collins and Company, who, in 1946, invited him to write about his personal experiences during the so-called Dirty Thirties.

Gray banged out *The Winter Years* as quickly as he could in his spare time. Six months later, Collins returned the manuscript with a rejection slip; the editor who had commissioned the book had left the company. While absorbing the humiliation, Gray learned from one of his colleagues in the press gallery that John Gray of Macmillan had recently been in Ottawa looking for new Canadian books. He sent off *The Winter Years* and, within a month, received a letter accepting the manuscript and inviting him to Toronto to discuss editorial changes. There, in early 1947, he watched in frustration as two Macmillan editors argued about the merits of the book: one wanted a dramatic story, the other, one that was more subdued. Until these conflicting views could be resolved, Macmillan refused to publish the work and returned it with a note of apology.

Gray, in the meantime, faced a bigger problem. That same year, he lost his job when the publisher of the *Free Press* reacted angrily to his coverage of Canadian trade policy. Making his way back to Winnipeg, Gray did freelance work for several eastern newspapers, CBC radio, and *Maclean's* magazine. He also struck a new deal to have *The Winter Years* published. He agreed to have the manuscript serialized in the Winnipeg *Citizen* in book-sized print, on the understanding that it would later be published as a regular book from the set type. But less than halfway through the project, all of *The Winter Years* type had to be melted down when the composing room ran out of lead one day for the linotype machines.

By this time, Gray had re-located to Calgary, where he edited the *Farm and Ranch Review* and then the *Western Oil Examiner* before joining the Home Oil Company as public-relations manager in the late 1950s. It was during a business trip to Toronto that he ran into John Gray of Macmillan who recalled their misadventures with *The Winter Years* and asked to take another look at the manuscript. An ecstatic Gray jumped at the opportunity. It was a chance to get back into full-time writing. It would also allow him to include material about the agricultural depression that he had absorbed while working on the *Farm and Ranch Review*. Gray consequently walked away from his lucrative position with Home Oil to completely re-work *The Winter Years*. He added 80,000 words, mostly on the rural west, and then fired off the revised manuscript. This time, Macmillan offered to publish the book, but only if the new agricultural chapters were dropped. The company was concerned about the length and also believed that Gray's own story would have greater appeal.

The Winter Years, when it finally appeared in 1966, was an instant best-seller. And it is easy to understand why. Gray's easy, lucid style made for an absorbing read. He also had the knack of telling a good anecdote: his description of boondoggling projects, in particular the dandelion-picking antics of relief crews, borders on the surreal. He could also find the perfect phrase, such as when he suggested that the twenty-cent daily allowance paid relief camp workers was "just the right size to be insulting." But the true appeal of *The Winter Years* was Gray's experience and observation as a relief recipient in Winnipeg. In the first chapter, appropriately titled "Our world stopped and we got off," he described how it took three tries before he could put his pride in his pocket and walk in the front door of a Winnipeg relief office. These and other incidents were all told with a deft touch, a kind of personal imprint on a decade that seemed to have turned the world upside down.

The publication of *The Winter Years* marked the beginning—at age sixty—of a prolific writing career. Over the next quarter century, Gray published twelve books, many of which became classics: *Men Against the Desert* (1967), his autobiographical *The Boy from Winnipeg* (1970), *Red Lights on the Prairies* (1971), and *Booze* (1972). There was a string of awards as well. In 1987, he was named to the Alberta Order of Excellence, followed by the Order of Canada the next year. He received three honorary doctorates, all from prairie universities (Brandon, Calgary, and Manitoba). And he was given the Pierre Berton Prize by Canada's National History Society for his role in popularizing Canadian history.

But despite the many accolades and personal success, Gray always remembered where he had come from, even during his final weeks in a Calgary nursing home. "The most important fact . . . about me," he once wrote, "is that I am a product totally of the Great Depression." This connection to the suffering and persever-ance of the 1930s explains why he continued to take such great pride in *The Winter Years* and all that it represented, both for him and his family. It was not something that could ever be forgotten, as evi-denced by the book's dedication to his wife, Kay, "who was so much a part of the surviving." And when Kay died in 1994, he lovingly buried a copy of the book under the tree he planted in her memory.

Bill Waiser
Department of History, University of Saskatchewan

INTRODUCTION

The era that began with the Wall Street crash in 1929 and ended with the invasion of Poland in 1939 more profoundly affected the people of western Canada than any other decade in peace-time history. This is the story of that decade—of 'The Depression', as it is remembered in Winnipeg; of 'The Dirty Thirties', as the people of Saskatchewan remember it. In the beginning, one clarification is essential. To refer to the era as ' *The* Depression' would be to misname it; and to ascribe its origin to the Wall Street crash would be to misdate it. Our depression in western Canada was actually three different depressions, separate in time and space, and different in cause and effect. The October crash was not in itself a primary cause but a synergist that set off a chain reaction within the other depressions and produced a greater total effect than the sum of their individual effects would otherwise have been.

Each depression eventually overlapped the others and was exacerbated by them. In the process, the boundary lines tended to blur. The farm-drouth depression began in 1929 and grew progressively worse until the complete disaster of 1937. The extreme drouth, however, was confined to south-central Saskatchewan and the adjoining corners of Manitoba and Alberta—the famous Palliser Triangle. While Saskatchewan choked in the Dust Bowl, areas of Manitoba and Alberta enjoyed good crop years.

The prices-debts-interest depression was worst in Alberta, where it gave rise to the Social Credit revolution of 1935. It was only partly the product of the Canadian collapse in prices that followed Wall Street's 'Black Thursday'. Equally important contributing factors were post-war inflation, the high cost of mechanization, exorbitant interest rates, and boom-bust-boom grain prices that kept the rural West in a turmoil throughout the 1920s.

Small-scale unemployment occurred periodically in Winnipeg and other western cities during the 1920s. It did not reach crisis proportions until late autumn 1930, and got steadily worse until 1933, when it levelled off to remain the most vexing urban problem for the rest of the decade. It did not, as many assume, dwindle into nothingness with the election of the Liberal Party in 1935.

For Winnipeg, the climactic date was not October 24, 1929, but August 4, 1914. On that day, the First World War ended the city's thirty-year construction boom; and the passage of the first ship through the Panama Canal laid an inexorable, delayed-action curse upon the very basis of the city's commercial prosperity. For a hundred years, as a trading-post and business centre, Winnipeg was a toll-gate on the only practical access route into and out of western Canada. Westward through Winnipeg a million settlers moved in a single decade. The freight trains that brought all the consumer goods and production machinery into the West were broken up in Winnipeg, and the contents were distributed throughout the huge complex of wholesale warehouses in the centre of the city. From there they moved out again into consumption in the wake of a small army of travelling salesmen who carried their order-books as far afield as the Peace River.

The wheat from steadily expanding plantings found its way to world export markets over the same railway system, while the wheat merchants of the Grain Exchange siphoned off their commissions. Winnipeg's slaughter-houses rivalled those of Toronto and St. Paul, and cattle from the West moved through the city's stockyards to southern, eastern, and United Kingdom markets. All this required several thousand skilled craftsmen in three mammoth railway shops to keep the trains moving. More thousands manhandled the merchandise in and out of warehouses. In the centre of it all, within a four-block stretch of Main Street, was the financial heart of western Canada. Here were the western head offices of all the chartered banks, trust companies, and insurance companies, in whose marble mausoleums other armies of clerks processed the outflow and inflow of credit that fuelled the western booms.

Winnipeg lived opulently on its exactions from the commerce of the West. Its new hotels and theatres were pleasant and palatial; its wealthy wholesalers, grain-brokers, bankers, and merchant princes went mansion-building along the banks of the Assiniboine River on Roslyn Road and Wellington Crescent, and in Armstrong's Point. Having easily survived a dozen small setbacks over the years, the city that fateful August was in the throes of the biggest real-estate boom of them all. The war brought it to a full stop, but everybody assumed that when the war was over it would start in where it had left off. Instead, everything went wrong.

The struggle between the militant British socialists and the arch-conservative craft unionists for control of the labour movement helped ignite the Winnipeg General Strike of 1919. No strike so big and comprehensive ever happened before in Canada, and it has never been equalled since. It set trade unionism back twenty-five years, severely damaged the city's economy, and tarnished the city's image to the point where the inflow of investment capital was seriously reduced. As the Panama Canal enabled Vancouver to take over the western markets Winnipeg had supplied, the doldrums gripped the wholesale business.

The opening of huge mail-order houses in Winnipeg and Regina, coupled with the arrival of the American chain stores, delivered a final one-two punch to the Winnipeg wholesale district and marked the small-town merchants and small city retailers alike for ultimate extinction.

The high good times of the pre-war West never came back to the Prairies. But, if Winnipeg's economic foundations were beginning to crack, no surface manifestations of the fact appeared in the 1920s. There has always been an ebullience about Winnipeg that the worst climate in Christendom could never suppress, a sort of what-the-hell optimism that keeps its attention permanently focused on the bright side.

Though they abominated the Grain Exchange futures market as a mechanism for selling their wheat, western farmers by the thousand could not resist taking an annual fling at the market—and losing in speculation what they had gained by sweat in their fields. There was a partial crop failure in 1924, and that fall the gambling farmers were joined by legions of city businessmen buying wheat futures. By late November every brokerage house in the Grain Exchange was jammed to the doors, and the telegraph lines brought an endless flood of buying orders from the farms. The price rose from $1.50 to $1.75 to $2.00 a bushel. Nobody cashed in. Instead, they used their paper profits to buy more, to pyramid their holdings from 5,000 bushels to 10,000 bushels to 100,000 bushels. When the crash came, hundreds of millions of dollars worth of profits were wiped out in a matter of days. Two years later, everybody was back for more of the same.

The discovery of wet gas in Turner Valley in 1924 turned the whole of western Canada into a happy hunting-ground for the oil-promoters. Companies like Royalite, Devenish, United, East Crest, Home Oil, C. & E., Turner Valley, and Anglo-Canadian, which sold for pennies in the beginning, sold for dollars before the end, making and unmaking paper millionaires several times in the process. In Winnipeg the big boom was in gold-mining shares as prospectors came out of the north loaded with mining claims to be processed into stock certificates. Such names as San Antonio,

Central Manitoba, Sherritt Gordon, Eldorado, Island Lake, God's Lake, and Howey whetted Winnipeg appetites for more, and the demand was filled by British Columbia and Ontario. For Manitobans, however, neither oil nor gold ever matched the attraction of the wheat-pit.

All this came naturally to a people who, if they had not been born gamblers, would never have come to western Canada in the first place. But they had come, in a round million before the war, from all over Britain and Western Europe. Seventh- and eighth-generation urbanites from London, Glasgow, and Liverpool settled confidently on homesteads in the hinterlands of Saskatchewan. Or they came with shiny new skills from the Midlands and the Clydeside, exuding wild-eyed ideas about how trade unions should be organized, and even wilder ideas about how the Canadian economy should be socialized. They came as pin-neat clerks from London and Manchester to monopolize the civil service jobs, as Highlanders to take over the police departments, as muscular Ulstermen to run the fire departments. And they came as Jews fleeing pogroms, as Ukrainians fleeing Czarist oppression, as fishermen from Iceland, as peasants from Poland, Russia, Germany, Galacia, and Ruthenia, with their worldly possessions in wicker baskets, to fill the settlement gaps left by the earlier migrations from Ontario.

They came, finally, on thousand-mile harvest excursions from Ontario to earn a stake on the prairies to keep them over the winter. Then, if they failed to run the gantlet of pimps, pickpockets, and bunko artists who infested the railway stations in Winnipeg, they never went home again. What did it matter if they were rolled of their wads in an Annabella Street brothel? Bush jobs turned up every winter and anyone who could drive a car could pick up a new stake running booze to the United States.

Jobs themselves were adventures to be savoured. Anyone who

5

became dissatisfied with his job could walk out of it into a new one. With wage rates largely frozen, it was fruitless to hang around waiting for raises in pay, so searching for jobs that paid better became a popular preoccupation. In many trades the boomers still followed booms from town to town and region to region. Boomer telegraphers, who never gave more than five minutes notice before quitting a job, turned the telegraph business into a long nightmare for straw-bosses. Building tradesmen followed the sun to the prairies in the summer and to California in winter. Most newspapers had one staff coming and one going, and no boomer reporter ever stayed longer in one place than was dictated by a quickly jading interest in the local fauna.

Whether they were itinerant telegraphers, drifting carpenters, or established entrepreneurs, risk-taking for the sake of the risk had an endless fascination for Westerners. It followed naturally that anybody with an idea could find Westerners willing to finance it, and the wilder the scheme, the easier it sold. Joe Hurst came all the way from New York's Tin Pan Alley to Winnipeg to set up a music-publishing business. His songs were tremendous and are still heard in the land, but the $500,000 he raised in Winnipeg went into the stock market and Hurst went to jail. Aaron Sapiro preached the doctrine of co-operation with such conviction that 50,000 western farmers immediately put up $40 million to finance three brand-new wheat-marketing organizations—the Prairie Wheat Pools—which they hoped would eliminate the Grain Exchange.

Money, to western people in the 1920s, was not just for spending on creature comforts. Money was for putting into things to make more money. It was for investing in oil stocks, mining stocks, vacant lots, paper plants, and power plants, and above all for 'getting into business for yourself'. The roster of home-grown Alger heroes—Ashdown, Robinson, Macdonald, McFarland,

McIntyre, McArthur, Burns, Bennett, Boyd, Shea, Lougheed, Aikins, Alloway, Cross, and a score of others—testified that, with luck and hard work, it was still possible for poor boys to become rich men.

These were the 'Roaring Twenties'. This was the super-confident, speculative environment, stretching back almost unbroken to the turn of the century, that gave birth to the 'Dirty Thirties'. For the West, the end of the era did not come in any such single thunderclap as the Wall Street crash. Instead, disaster came slowly, imperceptibly, like a descending ice age fastening itself upon the land. It was only after the Mardi Gras closed down that basic flaws in the economy began to show through. Wholesale and retail bankruptcies increased, the railway layoffs became more extended, delinquent accounts backed up from retailer to wholesaler to jobber to banker, and credit became more and more restricted. The need for retrenchment, which business had tried to ignore, could be ignored no longer. A healthy West might have been able to absorb the subsequent shocks from the world-wide depression, but the star-crossed Prairies of 1929 could not.

In the summer of 1930, the Right Honourable R. B. Bennett was swept into office on a promise to end unemployment or perish in the attempt. He perished. Before the West could recover, a whole decade would be swept under the rug of history and a world war would be raging. It was a decade that destroyed men's faith in themselves, mocked their talents and skills, blighted their initiative, and subverted their dedication to the cultivation of their land. It shattered the morale of our inland empire, replaced a whole people's proud search for success with a dispirited search for security.

In the vernacular of the times, this is how things were with the people of western Canada during those winter years. It so happened that, for two years, things were just about as bad for the Grays as for

7

anybody else. Much of the story is thus based upon our experiences on relief in Winnipeg. The balance was obtained at first hand in later years as a staff reporter for the Winnipeg *Free Press*, covering the events to which I was assigned. In one sense, therefore, this book might be described as a personal history of the depression; but it is history only in the sense that the books by John Reed, Vincent Sheean, Eugene Lyons, and Alexander Barmine were histories of Russia. Definitive histories are not written by participating witnesses and no exception is claimed for these observations on the follies of the 1930s. Also, definitive histories are mainly concerned with the long-term growth and decline of great political forces, economic developments, and social revolutions. This is a book about people and their problems, about a lot of ordinary, cantankerous, friendly, selfish, helpful, disenchanted, and irrepressible people on and off relief. It is a chronicle of their minor tragedies, hilarious adventures, small disasters, and ephemeral triumphs, none of which made much history and some of which were our own.

Mainly, however, this is a book about people, because it is the only kind I feel qualified to write. What craftsmanship I possess as a writer was acquired while we were on relief, and the quarter of a million unsold words I wrote then were predominantly about people—race-horse trainers, pioneer farmers, gamblers, labour agitators, labour exploiters, professional atheists, holy-rollers, stock-promoters. In later years, whenever I tried to edge into the precincts of the professors in the development of a global theme, my preoccupation with people inevitably intruded to spoil the pitch. I was never a successful political pundit because I was too often fascinated by politicians as human beings and bored by the lofty causes they espoused.

If this book has any viewpoint it is that the depression brought out more of the best than it did the worst in people; that people, if left alone, tend to work out their own problems for themselves; that expert advice, particularly in economic matters, is most useful when it is completely ignored; that so much was learned from the depression that it will never happen again.

CHAPTER I

OUR WORLD STOPPED
AND WE GOT OFF

From our home on Ruby Street in Winnipeg to the relief office at the corner of Xante Street and Elgin Avenue was less than three miles. It could be walked easily in an hour, but I didn't complete the journey the first time I set out, or the second. If I had not been driven by the direst necessity, the third trip would have ended as the first two had done. I would have veered sharply to the right, somewhere en route, to head down town in one last attempt to find a job. But on the third trip the truth could no longer be dodged by any such pointless manoeuvre.

We were almost out of food, we were almost out of fuel, and our rent was two months in arrears. At home were my wife and daughter, and my mother, father, and two younger brothers. Applying for relief might prove the most humiliating experience of my life (it did); but it had to be done, and I had to do it. The deep-down realization that I had nobody to blame but myself made the journey doubly difficult. In mid-February 1931 I was not yet twenty-five, but I could look back on ten years of psychopathic concentration on getting ahead in life. Then my number had come up and I was confronted with the ego-shattering discovery that there wasn't a single employer in all Winnipeg who would give me a job.

I had been out of work since the end of November, and I was already deeply in debt when my job disappeared. I canvassed the Grain Exchange, where I had worked, from top to bottom every week. I tried door-to-door selling, attempted to leave my application with department stores and the Post Office, but nobody was even taking applications, let alone dispensing jobs. There was no alternative to applying for relief.

At that moment, I was a fitting subject for a sermon on frugality and thrift. Ten years before, at fifteen, I had started out to make my fortune. In our family, the idea of any of us pursuing a higher education was never considered because it was naturally assumed that, as the oldest of four brothers, I would leave school to help support the family as soon as it was legally possible. If I had an educational goal, it was to go as far as I could as quickly as I could before I had to quit. I made it to Grade 10 and then got my first job in 1921 delivering groceries for $5 a week. From that I moved up to delivering engravings for $7 a week. When I landed a job as an office boy in the Grain Exchange at $10 in the early fall, I was convinced I was on the sure road to success. The Grain Exchange was synonymous with unmitigated affluence and was the status place to work in post-war Winnipeg. No one knew this better than I, for I had delivered morning papers to the baronial houses of wealthy Grain Exchangers. Inside these houses lived the men who had come west with nothing and made their fortunes in Winnipeg. If they could do it, I would some day do it. Spinning day-dreams helped take some of the sting from the cold winter mornings.

Money has an overweening importance to anybody who grows up in poverty, and our family knew nothing but poverty in Winnipeg during the First World War. From the time I was nine, and my brother Walter was six, we sold papers, ran messages, delivered groceries and laundry after school. If we never went hungry, there was never a time when what was wrong with our family could not have been repaired with $25 or $50.

The Winnipeg Grain Exchange in 1921 was on the threshold of its last great fling. The brokerage offices were crowded with speculators who bought and sold grain futures on margin. Outside, work was starting on a ten-storey addition that was to make it the biggest office building in the British Empire. The trading floor itself was a forest of temporary wooden beams and scaffolds, for it, too, was being enlarged. Here the shrieking voices of a hundred pit-traders created a din that, when the windows were open, could be heard clear over to Portage and Main. Behind the Monte Carlo façade was the actual business of warehousing, transporting, and marketing the western grain crops. Incidental to the frenzy of speculation, the wheat crops did get marketed. It so happened that the company I went to work for was actually engaged in the marketing business, and my employer never went into the wheat-pit. He was one of half a dozen vessel-brokers who obtained lake freighters for grain exporters and found exporters to charter the vessels.

My first job was running messages back and forth between our office and the telegraph offices on the trading floor. Soon I was helping with the books and learning eagerly how to run a typewriter, operate an adding machine, and make out insurance policies and invoices. The office opened at nine and closed whenever the day's work was done, usually along towards midnight. My job was as exhausting as it was exhilarating and at Christmas time I was amply rewarded with a $100 bonus. I ran all the way home clutching my envelope full of $5 bills.

When navigation ended on the Great Lakes in December, the vessel-brokerage business came to a dead stop. My employer went off to California; I enrolled in a correspondence course in accounting and picked up some extra money as a part-time bookkeeper in an option brokerage across the hall. Thereafter, promotions and pay raises came rapidly. By the time I was nineteen, there was nothing about the business I did not know or could not do, I was making $150 a month, and my Christmas bonus reached $500. Only experienced bricklayers made more, and most bank accountants made less. In those days the banks refused to permit their employees to marry until they were earning $1,000 a year, a level that usually took ten years to reach.

The success I achieved only whetted my appetite for more. I bought a half interest in a couple of race-horses, fell for one swindle after another, sent good money after bad to promoters of oil wells in Louisiana, gold mines in Colorado, and silver mines in Ontario. In between times I took losing fliers in the grain market. That I did nothing but lose never concerned me, because ultimately I would make an investment that would repay all my losses. Besides, by 1926, I was otherwise preoccupied. I had acquired a nearly-new Ford sedan, smoked two-for-a-quarter cigars, and was squiring one of Eaton's prettiest cashiers. Her name was Kathleen Burns, and by that Christmas we were so much in love that we could discover no reason for not getting married. We did so, and I had a further incentive to get on with my fortune-making. Instead of buying furniture or a house, we bought a race-horse, with my employer as silent partner, and for the next year I coupled horse-training with my Grain Exchange employment. As a horse-trainer I was a monumental bust, but it was great fun.

Our daughter Patricia was born in 1928, and her arrival gave me still another incentive. But somehow I had slipped into a rut. My salary had stopped going up, my employer had brought his brother into the company, and my position steadily deteriorated. When a group of grain-brokers decided to finance a new stock-brokerage office in Portage Avenue, I hired on as margin clerk, statistician, and general factotum. Not a single partner or employee knew anything about the stock market or the brokerage business. We even had to bring in employees of other brokers to train us in the simplest procedures such as computing margins. On the basis of this all-pervading ignorance, we were prepared to advise everybody in town how to make and manage investments in the stock market. In the logic of 1928, we should have been eminently successful, but the project never got off the ground and the business closed a full year before the crash.

Instead of going back to the Grain Exchange, I decided the time had come to get into business for myself. The first chance that came along was a candy franchise, and for the first half of 1929 I was in the candy business. I worked eighteen hours a day servicing the candy stands and Kay worked almost as long filling bags with candy. We went broke in six months and I returned to the vessel-brokerage business with a different employer. A few months after the Wall Street crash I was offered a much better job as manager of the grain department of a new brokerage firm that was opening an office in Lethbridge.

I arrived in Lethbridge just before the Solloway Mills scandal broke. Brokers were being arrested all across the country for 'bucketing' their customers' orders during the mining boom. They were more victims of circumstances than anything else. The banks would not lend money on mining shares, and this prevented the brokers from financing their customers' margin purchases at a time when the customers were clamouring for mining stocks on margin. So the brokers sold stock on the exchange against their customers' purchases, a highly illegal action for which they went to jail.

By the time Kay had sold our furniture and brought Patty to Lethbridge, I had discovered some highly unsavoury things about an oil company my employers were floating. The more I probed into it, the more certain I became that the investors would lose their money. I quit in a panic, for fear I too would go to jail, and went back to Winnipeg to the job I had quit only a few months before. It was not until much later that I realized how lucky I was to get any kind of a job then. The brokerage failures turned hundreds out of jobs in

Winnipeg. The break of the wheat market below a dollar and then below ninety cents brought hard times for the Grain Exchange, and, outside, the secondary effects of the stock-market crashes were becoming clear. But not to me.

That was the year of the miniature-golf craze. Like millions of others, Kay and I took up the game. The trouble was that the nearest course was miles away from home, and it was always crowded.

'You know,' I said, 'a guy could make a lot of money with a course like this near our place.'

Kay pointed out that she could act as cashier during the day, if my mother would look after Patty, and I could run it at night. Our overhead would be small, and, if we got a quarter of the business the pioneer course was getting, we could clean up. We talked ourselves into it in no time. There was a small impediment. We had no money, or relatively little, compared to the capital required. The original operator egged us on.

'Why,' he said, 'there's nothing to it. Do it on credit! Your course will cost you $2,000. You might even do it for $1,500, and all you need is a couple of hundred in cash. Right now I'm taking in better than $200 a day. You won't do that good. But you could figure on a minimum of $100 a day. In fifteen days you'll pay for the course and you'll be set for next year.'

It sounded wonderful. And it was as easy as that—almost. We rented a vacant lot, installed lights and a shack, and bought clubs and balls. No one demanded payment for the supplies. We were astounded at how good our credit was. Nevertheless, we spent all the money we had and borrowed more before the thing was finished. During the first week business was wonderful and we took in well over $500. Then came Labour Day, and nothing collapsed as quickly as miniature golf in September 1930. We closed the course in October with creditors clamouring for their money. So much of my pay was earmarked to repay loans that there was little left to live on.

Then the blow fell. On November 30 my employer went out of business. Nor was this all. By one of those queer twists of fate, two of my brothers were laid off on the same day. By a momentary stroke of good fortune, I managed to find a buyer for the golf course and he paid me enough to clean up most of my debts. But I still owed better than $300, which was more than I could have repaid even if I had had a job. And I had no job.

I have told this story in detail to make this point: I was a typical 'child of the Twenties'. What happened to me happened to everybody, more or less. What you became in life depended upon the job you settled into. You left school when you had to, though no earlier than fourteen, the legal limit. Then you got whatever extra education you needed at night schools or by correspondence courses. If your first job lacked opportunity for advancement, you quit and went elsewhere. It was not uncommon to make three or four false starts before settling into a permanent position, and no stigma attached to rolling stones.

Lack of education was no handicap in obtaining employment, and it was no bar to advancement for the eager and industrious youth of the Twenties. My educational attainments were at least equal to those of my contemporaries who rose to lofty eminence in Canadian banking and industry. Arnold Hart was fresh out of high school when he joined the Bank of Montreal at eighteen. A. T. Lambert reached the top of the Toronto-Dominion Bank by getting an early start at fourteen. At sixteen, H. G. Welsford got the job that led ultimately to the presidency of Dominion Bridge; James Pearson was only fourteen when he hired on at National Steel Car; G. H. Sheppard got to the top of IBM by starting as a fifteen-year-old office boy in 1929.

Harry Sellers parlayed a teen-age job in a Fort William grain elevator into the presidency of a dozen western grain companies. His feat was matched by K. A. Powell, who began as a minor clerk in the Grain Exchange. George McKeag made it from office boy to the head of Security Storage, western Canada's biggest forwarding enterprise. T. O. Peterson detoured from rural Saskatchewan through the Bank of Montreal to the presidency of Investors' Syndicate. W. M. Currie began as an office boy in Medicine Hat at seventeen and was elected president of the Canadian Imperial Bank of Commerce in 1965.

Rapid advancement was possible on ability alone. The so-called professions had not yet become government-sheltered monopolies, and professional unions were not yet blockading the avenues of advancement. Ours was a boot-strap economy in which you learned by doing. Young men became accountants by enduring the starvation wages of the banks for two or three years. They became mechanics by getting jobs in garages, became carpenters by carrying lumber around construction sites, became railway engineers by starting as wipers in the shops. If they were Harts, Sheppards, or Welsfords, they settled into their first jobs and made them their life work. If they were James Grays, who were driven to running before they could walk, they were willing to try anything once, again and again. There was nothing either in our experience or in our history that prepared us for the Dirty Thirties. Booms and busts there had been—four major depressions in the previous thirty years. But they had passed quickly; and the assumption everywhere was that this, too, would pass quickly. The Dirty Thirties were almost over before governments recognized that a hard core of unemployment had become a permanent fact of economic life. The Dirty Thirties were almost over, too, before the young adults of the Roaring Twenties realized that the world they had known was gone forever; that they had emerged from it equipped only to blunder and flounder through a pathless wilderness.

In the transition between the 1920s and the 1930s, the most persistent and widely held delusion of all was that unemployment was a temporary thing that would soon pass. As I walked to the Elgin Avenue relief office I believed it; the hundred-odd other applicants I found waiting in line believed it. It was a delusion that encompassed all governments and it was the foundation on which the entire system of unemployment relief was erected. The governments simply adopted whatever method there was in existence for dispensing temporary assistance and extended it *ad infinitum.*

The Winnipeg system, like that of all other prairie cities, was designed only to bridge the winter for those who were seasonally unemployed and could prove they were completely destitute. Those who were aided—a few hundred families each winter—worked off their relief sawing cordwood into stove lengths at the city Woodyard. The city Relief Department was an adjunct of the Woodyard—departmentally and physically. Cordwood from the tamarack forests was still a staple fuel in Winnipeg. The city brought it in by the trainload and stored it in great piles twelve feet high and six rows deep around the two city blocks that the yard occupied. At an open corner in the stockade was the yard office, to which the relief office was attached. Least adequate of all the Relief Department facilities was the building itself. It was shaped like a flattened, stretched-out U. The centre section was some sixty feet long and contained the office. At one end an extension, some thirty feet long, jutted out at a right angle and was used as a store-room. The waiting-room was another extension from the other end and it was about fifty feet long and twenty feet wide. Over a door at the corner was a sign:

RELIEF OFFICE

A crowd of several hundred milled around in the yard and I elbowed my way through to the shed. Inside, at the far end of the shed, were three doors leading into the main office. One was marked APPLICATIONS. The next was marked RENT AND FUEL, and a third was marked GROCERIES. There were long lines in front of each door and the APPLICATIONS line extended the full length of the shack and out into the yard. I found the end of it and huddled against the wall with a dozen others while we waited for the line to move up and let us inside. After half an hour in the shack, the one thing we wanted most was to escape into the fresh air, regardless of the temperature.

Winnipeg's North End was home to Canada's largest blocs of unassimilated immigrants, many of whom had only lately arrived. Because of the language barrier they were the last hired and the first fired, so it naturally followed that the bulk of the first applicants for relief were New Canadians. In addition to their arts, music, dancing, and literature, they brought to Canada a folk cookery based upon highly aromatic herbs and spices. Garlic, to race-proud Anglo-Saxons, was something to touch gently to a salad bowl. To the Galicians—a derisive generic term Winnipeggers applied to all foreigners—garlic was an anti-toxin, a medicine, a gargle, a liniment, and a confection to chew while waiting for streetcars. The Woodyard waiting-room that day swam in an aroma of garlic, to which was added the smells of stale tobacco, wet leather, perspiration, and singed rubber and wool from those who stood too close to the intermittently smoking stove.

Overpowering as the atmosphere became, it never reached a sufficient potency to drive anybody out of his place in line. Perhaps it was the narcotic effect of the air, but as time passed so did my panic about going on relief. The closer I got to the door, the more anxious I became to get the thing over and done with. It was as if some impersonal force was moving me inexorably to some mysterious fate. I relaxed and waited, almost impatiently, for the next adventure. The terrible aloneness of the long walk to the relief office was gone. Nobody was alone any more.

I was feeling a lot better when I reached the end of the line that afternoon and a harried clerk took my application and explained the system to me. I became entangled in the regulations before we even got on relief. When we returned from Lethbridge, Kay and I had rented a house with my parents and brothers. The clerk said I could apply for relief for Kay and Patty, but my father would have to apply for his own family. Nobody could get relief for relatives. I explained that my father was partly crippled and could not walk all the way to the Woodyard. In that case, he said, there was no point in his coming. Being unemployable, he was only eligible for social welfare, which was something different and dispensed by the City Hall. I answered that my father was perfectly capable of doing clerical work, only his legs were arthritic.

The clerk went off for a long conference with a supervisor. In the end the supervisor let me apply for everybody, and I went home to await the arrival of an investigator who would come around to inspect us. Two days later an investigator turned up, made a few perfunctory inquiries, and approved my application. He also took the time to make out a special form for my father to sign, scribbled his approval on the bottom of it, and said he would turn the form in at the office and the vouchers would be sent out by mail on a temporary basis. I was to take my approved application back to the Woodyard on Tuesday. Thereafter, save when sickness intervened, I was a regular Tuesday visitor to the Woodyard for the next two years.

When I arrived on the first Tuesday, the system had been somewhat reorganized from the week before. There was now a 'NEW

CARD' line parallel to the 'APPLICATIONS' line. The end of the line for new cards was again outside the shack and it took the better part of an hour to get in out of the cold. Eventually I reached the clerk who was handing out the cards. He took the slip the investigator had given men and laboriously copied the particulars onto a printed card somewhat larger than a driver's licence.

Across the top of the card were a number of headings, viz.: 'Groceries', 'Bread', 'Meat', 'Milk', 'Rent'. Under each the clerk inserted code numbers after I had named the store, bakery, meat market, and creamery with which we dealt. I spent the rest of the day going from line to line picking up vouchers. One qualified me to receive seven quarts and seven pints of milk, a second provided for seven loaves of bread, a third was worth sixty-five cents at the butcher's, and the fourth was for $2.38 in groceries. This was the new world of vouchers in which no cash ever passed from hand to hand.

In some cities a different system was used. Regina and Saskatoon gave out food supplies from a central depot. Edmonton and Calgary used vouchers. Regardless of the system, the allowances were about the same everywhere, varying naturally with the size of families. A family of three such as ours was allowed $16 a month for food and $10 to $13 a month for rent. Householders got a winter allowance of $6 to $10 a month in cordwood for fuel. It was possible to live on these allowances because of the collapse in the price structure. Indeed, as prices dropped even these relief allowances were reduced. Regina once cut the food allowance from $16 to $14 a month, until a near-riot changed the city council's mind. Any such episode naturally got economy-minded aldermen in other cities thinking about making similar reductions, 'in view of the drop in food prices'.

In the late winter of 1931, milk was ten cents a quart, bread six cents a loaf, chuck roasts sold for ten cents a pound, hamburger was nine cents, a rib roast was twelve cents, sausage was three pounds for a quarter, and potatoes forty-five cents a bushel. Even these prices would seem high a year later, when milk sold for six cents a quart in Winnipeg, bread was three loaves for a dime, butter sold for fifteen and twenty cents a pound, and eggs were fifteen cents a dozen.

For people accustomed to shopping with money, operating a household with vouchers took a lot of getting used to. Everything had to be bought in small quantities. If we had been given our grocery allowance for the month in a single voucher, instead of once a week, advantage could have been taken of quantity buying. But many months were to pass before the fact was recognized and allowances were distributed on a fortnightly basis. While becoming accustomed to voucher shopping was slow, people settled into the relief system itself with little difficulty. We had lived in a continuing food-and-shelter crisis for a month, and once these problems were solved by going on relief we were freed from the feeling of being incessantly driven. We relaxed and made a start at sorting out our family problems. On an invitation from relatives, my father and brothers emigrated via cattle train to Ontario to look for work in the textile mills. My mother stayed on with us until they could send her transportation. We found a house we could rent for the $13 a month the relief department would allow and settled down to wait for spring and a job. Two months later I came down with tuberculosis.

CHAPTER II

BEATING THE WOODYARD

Measured by what was to come afterwards, the unemployment problem in Winnipeg in the winter of 1931 was trifling indeed. Measured against anything the city had ever experienced before, it was a crisis of incomparable severity. The process of starving the other civic services to get money with which to pay for unemployment relief had not begun. But the Unemployment Relief Committee was well launched on its career as buffer between the provincial government, the city council, the taxpayers, and the grievance-ridden unemployed. It never succeeded in satisfying anybody completely, least of all the people on relief.

The fundamental error lay in trying to handle a growing army of unemployed with an apparatus geared to the needs of a platoon. The system was based upon providing temporary aid to the immigrant labourer. The rent scales, which allowed a maximum of $13 a month for a family of three, was what an immigrant could rent rooms for in a Winnipeg slum. The fuel allowance was calculated for that accommodation. The allowance for light covered use of two sixty-watt bulbs. When gas was used for cooking, the allowance fed the gas meter twenty-five cents once a week.

The ancillary regulations were designed to ensure that the immigrants who applied for relief were completely destitute. Rent was not payable until a family was two full months in arrears and had received an eviction notice. No payment was made for light and water until the utilities had issued final notices that services would be shut off. It was hardly possible for a family to reach all these stages while still possessing pawnable valuables.

25

People who could not speak the language and found themselves out of work in a strange land might accept such onerous regulations without complaint. Those who had grown accustomed to living much better did not, and their protests evoked endless turmoil at the Woodyard. The clerks were strictly bound by the regulations, while every third applicant insisted that a special set of circumstances made them inapplicable in his case. So there were long arguments, followed by trooping back and forth to the City Hall, where the relief committee sat as a court of appeal. Rejected there, appeals might be carried to the aldermen in their homes, to Premier John Bracken at his office, or to the Winnipeg newspapers.

The surging flow of applicants through the Woodyard from November 1930 until March 1931 had the effect of a snowball rolling downhill. It buried the relief administration in work. Yet no ameliorating step was taken until a crisis stage was reached, because when it came to the cost of administration the city's own money was being spent. The Dominion and provincial governments shared the cost of actual relief, but paid none of the costs of dispensing it. Having started with its own system, Winnipeg was stuck with it when the two senior governments joined in sharing relief costs. It was not only Winnipeg; the Winnipeg system was generally used as a yardstick by the other cities of the West.

The offices of the relief department became jammed with desks, filing cabinets, and clerks with no place to work, but the lines outside grew and grew. No one was concerned with the interminable waiting around by the unemployed at the Woodyard, except the unemployed. They were not going anywhere anyway, so what did it matter if it took the better part of a day for them to collect their weekly tickets? The delays, nevertheless, became a cause of trouble for the administration because the unemployed whiled away the time grousing about regulations, mis-interpreting the regulations, finding loop-holes in the regulations, and lying about the regulations. Getting on relief and staying on relief had become the end-all of existence that winter. Nothing was as important as the food, rent, and fuel vouchers; but nothing was as soul-satisfying as finding ways around the regulations without being cut off relief. 'Beating the Woodyard' the game was called. It was like playing Russian roulette with paper food-vouchers.

In no other area of life on relief did everything seem to work together for the worst quite as completely as in the medical care branch. There were 16,000 men, women, and children on family relief in the spring of 1931, plus an additional 5,000 single unemployed who were fed at a government soup-kitchen. If the unemployed and their dependants had been collected into one camp, they would have been the second largest city in Manitoba. Such a city would have required the services of twenty-eight doctors, thirteen dentists, and four chiropractors. For the entire unemployed population, Winnipeg provided one doctor and no dentists.

It was impossible for one doctor to serve the needs of 16,000 people, although the relief doctor did his best. He made no house calls, but he was at his office all day every day, and sometimes the line-up at his door was the longest at the Woodyard. Anything more than a rudimentary diagnosis was impossible, and patients with more than superficial illnesses were given slips directing them to the out-patient clinic of the Winnipeg General Hospital. Besides treating the sick, or pointing them in the direction of treatment, the doctor had several other functions that, in combination, made him one of the ogres of the Woodyard.

In addition to paying all administration costs of unemployment relief, Winnipeg was responsible for caring for the unemployable—the social welfare cases. The social welfare scale of assistance was decidedly inferior. When an employed man became ill and could not work, the senior governments demanded his prompt transferral to the city's Social Welfare Department. Eventually, the rules were changed so that when the husband took sick his wife became the eligible head of the house and the family stayed on relief. During the first years of the depression, however, families were shuttled back and forth between the Relief Department and the Welfare Department. It was the relief doctor's responsibility to certify the employability of the unemployed. Those he rejected were automatically transferred to social welfare.

As time passed and the unemployed discovered the difference between the relief and the welfare allowances, the line-up outside the doctor's office thinned perceptibly. An outbreak of reverse malingering swept the ranks. Rather than risk exile to the Siberia of social welfare, the unemployed with serious ailments would avoid seeing the doctor, while their aches and pains got worse and worse; or got better. Usually they got better. If they did not, they were given the best $35 funeral the city could buy. It included the service, a casket, recorded music, a hearse, two cars, and a cemetery plot. The employed paid much more and got very much less.

The relief doctor also had the responsibility for excusing the temporarily incapacitated from the enforced labour demanded of those on relief. Regulations required the unemployed to do short stints on various make-work projects. These 'boondoggles' consisted mainly of raking leaves, sweeping back lanes, digging ditches, etc. Eventually the labour requirements took on punitive overtones as recipients who violated the regulations were forced to do extra shifts on the work-gangs. The doctor, however, could excuse the reliefers on medical grounds, and epidemics of sore backs and sprained legs broke out with any sharp rise in relief work.

On the principle that every dog is entitled to one bite, the doctors gave every relief recipient one exemption. The first time around, he would write 'excused' across the slip and sign it without wasting much time on the complainer's catalogue of miseries. Let anyone turn up again too soon, however, and it would take a real illness to keep him from work. The doctor had a prodigious memory for work-dodgers. There is scarcely a more explosive temper than that of a malingerer caught with his symptoms down. Such tantrums were almost hourly occurrences around the Woodyard clinic, and a uniformed policeman was kept handy to manage evictions.

Less frequent, but more violent, were the angry outbursts of frantic fathers seeking medical assistance for their sick families at home. During the early years of 'Relief City', the only advice the relief doctor could give to anyone with a serious illness in the house was to call in a friendly doctor. As time passed, the doctors got wise to the racket and refused to take calls from people on relief. The regulations never contemplated pregnancy in women, impacted teeth in men, or colic in children. Anyone who awakened in the night with a pain waited until morning and walked the pain to the Woodyard or to the nearest hospital for charity service. About-to-be fathers could deliver their own babies, if they failed to find a way of getting their wives to hospitals. Phoning for a cab was out of the question, because no one on relief was allowed to have a phone.

Perhaps the most aggravating aspect of medical care was the realization that there were many 'almost available' facilities around. All the hospitals had charity wards, but the patients had to get to the hospitals. There were school nurses to visit sick children, but only after a delay of several days. The city Health Department employed nurses and inspectors to visit contagious disease cases, but only to disinfect the houses and nail up quarantine signs. None of these was available to the unemployed, but in most cases they never made that discovery until some emergency had arisen.

After rattling around on such a merry-go-round, the last stop for the overwrought father was the doctor's office at the Woodyard where the chemistry was right for an explosion. When the pent-up frustration reached its peak, the urge to slam the doctor's door on the way out was irresistible. Most of the time, the outdoor air took care of the exploder's hysteria, while nature took care of the illness at home. The relief administration cracked down hard on most temper tantrums around the Woodyard, but there was understanding patience with harassed parents seeking medical assistance.

All this I discovered by accident in the process of trying to finagle my way out of a work slip. Late spring of 1931 brought a small breeze of optimism to our economy. Most of us on relief felt that spring would be the end of the ordeal, that jobs would somehow turn up for us. So we shaved every day, kept a clean shirt handy, and started making the rounds in search of steady jobs. My turn for a work slip came up in early April, and I decided to try to con the doctor into excusing me. I had developed a heavy cold in February and it seemed to be getting worse instead of better. With the cold for an alibi, I hoped to be excused from the work-gang and freed to continue my pursuit of a regular job. So I joined the line at the doctor's door.

The relief doctor was surprisingly friendly and gentle, a type-cast family doctor from a hundred movies—fiftyish, paunchy, stooped, and watery-eyed. He put me on the scale listened to my heart and lungs, asked about coughs and night-sweats, and gave me a slip to report to the General Hospital. It must have been quite some time since he had encountered such a walking skeleton. I was five feet eleven inches tall, and I weighed 118 pounds with most of my clothes on.

No one who had ever gone into the out-patient department of the General Hospital could have any doubts that it was the charity department. Enough obviously sick people sat on antiseptic benches, fearfully holding white pieces of paper, to give any half-healthy individual a whole new set of symptoms. My examination, when it came an hour later, was amazingly thorough. Amazingly, because this was the first time in months that anyone had taken an interest in me as a person with a problem. The doctor thumped my chest and listened. He asked questions and wrote down the answers. He ordered X-rays and blood tests, and he gave me a huge bottle of cod-liver oil.

Three days later I returned to the hospital and got the bad news. The doctor was completely off-hand about it. There was an early tubercular infection in the upper corner of my right lung. Nothing serious really, he said, and nothing to worry about. A few months of complete rest and an adequate diet should fix me up as good as new. Anyway, he said, the thing to do was to go home and go to bed and stay there until the city health nurse called in a few days, and not to worry.

I reacted in the only way people ever react to advice not to worry: I went on a veritable binge of worrying. It was spring, things had to improve, and I had to get a job. With me sick, what would happen to Kay and Patty and my mother? They took the news much better than I did, and the city health nurse added her comfort. Her advice was to go into the King Edward Sanatorium for a few months, where they would make a new man of me. I rejected this advice in favour of staying in bed at home. I won my point, but only temporarily.

The Relief Department nudged us into the Social Welfare Department. We thought but little of the change until a box of groceries arrived to keep us for a month. The echoes from the indignation meeting in the kitchen lured me from my bed on the verandah. I have forgotten all that was in the box, but there were bags of dried peas and beans, lentils, dried apples and apricots, and salted meat.

This box of social welfare groceries, and the idea of living on such a diet, made up everybody's mind. Mother decided to sell off what furniture she had left and use the money to join my brothers, who had obtained work in Ontario. Kay and Patty would go home to her family, and I would go to the King Edward Sanatorium. It was all decided in five minutes, and the decision was one of the best we ever made. It ended an intolerable ordeal for my mother, gave Kay a two-month respite from life on relief, and made a new man of me. Not only did the hospital rebuild my health in short order, but a dying Ukrainian second cook straightened out my thinking so effectively that the next eighteen months we would spend on relief would be the most rewarding of my life, as it was, indeed, for many, many others, though few recognized it at the time.

As it turned out, somebody at the General Hospital had either misread my X-rays, or my lung trouble had cleared up before the sanatorium staff got around to taking their own pictures. Within a month I was pronounced cured of tuberculosis and my trouble was diagnosed as a stomach-acid deficiency. They kept me in for an extra couple of weeks to fatten me up, and got ready to turn me loose. It was then that I made this shattering discovery: as long as I was a broken-down liability to our society, I got lavish attention. Once I was restored to the status of a healthy asset, able and willing to work, nobody wanted me, and least of all the Relief Department.

When the time came to be discharged from the sanatorium in late July, I arranged to stay on for an extra week while I negotiated my way back onto relief. It took most of the week. The shift from unemployment relief to social welfare had been automatic, but there was nothing automatic about going back. Instead, I found myself completely entangled by the regulations. We had been off relief for two months, which made me a new case. As such, I could not get relief until I had reapplied and an investigator had made his report. Kay and I had to be reunited in our own room, however, before we could be investigated. We did not yet have a room, although Kay had made arrangements to rent one. The landlady had agreed to accept the $13 relief rent. All I had to do was bring around the voucher for her to sign. The Relief Department clerk pointed out that he could not give me a voucher, nor could the rent be paid, because our rent was not two months in arrears. We became so deep in argument that he suggested I return the next day and see the superintendent.

The superintendent agreed that I was entitled to relief, that what I said was right, and what the clerk had said was also right. In such a circumstance, it was up to the Relief Committee itself to decided what to do. The following day I caught the Committee in an unfriendly mood, perhaps because I presented them with a brand new problem, and once they understood it they were reluctant to believe it. In any event, discussion got sidetracked onto relief eligibility and away from the crucial question of paying our rent. They authorized the department to reinstate us on relief, but boggled at paying our rent until we were in the required arrears. This crisis was solved by Kay's family, as our crises often were. They lent us the money to pay our rent for the qualifying period, and thus enabled us to buy our way back onto relief.

Within a matter of months, when the Woodyard started rigidly policing the earnings of everybody on relief, the whole procedure was reversed. The rule became, once a reliefer, always a reliefer, so that the unemployed who got jobs had to account to the Relief Department for how they spent their wages no matter how long they were off relief. Ultimately, the pressure of human numbers upon inadequate facilities brought other great changes to the relief system. Medical care for the unemployed was recognized as being as much a necessity of life as groceries. Nevertheless, Winnipeg had to shoulder the burden alone until 1934, when the General Hospital got into deep financial trouble and temporarily shut down its outpatient department. That brought the province into the picture, and thenceforth medical care was provided for the unemployed and their families. A panel of doctors with offices scattered over the city was recruited. They were paid $1 a visit for treating the unemployed and were empowered to prescribe medicine to a maximum of $6 a month, for which the Relief Department also paid. A panel of dentists was organized to make extractions for a payment of $1 per tooth, but fancy filings and inlays were excluded.

The regulations were amended to remove the wilder lunacies with which they were punctuated, but all the changes came with glacial slowness. The staff was doubled and redoubled, the Woodyard offices went through a process of addition, subtraction, multiplication, and division. But none of the changes ever caught up with the congestion for long or assuaged the fraying tempers on both sides of the Woodyard wickets.

CHAPTER III

THE *SINE QUA NON* WAS $1.50

The atmosphere in which I grew up in Winnipeg was the most revolutionary the community had experienced since the days of Louis
Riel. To the militant Marxists of the labour movement, whose
attention was focused on the toppling monarchies of Europe, the
end of capitalism was at hand. Among my father's friends were several who were openly impatient to get on with the business of
storming the barricades. I remember vividly as a small boy in 1917
going with my father to an anti-conscription rally, in the old Grand
Theatre, which was turned into a riot by invading soldiers. In 1919,
I stood on the fringe of the meetings in the old Victoria Park and
heard orators like Bob Russell, Fred Dixon, and George Armstrong
recharge the enthusiasm of the general strikers. Portage and Main,
that June, was the centre of a no-man's-land that stretched from the
Labour Temple on James Street to the Industrial Bureau on Main
Street South, the main base for the Chamber of Commerce vigi-
lantes, the 'Committee of 1,000'. Members of the committee,
armed with baseball bats, patrolled the business district on horseback. Bruises from the bats were worn as badges of honour by the
strikers. Though I understood little of the message, I saw and felt
the emotional impact of impassioned speeches on receptive crowds.
There were men abroad who could move crowds to action, and they
were crowds that could be emotionally aroused.

The economic distress of 1919 was as nothing compared with
1932, but in the interval the revolutionary fires had gone out. The
closest we ever came to re-capturing the spirit of 1919 was in a small

riot at the City Hall, when a few rocks were thrown and a few rock-throwers were clubbed. To anyone who had known Victoria Park, and could remember a streetcar being burned on Main Street, it was an anaemic imitation of the real thing. The revolutionary spirit that had been a Winnipeg hallmark had melted into an all-pervading political apathy.

The change was partly explicable on ideological grounds. The Menshevik-Bolshevik split in Russia had its counterpart in the global Socialist-Communist cleavage. In Germany, the Communists were bent on destroying the Weimar Republic and its Social Democrat government. In Winnipeg, they concentrated their venom on the 'labour skates' of the Independent Labour Party, the forerunner of the C.C.F. In their spare time, they worked tirelessly to organize the unemployed, but the unemployed could not bother being organized. Even when there were over 8,000 families on relief and the congestion at the Woodyard reached its peak, neither the Communists nor the Independent Labour Party could recruit much enthusiastic support. The I.L.P., to which I belonged, was shocked to discover in the 1932 provincial election that it had made the least headway in polls where almost everybody was on relief. The Communists did scarcely any better. Their interminable efforts to organize marches on the Legislature seldom brought out more than 2,000 to 2,500 hard-core followers.

Every effort to organize the unemployed foundered on the shoals of apathy; and yet it was more than that. We had been forced by the relief system itself to hammer out a whole new set of values. Everybody had the most pressing personal problems that required constant attention, and they were problems without the remotest connection with the public issues or grievances about which politicians made speeches, or about which the Unemployed Association could stage demonstrations. There were the usual vexations about clothing and shoes and landlords, which everybody had all the time, things one could worry about when there were no worse problems at hand. There usually were worse problems, all of which revolved around how to get hold of $1.50 in cash every week. Some people needed $2, others could manage on $1, but getting what was needed became the *sine qua non* of our lives. It was this driving need that made us a real and continuing threat to the wage standards of those who were still employed.

We received no cash in relief, and for the first year no clothing whatever was supplied. Relief vouchers covered food, fuel, and rent, and nothing else. But we needed other things—many other things like tobacco and cigarette-papers, tooth-paste, razor blades, lipstick, face powder, the odd bottle of aspirin, streetcar fare, a movie once a week, a pair of women's stockings once a month, a haircut once a month, and a permanent twice a year. Most people tried to find twenty-five cents a week, every week, for a newspaper. Unexpected needs continually cropped up, like needles and thread, darning wool, a bit of cloth for fancy work, a pattern for remaking a dress, a half-dollar every other month for a co-operative half-keg of beef for a neighbourhood party at which the Woodyard could be forgotten. The catalogue of essential trivia differed from family to family, but it seldom added up to less than a rock-bottom minimum of $1.50 a week.

The chain stores, in a drive for the business of the unemployed, began to stock toiletries so that we could get tooth-paste, lipstick, razor blades, etc. on our grocery vouchers. But as this only meant we would have less to eat, it was really no solution. We could, of course, have got along without any of these items. We could have stopped smoking, cleaned our teeth with hand-soap, walked wherever we had to go. But there was such a thing as morale, even for the destitute, and we at least had to try to put up a front to ourselves. So morale was built by taking the children to the zoo to feed the bears, by taking a streetcar ride down town to wander through Eaton's and The Bay, as women did by the hundreds just to get away from their rooms for an hour or two. The monotony of an existence without money created strains that had to be worked off. In that sense, a movie a week was as necessary as an occasional ice-cream cone for the children, or twenty-five cents worth of ribbon with which to retrim a hat.

The most trying experiences were when household articles wore out or broke and had to be replaced. It was often the most trivial problem that precipitated a family row. In any rooming-house, these spats could be heard erupting like firecrackers. The springs in window-blinds lasted forever for people who were not on relief, but, for those who were, blind springs were excessively fragile. When they broke, somebody had to climb on a chair, night and morning, to wind down and to wind up the blind, and every time the climb was made it was a reminder of being on relief. Even such a simple thing as the burning out of a light-bulb could blow up into a storm.

It was the burnt-out light-bulb that most sullied the reputation of the unemployed with the janitors of the city commercial and apartment buildings. Whenever someone on relief came up with a new idea, he set it adrift at the Woodyard and it soon permeated the unemployed community. One such discovery helped unemployed Winnipeg solve its light-bulb problems by embarking on the old army game—finding light-bulbs burning unguarded in a public place and liberating them. Another widely circulated trick was how to open a metal toilet-paper holder with a piece of wire. It kept many a family from using its grocery allowance for the purchase of paper. Both capers became increasingly difficult as time passed. Washroom doors in public buildings were kept locked and janitors covered their lights with wire screens that required a special screw-driver to remove.

In pursuit of the almighty buck and a half, especially for the first months on relief, everybody thought of the usual things first. Men with lawn-mowers wandered around the town looking for lawns to cut. It was not uncommon for a man to push a lawn-mower from the North End out to River Heights, a distance of four miles, get four or five hours' work, and return home at the end of the day with fifty or sixty cents. In the fall there were storm windows to be put on if anyone could be found to pay for the job. The standard rate was ten or fifteen cents a window for washing the storm windows and the outside of the house window. The rub there was the house-holder's wife, who would say:

'Just do these and these. John will do those small ones himself and put them on later. We don't want them put on yet.'

Thus, the small windows, which made the job easier and prof-itable, were culled out and only the large windows and those in the most inaccessible spots were farmed out for washing. To do the job, incidentally, required at least enough capital to buy a fifty-cent chamois. Sometimes cleaning and hanging storm windows could yield twenty-five cents an hour, but window glass broke easily and a dropped window could wipe out most of a day's pay.

People who lived near cemeteries could cadge jobs cutting the grass on the graves, at so much per grave per season. However, it was a sadly overcrowded field of enterprise, and unless a prospective grave attendant was at the door soon after the funeral he would dis-cover a rival had taken the job. Considerate people who hesitated to barge in on the sorrowing survivors did poorly in this business.

Every winter dozens tried their hands at fishing through the ice on the Red River, but the hazards far outweighed the few cents a day's catch would yield. The only satisfactory place to fish was near open water at sewer outlets. Any sharp change in the temperature of the water made the ice unsafe. A lot of time was lost by the fishermen having to halt operations to fish one of their competitors out of the river. One dip in the Red River in January, however, was likely to discourage the dippee from further operations for the year.

Those living on the fringes of the wealthier south end of town could earn odd quarters shovelling snow off walks and driveways. The house-to-house canvassing racket played out early in the depression, but not before the unemployed by the thousands had taken a crack at it. Everything that could be carried—from home-knit socks to wax flowers, pastry, dill pickles, embroidery, patented can-openers, and shoe-laces—was hawked from door to door.

A warning posted in the Woodyard ended a project, on which I had counted, to put some cash in my pocket. I was looking forward to the return of the horse races for two reasons. I was sure that I could earn a couple of dollars a day walking the horses as they cooled out after the races. I had also hoped to do some ticket scavenging in the betting ring, to retrieve winning tickets that bemused bettors occasionally discarded by mistake. In my last year at school, I had sometimes recovered $30 or $40 worth of such tickets in a week. The Relief Department served notice that any recipient seen at the race-track by its investigators would be cut off relief.

The shutting off of another source of income illustrated the thoroughness with which the Department scrutinized the lives of its clients. I still had a liquor permit at that stage and was sometimes able to pocket a fifty-cent tip by getting a bottle of Scotch from the vendor's for a hung-over Grain Exchange broker. One day when I went to collect my grocery vouchers, I was sent to the investigation department. Over a period of a month, three bottles of Scotch had been purchased on my permit. How come? I explained I had bought it for a friend in the Grain Exchange. The investigator demanded the name of the broker, so he could phone to confirm my story. He went off and came back satisfied. Then I had to go home, get my liquor permit, and bring it back to the Relief Department. After that was done, I got my relief allowances, but I was out of the liquor-running business for good.

The desperate need for small change set off a minor, though hardly profitable, boom in the auctioneering business. Homes all over town were ransacked for odds and ends of clothing and household goods that could be sold. While one group of unemployed was selling off their winter clothes, another was selling anything of value, and not urgently needed, for money to buy second-hand winter clothes. Prices were understandably low, for bids seldom started at more than a dime, but if the bundle was big enough it might bring $2 or $3, which was always enough to get over a crisis.

People with special skills—plumbers, carpenters, mechanics, and painters—could pick up odd jobs more easily than clerks or salesmen, but they could do so only by working for a fraction of their regular rates. This brought two completely contradictory public opinions into head-on collision at the Woodyard, and complicated the problem of earning the small sums we needed. One was the force exerted by employers, complaining taxpayers, and householders to compel us to accept any jobs offered, regardless of wages, or be cut off relief. The other came from employees and trade unions, who were determined to prevent the unemployed from working for near-nothing and destroying the wage scales of people with jobs.

In thrashing around to relieve the pressure, the Relief Department adopted a set of rules that antagonized everybody. Recognizing that it was impossible to hold 8,000 families responsible for every penny they earned, it allowed each family to earn up to $6 a month for minor necessities. This concession opened the gate for chiselling employers to hire men on relief to work a forty-hour week at fifteen cents an hour. They would work one week a month and be laid off. A new crew would be hired the following week and the process repeated, week after week, until the original crew's turn came up again. This racket became such a public scandal that the Department eventually ruled that anyone on relief who took a job had to earn at least twenty-five cents an hour at it.

At the other end, men who obtained longer employment at regular wages found themselves severely penalized. A carpenter who obtained a week's work at fifty cents an hour would earn $24. If he had been on relief for any length of time, there would be a dozen places for that money to go. By the time he bought some new bedsheets, got his wife a new dress and his children new shoes, he would be broke again. When he reapplied for relief, he had to explain how he had spent his earnings. He would not be eligible to receive any relief until sufficient time had elapsed so that his earnings equalled what he would have received on relief. A man who got a job for a month and earned $80, and who had been receiving a total allowance of $40 a month in relief, would have to maintain his family for two months on his earnings. This was subject to certain minor modifications, such as the $6 incidental allowance, plus fifteen cents per day for carfare and ten cents per day for lunches during the working period. Hardest hit by the earnings rules were the railway and mail-order workers, who might be on and off the payrolls several times a year.

If the government had set out deliberately to discourage people on relief from trying to get work, it could hardly have done better. A job that lasted a week could cause more trouble than it was worth. After four or five months on relief, the physical assets of any household deteriorated rapidly. Only constant patching could keep the props of ordinary living functioning. Because there was no money for small repairs, items that might have been fixed had to be thrown away. Under such conditions, people on relief developed queer fixations. Seldom a day would pass without someone blurting:

'I know what the first dollar that comes into this house is going to be spent on . . .'

It might be a new tooth-brush, or a coffee percolator, or a frying-pan. If it was a percolator—that a new one was needed would be noted with increasing vehemence at every meal. If it was a tooth-brush, there would be muttering every time teeth were brushed. So when there was folding money on the table for the first time in months, it was almost impossible to resist the temptation to rush out and buy the things that had become obsessions. The temptation to have some sort of outlandish celebration was almost too much to resist. Some would celebrate by having a meal in a restaurant. Others might buy a case of beer. Others might go to an uptown show or a dance, or buy a hat. But always the piper who drew the regulations had to be paid.

Relief recipients who earned money had to bring signed statements of their earnings from their employers. This was an embarrassment to the sensitive, who were not anxious to have the employer know they were on relief. Occasionally, an employer, knowing something of his employee's difficulties, would turn in a voucher falsifying the amount of the payment. There was, in fact, not a single regulation that was not constantly being broken by collusion of one kind or another. Some landlords, particularly in the least desirable districts, kicked back small amounts from the rent to the tenants. In order to prevent the spread of chiselling, the department expanded its investigation department, which seemed to be in constant communication with half the community. The other half, of course, was happily scheming to help relief recipients circumvent the regulations.

Gradually the existence of the relief system began to work subtle changes for the worse in the paternalism of the business community. Before the depression, it was the accepted business practice to keep staffs intact during dull periods as compensation for working hard during busy seasons. Besides, good employees laid off temporarily might obtain permanent employment elsewhere. Moreover, such layoffs might cause unnecessary hardship to lower-paid workers. Rank did impose obligations, and the obligations were accepted.

When the large employers—the railways and mail-order houses in particular—set the fashion for laying off staff *en masse*, other businesses followed the leaders. There was no longer any risk of permanently losing good employees to other jobs. There were no other jobs. So long as unemployment relief was available, there need be no concern about hardship to laid-off workers. When business picked up again they could be called back, so the cost of keeping a staff over slack periods became charged to the taxpayers instead of against company profits. Though the city council railed against the practice, it spread and spread, and the process gave rise to other practices that sharpened the unemployment crisis.

Chain and variety stores discovered means by which the lay-off system, if it could be called that, could be imaginatively refined. They turned more and more to women, whom they would employ only on two or three of the busier days each week. Other employers made it a practice to employ men at boys' wages, and stretch the 'learning' period of employees so that skilled workers were only paid apprenticeship wages. Thus, while the relief administration was continually changing its rules, it was being continually confronted by new conditions deriving from a deteriorating social consciousness.

The regulations discouraged job-seeking—of that there was no

doubt. But what was the solution? There was none. Any liberaliza-
tion of the rules would have led to wholesale abuses. The unemployed constituted such a threat to the standard of living of those
still employed that the perfect solution from the latter's point of
view, would have been to somehow freeze the unemployed on relief
and permanently out of the labour market. We were like termites
that had taken up residence in the wage structure of the community. We were so many, and our nibbling was so consistent, that
eventually we would bring the whole structure crumbling into
ruins. This was, in fact, what happened.

Many of those who had jobs during the depression were better
off than they had been before the depression. Their food costs were
down, their rent was down, the prices of everything they bought
was down. Their real standard of living, *ergo*, must have risen.
Many others, however, were still paying debts incurred in 1929 and
1930. Those who in 1929 and 1930 had bought cars and electric
stoves and fur coats and radios on the instalment plan—and who
didn't?—were in desperate straits after their salaries were cut ten
and even twenty per cent. The mortgage interest on their home,
bought at 1929 prices, was still eight per cent. The principal payments, which had been possible to meet on a 1929 income, became
millstones in 1932. The people on relief had lost their cars, radios,
and other instalment-bought goods to the bailiffs, or had sold them
before going on relief. But the employed were still being hounded
by bill collectors while they tried to adjust their lives to salary cuts
and short work-weeks.

The lives of the employed were hardly less unnatural than those
of the unemployed. The average worker lived close to the edge of his
income, no matter what it was. He looked forward to the next pay
increase so that he could afford something more or something better for his family. But in those days no one in western Canada could

look forward to a raise. The workers had to adjust their lives to the possibility of more salary cuts and more lay-offs—not to raises in pay. No matter where they worked, they were conscious of a stream of people coming in every day looking for jobs—their jobs! A $20-a-week job may not have been any bed of roses, but they knew, and their bosses knew, that any $20-a-week job could be filled a hundred times over in a single day for $15 a week.

If the people on relief would only have stayed there and not tried to find jobs, they might not have engendered so much fear. But we did try to find jobs, and the people who had them naturally resented the fact. Under such circumstances, it would have been ridiculous to expect them to understand our problems, for we did not understand theirs. On the one hand, they often regarded the unemployed as a lot of lazy louts who were content to spend their lives in idleness while the rest of the community kept them. Yet they would insist, in the same breath, that the regulations should be so drawn as to make it as difficult as possible for us to have anything above the mere relief allowance if we managed to get jobs.

I have said that men who had some special skills had an edge in the search for casual employment. That was only partly true. A great many were disillusioned with their own particular trades and were trying to find new ways of making a living. A railway machinist might try his hand at auto-mechanicking. An auto mechanic might turn to painting or carpentering. Anyone who could drive a nail and hold a saw passed himself off as a carpenter. Anyone who could wield a paint brush, no matter how inexpertly, had no compunction in undertaking a paint job. 'Hammer-and-saw' mechanics made a shambles of the whole wage structure of Winnipeg and reduced the building-trades unions to complete impotence. Union carpenters were forced to take jobs at contract rates that yielded an hourly income that would have got them expelled from any union.

The flat hourly wage-rate disappeared from the prairie economy. Almost all the work that could be found, whether on a new house or the fixing of a fence, was on a contract basis—so much for the job. It remained so through the entire decade. When the Bracken government in 1934 established a minimum wage of twenty-five cents an hour, the minimum became the semi-skilled labour maximum. Naturally, on government contracts and where unions were a factor, higher rates prevailed for skilled tradesmen. But over a far greater area of the economy the employers who paid the minimum wage regarded themselves as exemplary citizens a full cut above the common herd.

CHAPTER IV

THE GOLDEN AGE OF BOONDOGGLING

Many millions of dollars were spent on public works in western Canada in the first years of the Bennett administration, but few of us on relief in Winnipeg ever got any of it. Post-offices or federal buildings went up in most of the cities, and Winnipeg obtained a new auditorium. These projects, however, gave work to only a few building tradesmen, and the idea of combating unemployment with a public-works program was an early casualty of the campaign of organized business for balanced budgets and lower taxes.

The closest any of us on relief ever got to socially useful labour was sawing cordwood, but we were drafted periodically for all the make-work projects, like raking leaves, picking rock, digging dandelions, and tidying up back lanes. These 'boondoggles', as the Chicago *Tribune* was later to christen them, were devised to enable us to work off the assistance we received, and our services were demanded for a couple of days once a month. It was all justified on the grounds that the exercise would be good for us, that working would improve our morale, and that, by providing us with a token opportunity to work for our relief, we would be freed of the stigma of accepting charity. None of these dubious propositions had much validity. The fatuous nature of the projects the authorities invented quickly brought the entire make-work concept into disrepute.

My first boondoggle assignment came with the first issue of relief I collected. A printed work-slip instructed me to report to the Woodyard foreman to work for three afternoons. The foreman explained the system. There were 4,000 or 5,000 cords of wood in the piles, which extended clear around the yard on four sides. Strung

49

out down the centre of the two- or three-acre courtyard were a dozen saw-horses, or 'saw-bucks' as the foreman called them. Beside each saw-horse was stacked half a cord of wood in four-foot lengths. This wood was to be cut into three pieces—stove-lengths. Half the work-gang would saw and the other would load and pile. The pilers would pick up the cut wood and throw it on a heap in front of the saw horses. One piler would serve two cutters. The rest would help load cordwood onto the horse-drawn sleighs. When the cutters finished their quota, they could go home. Everybody else would stay until 4:30 to load the trucks with cut wood, for the social welfare families, and the sleighs with cord-wood, for the unemployed on relief who were supposed to saw it themselves. After my experience with a buck-saw the first afternoon, I never did. We always managed to have seventy-five cents on hand with which to hire a truck-mounted circular saw that followed the wood sleighs around the city.

When the foreman finished his instructions, my instinct was to choose the piling job. Not only had I never held a cordwood saw in my hands, I had never done any manual labour. But I became somehow caught up in the rush for the saws, and almost before I knew it I was headed for a saw-horse with a saw in my hand. This was one of the crowning blunders of my life, a fact that must have been obvious to any half-observant beholder. From any angle, I cut a ludicrous figure as I moved towards the field of combat. I was costumed in a soft felt hat, silk scarf, and form-fitting overcoat with a small velvet collar. I wore light chamois gloves, silk socks, and light oxfords. I could not even carry a buck-saw gracefully, let alone saw with it, but I located a vacant saw-horse and went to work.

How far below zero the temperature was that day, I never knew. I remember only that a cold wind was blowing and there were gusts of snow in the air. The first piece of wood fell from my log, and the second. Soon I was gasping for breath, and my arms started to ache. I tried resting, but that was no good, for the wind fanned the perspiration into ice on my hair.

It was while I was catching my breath that I saw the discarded gasoline-powered circular saws standing in the corner of the yard. Either machine could have sawed as much wood in an afternoon as our entire work-gang. The two machines, in a couple of days, could have cut all the wood the welfare families consumed in a week, perhaps in a month. But they stood idle in silent mockery of our puny efforts as the administrators of unemployment relief repudiated the machine age and set their course back through history in the general direction of the stone age.

My hands and feet were numb with cold before I discovered it was permissible to leave the saw-horses and go into the shack to get warm and have a smoke. Darkness fell, and I was not half through my pile. All the other buckers, save two, had long since finished their stint and departed. At 4:30 I was more dead than alive, and then the foreman unveiled another rule. Those who failed to finish their piles would have to come back the following morning!

'And look, you,' he said, meaning me, 'when you come back, put on some work clothes. Don't come around here all dressed up like a dude to buck wood!' His disgust was awesome, and I was almost too exhausted to reply.

'These,' I said, '*are* my work clothes. I've been going to work all my life in clothes like these. They're the only clothes I have.'

'Then for God sake get yourself some rough clothes.'

I got mad.

'Look, damn it, if I had money to buy work clothes with, I wouldn't be on relief. And anyway, what clothes I wear is none of your goddam business!'

The other less printable things I said taught me my first lesson in relief deportment—never, under any circumstances, swear at a straw-boss who is ordering you around. He rode me continually the next two days. That foreman's name was the first I put down on my son-of-a-bitch list of men with whom I would some day settle some scores. The list grew and grew during the next couple of years. The day I got a job again I forgot them all.

I completed my wood-sawing assignment the next morning and in the afternoon switched to the piling department. It was no soft touch either, because I picked a couple of men who were obvious experts. They brought their own 'Swede-saws' with them, and the first one, clearly a refugee from a lumber camp, was through in little over half an hour. The other was done within an hour. By then I had aches in new places in my back from rapid stooping and lifting and throwing.

The next day, I discovered the age-old dodge of beating straw-bosses. They could not stop you from going to the outdoor privy or into the shack once an hour to get warm. The third afternoon was endurable.

By long odds, the most imaginative boondoggle of them all was the Exhibition Grounds clean-up. Winnipeg once had a summer exhibition on a 100-acre site in the north-west part of the city. There had been a race-track and the usual exhibition buildings, but these were all torn down, or had blown away, after the First World War. The grounds had been vacant ever since, though a section was sometimes used for tourist camping. It was the sort of place that periodically attracted the attention of aldermen, and one summer they decided the time had come for a clean-up. A small army of us went off with a batch of wheelbarrows and picked up all the old tin cans, bottles, shoes, rags, paper, and other junk that had collected on this spot of prairie over twenty years. There was not as much as might have been expected and the pile we collected was perhaps ten feet across and three or four feet high at the crown. Trucks from the engineer's department took the debris to the city dump.

When we arrived on the second day, a supply of shovels, rakes, and picks had been laid in. The foreman distributed them among us and led us over to a corner where he measured off an area about ten feet square. He said he wanted a hole dug three or four feet deep. While we were digging, other men with the wheelbarrows scoured the area for field stones and dumped their loads beside our excavation. Naturally, as we dug, we pondered the nature of our project. The consensus was that we were preparing the foundation for either a tool-shed or a flag-pole. No one came close to guessing the real nature of the project. Before we finished digging, the foreman came over and revised his calculations. We were deep enough, he said. Now we should take the pile of stones that had been gathered and put them in the hole. One fellow needed better direction. How precisely did the foreman want them piled?

'Piled? Piled?' the foreman answered. 'Who said anything about piling them. Throw the **** stones in the **** hole. Then we'll cover them with dirt and scatter the rest of the dirt around on the low spots.'

Somebody laughed. Several swore. The foreman exploded:

'All right, all right, come on, let's get to work. This ain't my idea. I don't get paid to think. I get paid to do as I'm told, and this is what I was told to do. Maybe this afternoon, when we run out of rocks, we will just dig two holes and transfer the dirt.'

And this was almost what we did. We went around the grounds with shovels and rakes, levelling off imperceptible high spots and scattering the earth into imperceptible low spots.

It was invariably the same on these boondoggles. The foremen in charge seemed to resent the work more than the people who had to do it. It offended their sense of the fitness of things, and they took pains to assure us that what we were about to be employed at was not their idea. They would much rather have been engaged in building something big and permanent and useful. Yet such projects as these at least had the merit of transparency. No one tried to disguise them or make them into anything except what they were—organized time-wasting. There were others, equally useless, that were dressed up to look useful.

Many streets and lanes in the outlying sections of the city needed ditching and grading. This work, however, could only have been done if the cost was charged to the frontage property, and regular employees of the city would have had to do the work for regular wages. The taxpayers would not pay for it, and regular employees would not permit the work to be done by the unemployed. The net result was that the work was not done, and regular employees of the city were laid off and went on relief. Nevertheless, we were put to work digging ditches and grading streets, but deep in the woods where nobody lived.

I worked on a couple of these projects. Surveyors went far out into the bush in south Fort Rouge, hundreds of yards from the nearest house, and farther from sewer and water. A street a couple of blocks long was laid out. We went out first with axes and grubhooks and cleaned off the brush. Then we got picks and shovels and dug ditches. We threw the mud from the ditches onto the road. We levelled the road and graded it with hand tools. The job took relief gangs working in relays all summer in 1932. When we were finished, it was a nice mud road that started nowhere, led nowhere, and, for all I know, still leads nowhere.

The project that probably will be longest remembered by all reliefers as the zaniest ever devised was the great anti-dandelion offensive of the summer of 1931. When I returned to relief, after my discharge from King Edward Hospital, my first work-slip directed me to report to a Parks Board foreman in River Heights. There were several differences between this work-slip and the one given out during the winter. It was for three days instead of the then-normal two, and our grocery allowance was increased by thirty cents. This was to compensate for the extra cost of taking a lunch to work. They had figured it pretty fine. A pint of milk was five cents, and a couple of eggs for sandwiches, with four slices of bread, absorbed the other nickel.

Before we set off for the job the first morning, the foreman stood on a tool-chest and made a little speech.

'Men,' he said, 'when we leave here we're going to walk over to the top of Niagara Street and start cleaning the dandelions off the boulevards. If everybody will co-operate, we will get along just fine. Nobody expects you to bust a gut on this job, but, if you sort of set yourself some sort of goal, time is bound to go quicker. There is only one rule: You can kneel down, sit down, or lie down, but I don't want you standing up. Standing up will attract the attention of the people on the street, and if they see you standing around doing nothing some of these dames will be phoning in to raise hell. Then I get hell, and if I do I'll dish out some myself.'

We moved in on the dandelions in column of route, armed with a weed-sticker and a waterproof sack on which to kneel. River Heights in Winnipeg is laid out with twelve-foot grass boulevards separating the pavement and the sidewalks. A half-dozen of us lined up on either side of the street and the anti-dandelion offensive was on. It was a beautiful August morning, and the first hours passed quickly. The grass was rather thickly infested with dormant dandelions. We jabbed and pulled and jabbed and pulled. In an hour we travelled about 250 or 300 feet, leaving trails of dandelion-tops behind us. A couple of men were detailed on each side to rake up the harvest and put it in sacks.

Even in boondoggling, individualistic streaks began to emerge. The innately methodical edged ahead of the line. Some would be thorough and spare not the smallest weed. Others would take only the larger weeds and ignore the rest. Still others would work carefully in an effort to get the root out intact. A contest developed to see who could extract the longest root.

We had been working for an hour or so when two fellows on my immediate right got into a squabble. Over what? Over this: John accused Joe of chiselling on his territory. Joe, said John, was covering the narrowest front of anyone in the line. But when he pulled out his dandelions he pushed them over on John's side. This would give the impression to the foreman that John was lead-swinging while Joe was cutting a wide swath. Joe, of course, denied and said John was crazy. They loudly exchanged insults until the foreman put the width of the street between them.

What did the rest of us do? Laugh at them? We did not. We looked back down the trail of dandelions behind us, and several other arguments of a similar nature broke out. When lunch-time came, the dispute became the subject of lively controversy. I was on John's side—mainly, I suspect, because he seemed a nicer guy than Joe.

'Naw,' said another dandelioner, 'that John is always pulling something like that. Always arguing with everybody. I've been on work-gangs with him before. Once he was water-boy and belly-ached because we threw half a dipper of water away when we were through drinking. And he wouldn't leave the water in the shade so we could wander over and get a drink. No, the bastard, he had to keep it right on the road where it got hotter than hell and full of dust. Naw, take it from me, that guy John's a screwball.'

Weren't we all!

By the time we were at work for an hour after lunch we had

squeezed every conceivable blob of interest out of the job. We kneeled and jabbed dandelions, we sat down and jabbed dandelions, we lolled full length and jabbed dandelions. We sharpened the blades of the knives. We swapped experiences. We watched housewives going shopping. Then a band of ten-year-old boys materialized out of nowhere. Some were friendly. Some wanted to show off. Some just stood and stared. Despite the efforts of the foreman to drive them off, they got in our hair. One little fellow was full of questions.

'How much do you get paid? I could do that. Could I get a job?'
I told him we didn't get paid.

This he refused to believe, and he tried to trip me with other questions. That men would go to all the trouble of clearing his boulevard of weeds without getting paid made less sense to him that it did to us. He went off to discuss the mystery with a couple of friends.

'Of course they don't get paid,' said one of them. 'Don't you know they're all crooks. My mother said they're prisoners from Headingley Jail, and they are working out here now because they got the Parliament Buildings grounds all cleaned up. Prisoners don't get paid, you dope.'

'Aw, you're nuts,' said another 'I saw those prisoners at the Parliament Buildings and they were all wearing yellow pants.'

'G'wan, they weren't either. Some wore blue pants and blue coats, just like those guys over there!' The argument went on and on.

I don't know how the others felt. Perhaps I was feeling sorry for myself, but I was slowly developing an antipathy for small boys. It wasn't their fault that we were on relief and picking dandelions. Yet I looked at these kids and felt a great compulsion to go some place— to the City Hall or the relief office, or the Parliament Buildings— and punch somebody in the nose.

It was just before five o'clock when a dandelioner from the other side of the street exploded. A group of boys had been fooling around. I don't know what touched off the explosion. In any event, he leaped to his feet and, turning to a group of women on a near-by lawn, waved his dandelion sticker menacingly, and shouted:

'Goddamn it, somebody get these little bastards the hell out of here or I'll bury this in their guts!'

The sound of his voice seemed to frighten him. He sat down as quickly as he had risen, shaking and jabbing his knife into the ground, as if to try to dig a hole to crawl into.

The effect of his outburst was instantaneous. The kids were called home and you could see the women in angry discussion. All of us expected there would be trouble, because someone was certain to report us to the relief office. Conceivably, the man might be cut off relief. We agreed to tell whatever lies were necessary to protect him. However, nothing happened as far as we could discover, for the culprit stayed with the gang for the next two days.

On the second day, the heat in the early afternoon was terrific, and it was our bad luck to be working on a street where the trees were young and the shade was sparse. Along about 3:30 we got a pleasant surprise. A young woman came to the foreman, spoke to him for a few minutes, and went back into her house. A half-hour later she called the foreman over. He emerged from the house carrying a large earthen ten-gallon pickle crock containing a block of ice. The woman followed him with a large glass pitcher, full of lemonade that she emptied over the ice, and then she returned to the house. When the lemonade was finished, we took the jar back, rang the bell, and waited, because we did want to thank her. But, though we had heard movement in the house, she did not answer. We left the jar and went back to the dandelions.

The gift of the lemonade itself elevated our spirits far more than a mere cold drink on a hot day ever could have. Perhaps there was a touch of gin in it. Anyway, good humour exuded from the gang. For perhaps an hour, none of us hated anybody or anything. Then something happened to take the edge off.

A car drove up and stopped in the middle of the street. None of us paid much attention until we heard the voice of the driver.

'By God, this is the last outrage!' roared the voice. 'Here is what I sweat and slave to pay taxes for! To pay all the lazy bums in Winnipeg to sit around on the boulevards! Well, by God, I've had enough. I'm going to the mayor. I'm going to the newspapers! Who's in charge here?'

The next thing any of us knew, another voice was doing the shouting. It came from one of our gang. He had grabbed the taxpayer's tie and pulled his head through the open window of the car. Their noses were perhaps a foot apart and a dandelion knife was pointed at the taxpayer's chin.

Months of pent-up resentment against life on relief was exploding in a torrent of curses and threats. For artistry in cursing and variety of epithet, it was a *tour de force*, incapable of expurgation.

He was not, he said, a bum. He was a railroad fireman, but because the country was being run by **** stupid people like this **** taxpayer, he could not hold even a **** wiper's job in the **** shops. And we were not being paid, not one **** dime. We took jobs like this because we were afraid of getting cut off relief.

The taxpayer's indignation turned to panic. He tried to loosen the grip on his tie, but our champion jabbed his hand with the dandelion digger and his resistance collapsed. Our man went on:

The taxpayer was not going to report anyone to anybody. He was going to get the hell off the street, and if he so much as let out a peep to anyone, there were twenty guys here who would have his licence number and who had all the spare time required to make him live to regret it.

59

He released the taxpayer and gave his face a vigorous push back through the open window. As the car moved off to a chorus of loud jeers, he held his dandelion knife firmly against the body. So far as I know, the incident was never reported. None of us were as tired when the foreman came around and handed out the car-tickets that night.

It rained the next day, so we were sent home early. That was my one and only experience on the boulevard sector of the dandelion offensive. Apparently there had been trouble on other streets, for the boulevard campaign was ended and a new front opened in the city parks.

None of us minded the park work. Assiniboine Park was always a wonderful place to spend a day. After Labour Day it was almost empty of visitors and we had the place to ourselves. Later on, when the frost came, we exchanged our dandelion knives for rakes and turned our attention to the leaves. We raked enough leaves that fall to keep the park in compost for years. Raking leaves was a pleasant pastime, and whenever the foreman wasn't looking we'd start a bonfire and toast our posteriors while we enjoyed the aroma of burning leaves. Leaf-raking was not without its compensations.

One of the more curious aspects of the state of mind behind the boondoggles was the limited scope of the imagination. Weird and wonderful schemes of organized time-wasting were dreamed up for the manual labourers, but there was nothing for anybody else. Labourers had certainly been in the majority in the beginning, but they were eventually superseded by skilled artisans, clerks, bookkeepers, and white-collar workers in their infinite varieties.

On the work-gangs and at the Woodyard, we kidded around about being discriminated against. Why not some work for us to keep in practice, like adding up the numbers in telephone books, or keeping books in invisible ink? Low-grade satire it might have been, but from what transpired it was easy to suspect that somebody had been eavesdropping. One day in 1932 we were solemnly directed into a new line at the Woodyard. It ended at a table at which a battery of clerks were seated. Each of us was handed a printed promissory note in favour of the City of Winnipeg. We signed the note, solemnly promising to repay the city for the full cost of relief being given us. The clerks duly witnessed our signatures and deposited the notes in a large drawer.

The episode was of course treated as a huge joke, which it was. Bales of notes were collected and I often wondered what would have happened if the city treasurer had taken them into the bank and offered them as security on which to borrow enough to pay the bill for printing them. There is little doubt what the answer would have been. The notes were filed and forgotten and that was the end of them. But it was far from the end of the boondoggling, which lasted as long as the Depression itself.

CHAPTER V

FUN WAS WHERE
WE FOUND IT

It was mid-afternoon in August 1932 when one of the supervisors at the Lord Selkirk school-yard playground strode onto the pitcher's box, blew her whistle loudly, and made a short speech.

'If this happens again,' she screamed at us, 'I'm going to call the police! This playground is for children! If you men want to play baseball you will have to do it after supper, because I won't have you big louts spoiling the fun for all the children on these grounds. Now get off this playground and stay off or I am going to call the police!'

As she angrily gathered up the balls and bats and waited for the school-yard to clear, it was apparent that her complaint was justified. There had been at least three baseball games going on, all composed of grown men whiling away a pleasant afternoon. The children were hived off in corners, or trying to dodge the hard-hit grounders from the adult games. One boy had zigged when he should have zagged and had run crying to the supervisor with a bruised head. The episode was a perfect answer to the question that was forever being asked: What do you do with your time on relief? We did anything and everything that came along.

The authorities assumed that the unemployed on relief spent their days loafing around their homes. Their make-work projects seemed mainly designed only to get the unemployed away from home for a couple of days. The truth was that any kind of home the unemployed could afford could offer little attraction even for the most confirmed home-body. In most cases, home was a single room in a rooming-house, in which a family of three or four was expected to eat, sleep, and be happy. Happiness, for most, was achieved by spending as little time there as possible. On the afternoon in question, I had been *en route* to the public library with an armful of books when I discovered the baseball games and immediately invited myself in.

With boundless leisure, there was an almost infinite variety of things to be done. Along north Main Street, all the neighbourhood stores were equipped with chess tables, and the unemployed Jews and Ukrainians in the stores outnumbered the customers four and five to one. In the summer everybody had a garden, and puttering around a garden could kill the better part of a day. The service stations around town operated with staffs who were mainly volunteers—men who filled gas-tanks because they had nothing else to do.

As it did for so many others on relief, necessity turned Kay and me into inveterate walkers. From having to walk wherever we went, walking became a pleasure, and we seldom went to bed without a stroll around the neighbourhood. Rooming-house living had given us both an obsession to own a home of our own, which in our rambles developed into an insatiable interest in houses under construction. We frequently spent the evening making the rounds of construction projects and in the process developed a proprietory interest in the houses we liked. Very few homes were being built, so it was a long walk between houses, but we thought nothing of trudging a couple of miles in search of new construction. Early in the game I got a book on house-building from the library. We studied up on carpentry and, in following the course of construction on a dozen homes, gradually acquired a knowledge about building practices, and even felt qualified to identify and criticize unsound methods. A few years later, we thought so highly of the know-how we had acquired that we built a house of our own without a general contractor. It was a great success. The plans I drew passed National Housing Act inspection and, when the house was finished, a professional builder came around and bought the blueprints for $50.

Walking itself became great fun. So was hunting mushrooms, which we did after every rain; so was sitting in the park where Patty played in a wading pool or made castles in the sand. Kay was an indestructible movie-fan and would go to occasional shows with her mother or sisters. Sometimes we would go up town and drop in at auction sales. The sales were not only an important source of revenue for people on relief, but they constituted a popular form of entertainment as well. There was one auctioneer on Carlton Street whose store was always jammed. So many people came to be amused, however, and so few came to buy, that the enterprise eventually went broke. The auctioneer worked harder to get a ten-cent bid than most of the tribe worked to get a dollar.

He was a fattish, unkempt Englishman, with a Cockney accent and the Cockney's irrepressible humour and showmanship. His approach to every new bundle was one of well-simulated enthusiasm.

'Oh ho,' he would cry, pulling out a pair of men's combinations. 'What have we here? Why, it is none other than a genuine old-English hunting costume. All you have to do is dye the top half red and you can go out on a fox hunt tomorrow in the height of fashion. When you ride up in that, people will say: "Egad! 'Arry! 'Ere comes the Prince of Wiles."'

All the while he would be grimacing, leering, and winking at his customers and generally hamming up the performance. Though his gags wore thin after the third or fourth visit, he played to a packed house every night. No matter what he offered, the first bid was usually the same—ten cents. Towards the end of the evening, when he had polished off several bottles of spiked soft drinks from the back room, his tongue would thicken and this temper would come unstuck. Then a bid of a dime would send him into a towering rage at the bidder, his audience, and the world in general.

'What the hell are all you people doing here anyway?' he would shout. 'What did you come here for, to buy something or to get away from your wives? And you dopes over there in the corner—if you want to hold a meeting, go to the auditorium! Joe! Clear that gang the hell out of here! Not one of them has made a bid all night and I can't hear myself think above their chatter. And you, lady! If you make one more ten-cent bid tonight, I'm ready to dump you in that washing-machine over there and turn on the juice!'

Having bawled out everyone in sight, he would return to his auctioning, 'Now, how much am I bid?'

'Ten cents,' the lady in the front row would shout gleefully, the crowd would roar and rock, and everything was back to normal.

How people killed time depended on individual tastes, and perhaps those with the worst luck were those with a too-well-developed taste for beer. Beer addicts talked of nothing else, and could talk unceasingly about varieties of beer, how to make it, where to drink it, when they last had it, the difference in taste between Canadian and American beer, the superiority of beer over whisky, of one brand over another. Such men spent the whole day wandering from one beer parlour to another, searching for a chance acquaintance who would buy them a beer. Beer addicts knew when all the local enterprises had pay-days and which beer parlours were best on the fifteenth of the month and the first, which were best on the fifth and twenty-fifth.

Gamblers still found ways of gambling. Throughout the depression there was a jungle off Higgins Avenue where outdoor poker games and crap games operated from dawn to dusk. The poker games were for pennies, and the players were as serious as if they were playing for dollars. Sitting in the shade of a tree or a fence, they played with cards so dirty and so worn that the symbols on them were almost unreadable. Crown and Anchor was also played for pennies, but the crap game was strictly for silver. Two or three times a day a police cruiser car would sneak up in an effort to round up the crap-shooters and card-players. But they seldom caught any of the gamblers, perhaps because they never really wanted to. The morality-squad officers who staged the raids were usually the fattest, footsorest, and slowest in a department that was a notorious repository for out-of-condition policemen.

At the bottom of the depression, the downtown book-makers were taking twenty-five-cent bets on the horse races. One of our neighbours was an incorrigible horse-player, who would work frantically to earn a dollar and head for the nearest bookie joint. He would have been better off to have spent the money on beer or tooth-paste, and he admitted as much. If he had saved all the money he lost on the races, he might have had $10 a month. The rub was that small change could never be saved; it was always frittered away buying minor essentials. He preferred to donate his quarters to the bookies in the hope that, when he occasionally won, he would have some important money to spend. Once, after a long stretch of bad luck, he hit a winning streak with a series of complicated wagers and won $25.

'That's luck for you,' he moaned. 'Here I am with ten-to-one shots coming home in parleys and all I have riding is lousy quarters. Why, if I'd been betting real dough today, I'd have made 200 bucks at least!' A typical horse-player's reaction! He and his wife went on a shopping splurge with his winnings and a couple of days later he was back betting quarters.

The pool-rooms and brokerage offices were all crowded throughout the depression, though seldom with customers. The brokerage offices supplied free newspapers and the pool-rooms furnished both recreation and heat. In the downtown rooms, the unemployed congregated in such numbers that the players often had to complain to the management in order to get elbow room for their cues.

Recreation, like almost everything else, depended a great deal on where the people lived. There was one fellow who, from the way he told it, spent most of the depression standing on the Arlington Bridge, watching box-cars being shunted over the hump in the C.P.R. assembly yard. He said he had become such an expert in gauging the speed of the cars that he could guess within a yard where they would stop. He used to wait around the Woodyard in search of someone to walk home with him so he could demonstrate his skill.

Those who lived within walking distance of the city police court never missed the morning show in court. Their boast was that they could forecast the sentences that would be passed out each morning by the magistrate's appearance when he came on the bench. If he walked slowly he was in good humour. If he walked quickly he was in a bad temper, and God help the drunks that came before him that day! The high court criminal cases at the law courts drew upon a city-wide audience. Some spectators would catch the case first at the coroner's inquest, attend the preliminary hearing in police court, and move on to the law courts when the case came to trial. Sex cases and murder trials naturally got the largest crowds, and those who got pushed out of one court would fight their way into another.

Most of the criminal-court spectators were self-appointed critics, and at recesses the corridors buzzed with arguments over the ability of the lawyers and judges. Like all grandstand quarterbacks from the ancient Romans onwards, they were prepared to sit in instant judgment on the performance of the gladiators at the bar, second-guess judicial rulings; and evaluate the testimony of the witnesses.

What they were seldom prepared to do, in police court or high court, was to concede that there was much real justice in the administration of Canadian law, and the more seniority they rung up as spectators, the more critical they became. This attitude can partly be explained by the fact that in any contest between the police and the individual, the spectators identified with the accused. The more hopeless the prisoner's case became, the more intense was the sympathy of his cheering section. Even hardened police reporters occasionally got carried away by the plight of an accused, although they usually identified with the police. For the spectators, taking sides kept the proceedings from becoming a colossal bore.

Life itself could never be a bore as long as there was a working radio within earshot. Radio-listening was a passion that the unemployed shared with the employed, the rich shared with the poor, and all the rural West with all the urban West. For the farm families, a radio in working order was a categorical imperative. It broke the barrier of isolation that had held the prairie West in its grip for almost fifty years. The radio was not only entertainment, it enabled the farm people to shut themselves away from the depression itself, from the dust, and from the wind that blew night and day with its incessant, deranging whine.

For them, day-time serials to which they listened were far from the badly contrived 'soap operas' that the critics scorned as 'washday weepers'. The radio was more like the telephone party-line on which real people discussed real problems of heartbreak or triumph. It was not uncommon for the difficulties of Papa David or Rose or Claudia to be critically appraised at a quilting bee or church social as well as in the beer parlour.

There were at least a dozen soap operas every day on the American radio networks, and half of them were carried by Canadian stations. Each program, including commercials, lasted fifteen minutes, and Procter and Gamble ran four of them off, one after the other, following the noon-hour. Others were spotted throughout the day to catch the housewives at moments of relaxation.

The characters in all programs teetered interminably on the sharp edge of disaster. When an author came up with something new in the way of a crisis, he milked it unashamedly. A minor mishap in Central City could have Dr. Brent preparing for surgery for days without getting a finger on a scalpel or sponge. *Ma Perkins, Pepper Young's Family, Big Sister, Road of Life, The Right to Happiness,* and *Guiding Light* went on forever from one disaster to another, although the casts were constantly changing. As actors and actresses absconded, got drunk too often, got married, or became pregnant, the characters were killed off and new parts introduced. More people died in imaginatively contrived accidents on radio than television violence thirty years later was ever able to dispatch.

The soap operas were the dross of radio, but there was much that was pure gold. It was possible at any time of an evening, any day of the week, to turn on the radio and escape from the depression into a world of beautiful music, comedy, and drama. It was the heyday of the big bands—Whiteman, Lombardo, the Dorseys, Crosby, Spitalny, Wayne King, Miller, Goodman, Gray, Waring—and sponsors fought to get them on the radio.

Simply to list the programs is an indication of the great variety of entertainment that was available.

Sunday evening began with the 'Eddie Cantor Hour', featuring Rubinoff and his violin, comedy skits, and superb singing. The 'Chase and Sanborn Hour' followed with Edgar Bergen and Charlie McCarthy, Dorothy Lamour, Nelson Eddy, and Don Ameche. Eddie Cantor and Edgar Bergen did more to destroy Sunday-evening church services than automobiles and golf combined. On the evenings in the rest of the week, there were Bing Crosby and the Kraft Music Hall, Rudy Vallee and his Connecticut Yankees, Glen Gray and his Casa Loma Orchestra, Guy Lombardo and his Royal Canadians, Fred Waring and his Pennsylvanians, Ben Bernie and all the Lads. There were vocalists in infinite variety: from John Charles Thomas to Dick Powell to Kenny Baker; from Lily Pons to Kate Smith to Harriet Hilliard. And they played and sang in the golden age of American music, in which Berlin, Kern, Porter, Gershwin, Rodgers, Carmichael, and half a hundred others filled the nights with lilting tunes and joyous lyrics.

Many dramatic programs were superbly done. The best legitimate actors and actresses appeared regularly in radio dramatic productions, and the best modern dramatists, up to and including Eugene O'Neill, were produced on radio. And the clowns! Fred Allen, Fibber McGee and Molly, Jack Benny and Mary Livingstone, George Burns and Gracie Allen, Lum and Abner, Fanny Brice as Baby Snooks, Joe Penner and his duck, Red Skelton, Ed Wynn the Fire Chief, Duffy's Tavern, Amos and Andy, the Easy Aces.

Canadian national radio was a toddling, often squalling youngster, but by 1936 it was moving out of its infancy. The problems of the world, the nation, and the provinces were being discussed by perceptive and articulate commentators like George Ferguson, B. K. Sandwell, Willson Woodside, Watson Kirkconnell, Frank Underhill, and professors and editors in growing numbers.

With such attractions and unlimited leisure, it was small wonder that radio-listening became the major amusement of the people of the Prairies. For the farm population, keeping the radio operating became a major preoccupation and crowning frustration. Lacking electricity, farm families had to rely on battery sets, some old models of which required three different types of batteries. Most required both dry cells and storage-type batteries; the first went dead and the second became uncharged. Farmers on relief could get their thirty-five-cent dry cells on their relief allowance with a minimum of skullduggery. In the bitterness of winter, trips into town for the usual necessities could be postponed, but when a radio battery conked out, a compelling new force came into play. Faced with a choice of missing *Fibber McGee and Molly*, or making a ten-mile round trip into town in thirty-below weather, there was no question that the choice would fall on making the trip.

The weirdest pastime I ever encountered on relief might well have derived from Allen's Alley or an adventure of Charlie McCarthy or Mortimer Snerd. Its central character was an automobile nut who didn't let his being on relief interfere with his compulsive shopping for used cars. We got our relief vouchers the same day, and I often ran into him at the Woodyard. He always had exciting new stories about his adventures among the used-car lots, some of which were probably true. There were dozens of used-car lots around, and he used to wander from one to another having the cars demonstrated for him by eager salesmen.

'Boy, are those guys persistent!' he said one day. 'I made the mistake of giving one of them my right address and was he tough to shake! Used to come around to the house and pester me and pester me. One day I got my landlady to tell him I had moved to Regina. He was sure disappointed. But I wonder what he'd have done if he knew I was on relief!'

One day he ran into a salesman who looked familiar. It was while they were out for a demonstration that the salesman recognized him.

'Say,' said the salesman, 'I know where I've seen you. You're on relief! You were at the Woodyard a couple of weeks ago, so how the hell can you afford to buy a car? I'll bet you're still on relief!'

They had taken the car out into the country for a road test. The salesman, wild with rage, cursed his customer, opened the car door, and pushed him out to get back home as best he could. Then, a few minutes later, the salesman came back, apologized, and picked him up and drove him home.

'Boy, what a sucker that salesman was! You see, for him to have recognized me from the Woodyard he had to be on relief himself. So when he's half way back to town he realizes I could turn him in to the investigators, so he gets in a panic and rushes back to pick me up. And now have I got that guy in a hole! When I feel like going for a ride at night, I just call this guy up, tell him I want to go for a ride, and believe me, I go for a ride! I sure as hell hope that guy don't sell enough cars to get off relief, 'cause I have a hunch when he does I'm going to get my can knocked off! But in the meantime, it's sure a wonderful feeling to have a car come and pick you up whenever you want it. One of these days I'm goin' to call him and have him chauffeur me out to the Woodyard for my groceries!'

His story should have been true, but it probably was not, because telling lies was also a popular recreation, and more lies were told about the relief administration and the Woodyard staff than about anything else. Perhaps 'lies' is too strong a word for the conversion of a story from third person to first person. The original episode might have centred on a minor triumph of a relief recipient over the investigation department. Once launched, the story grew and grew as one reliefer after another took possession of it, cast himself in the hero role, and put it back in circulation with embellishments. For most of us, living a colourful lie once in a while was much to be preferred to living the dull truth that imprisoned us.

CHAPTER VI

LANDLADIES AND A
WANT-AD HUSBAND

The Winnipeg unemployed and everybody remotely connected with them were in a constant uproar about housing. The rental allowance varied slightly according to the size of the family. Kay and I and Patty qualified for $13 a month, which meant we could rent one unfurnished room. A large family might get up to $18 a month, but the allowance was never sufficient to pay the rent on a modern house. This meant that no family living in a rented house could stay in it when they went on relief. It meant that people buying homes lost them, because the rental allowances were insufficient to keep up the payments and taxes. Eventually, the home-buying class got a small break. When the debt-adjustments boards became operative, foreclosures were stopped if interest was paid. In some cases the unemployed were able to draw enough relief-rent to pay interest and taxes, if the house was very small and the family very large.

The economic results of relief rents were depressed housing values, and stagnation in the house-building industry. The social consequences were worse. Neuroses became endemic faster than psychiatrists could find labels for them. Hundreds of broken homes would have resulted from rooming-house congestion had it not been for relief regulations that discouraged separations. Husbands and wives, after a year on relief, might reach a stage where they could barely abide the sight of each other. But they went on living together because there was no practical alternative, except for the husband to hop a freight-train and leave the country, which frequently happened.

The rental department at the Woodyard was under continuous siege by landlords seeking to evict tenants, by tenants wanting permission to move to new quarters, by tenants looking for help to bring rooming-house feuds under control, and by optimists trying to persuade officialdom to make exceptions in their cases.

The delusion that it was possible to make a living by renting rooms was one of the most persistent of the depression. Every third house outside the better-off districts was adorned with a card advertising 'Unfurnished Rooms for Rent'. The signs never came down because the unemployed family that moved in this month would probably be moving out the month after next. Our landlord in the Furby Street house could have stood as the epitome of all the star-crossed landlords of the depression. The house contained seven rooms and a bath, and, by using some beaver-board partitions, he was able to cut the living-room in half and come up with seven rentable rooms for seven individual families.

The landlord and his wife slept on a cot in the kitchen. Kay and I and Patty had the largest bedroom, on the second floor. When we got a double bed, a bed for three-year-old Patty, a dresser, a kitchen table and three chairs into a twelve-by-twelve room, there was little room to move. In this room we cooked and ate and slept, as, of course, did all the others in their rooms. Everyone in the house, save the landlord, cooked on electric plates. When the storm windows went on, it was easily possible, on entering the house at meal-time, to tell what everyone was having for supper. The trick we discovered was to eat early, for if you waited until everyone else was eating, the conglomeration of odours jaded even the best appetite.

Our landlord lived in a state of perpetual hyper-hysteria. He was discovering, as hundred of others were discovering, that running a rooming-house was a sure route to pauperism, if not to insanity. It was a matter of simple arithmetic. He paid $25 a month rent for the house, and his income from his seven tenants was $80 a month. At best, he had his rent free and $55 a month on which to live. His $55 surplus, however, was illusory from the beginning. Six families cooking on hot-plates and using electric irons ran his light bill up to $25 a month. He had to buy fuel, which in this non-insulated barn of a house ran to $35 a month in winter. He had to pay another $3 or $4 a month for water. The very best he could do was to go behind $10 a month, if he and his wife didn't eat.

It was worse than that, however, because one of his tenants had stopped paying her rent. She was a prospective mother who lived in the tiny room at the back. No longer able to work, she was engaged in a seemingly hopeless campaign to get the soldier father of the impending child to marry her or at least support her. The other tenants fed her and tried to comfort her and for a while her plight occupied much of everybody's attention. The landlord, who was essentially a kindly man, was sympathetic, too. But, when the economic pressure on him became unbearable, he would rush up to her room, pound on her door, and demand his rent. Eventually, the army got the marriage arranged and the women in the house went on an orgy of trunk-ransacking in order to give the girl a proper send-off.

We all kept to ourselves, and we got along fairly well until winter set in, when the strain involved in keeping children cooped up in a rooming-house began to tell. Patty had a five-year-old playmate who lived downstairs. When they played together it had to be in the halls and on the stairs. When they played they naturally fought and cried, so the other tenants complained and shooed them out of the hallways. In an effort to keep peace in the house, Kay and I took turns riding Patty around the block in her sleigh, a Spartan regimen in a Winnipeg winter.

There were other, more difficult problems for which there was no such easy solution, problems common to all the rooming-houses in the city. There were hundreds of similar houses—old, old houses with broken-down furnaces and fouled-up hot-water systems. Life in the Furby Street *ménage* was complicated by a washing-machine, for the use of which the tenants paid twenty-five cents a week. The landlady could never keep track of who had paid and who still owed, and the faulty water-heater disrupted wash-day schedules. Such wash-day anarchy developed that by nightfall on Mondays half the tenants would not be speaking to the other half, and nobody would be talking to Mrs. Landlord. As winter deepened, arguments over lack of heat and hot water intensified. Shouting matches could develop in a hallway and turn the house into bedlam. There was no such thing as a private argument in our rooming-house.

We spent the worst Christmas of our lives in the Furby Street house and decided to move. We then discovered landlords typical of another very large group—still-employed persons trying to overcome salary cuts by renting rooms. Kay located a room in a private home on Kelvin Street, but we were barely moved in before the landlady was pounding on the door demanding that we leave. She accused Kay of lying to her about Patty, of assuring her we had no children. She would positively have no children running in and out of her house, tracking in mud, soiling her wallpaper. We could stay the night, she said, but we would have to get out in the morning. Not on relief, we couldn't!

We reminded the lady she had signed a form to accept the relief rent, so there was no way in which we could be moved until at least a month was up. She stopped shouting at us and ran to the phone. She phoned the relief department, then she phoned the police, but she got no satisfaction anywhere. When her husband came home, the argument broke off for supper.

In the hiatus, Kay and I discovered that the room was hopeless anyway. Our bed, the dresser, and the kitchen table took up so much of the floor space that there was no place for the chairs. We sat on the edge of the bed to eat, with the chairs piled on the bed behind us. To sleep, we transferred the chairs from the bed to the top of the table. There was nothing for it but to find a much bigger room, if the Woodyard would let us move so quickly. Our conditional surrender only angered our landlady.

The woman's husband drove a delivery truck and they were early risers. Our room was on the second floor and there was an unoccupied third floor. At six o'clock next morning the lady put on a pair of heavy shoes and went into a tramping and stomping routine above our heads. While her coffee was boiling, she pounded back and forth with a clatter that rattled the windows and shook the ceiling. When we got up the bathroom door was locked, and it was a full hour before we discovered it was locked from the outside. I tried to pacify her by repeating our decision to leave as soon as we could and asked for the key to the bathroom. She let her blood pressure rise slowly before shouting that the bathroom would stay locked as long as we were in the house and so would the front door if we ever left.

I found a skeleton key and opened the bathroom door. Thereafter, every time we used the bathroom we left the hot water running. This brought the landlady rushing up the stairs, two at a time, to shut the tap and lock the door. That night when her husband came home, we arranged a truce by agreeing to move as soon as we could get arrangements made with the Woodyard. But as long as we stayed the landlady did the clod-hopper dance over our beds in the morning.

There was a plentiful supply of rooms for rent during the depression; the only trouble was that they all tended to rent for the same price, regardless of size, location, or condition. At first relief tenants were regarded with suspicion, but they were quickly transformed by economic conditions into a preferred clientele. Rooms that might bring $10 a month or less from cash customers yielded $12 to $13 from people on relief. The first bit of information landladies always elicited from prospective tenants was whether they were on relief. The payment of relief-rent might have been slow, but it was sure, and that was unlikely to be true of some non-relief renters who paid cash but fell far in arrears. So eager did some landladies become to get relief tenants that they would offer to kick back a dollar or two a month to the tenant out of the relief rent.

Few people on relief were ever much more satisfied with landlords than the landlords were with tenants. Discussions of housing and landlords bulked large in any gathering of the unemployed. There was a deadly sameness to the stories that were told and underlying them all was the yearning for the perfect landlady. We eventually found her in an old cottage on Chalmers Avenue. She was seventy-seven years old and had lived all her adult life in this little house, which her first husband had built. Though she had come out to Canada in the '80s, there was still a trace of the English Midlands in her speech. She was a handsome and well-preserved old lady.

The house itself was badly run down. The almost flat roof was high at the front and sloped towards the rear. One storey in height, the house had no foundation or basement and was simply set on beams resting on the ground. It had last been painted perhaps twenty years before, and the paint might have been red or orange or yellow. It was simply a nondescript rust colour when we moved in. The original structure had probably contained two rooms, but more rooms had been added as time passed until it contained five. What sold us on it was that we could have two rooms, one to eat and cook in and one to sleep in. Another advantage was the yard, where Patty could play. We had the exclusive use of the front door, which opened into our kitchen-living-room.

Our landlady lived alone on the old-age pension and had been married at least twice and perhaps three times. She had little equity left in her house for it was plastered with hospital liens and she was several years behind in her taxes. From her $20-a-month pension, repairs were out of the question. We had this brought forcefully to our attention soon after we moved in. The toilet was located on the west side of the house in a little closet off the kitchen. The door from our kitchen into her living-room was also on the west side of the house. But the door leading from her living-room into her kitchen was on the east side. To get from our quarters to the kitchen it was necessary to cut diagonally across her living-room. The old lady always went to bed soon after dark and slept in a room off the living-room to the east. In order to ease our passage through her room, she had moved all her furniture to one side. We learned to make the journey in the dark and so got into the habit of closing our door quickly to keep the light from awakening her.

On the night in question I had taken off my shoes and was heading for the toilet in the dark. It was raining heavily. On my second step my foot landed in a pan of water. I swore, thrashed around, and my other foot kicked a jam-pail full of water. In the stillness of the house I must have sounded like an invading burglar. The old lady awoke and came out of her room full of apologies.

'Oh, I forgot to tell you about the pails. How stupid of me! Did you hurt yourself? Now, how did I ever forget to tell you about the pails?'

It transpired that the roof had been leaking for years. Unable to make repairs, she had done the next best thing—caught the water as it dripped through. She knew where every leak was located and when rain threatened she took down half a dozen empty jam-tins and a couple of pans. She knew so precisely where to set each tin that she seldom had a drop of water to wipe up after a rain.

This house, we were to discover that winter, was one of the most uninsulated houses in the city of Winnipeg. For both heating and cooking we acquired a small kitchen range with burned-out grates. The stove would boil water and fry eggs, but the oven was almost useless. When winter came, we were in trouble about heat. The only fuel we were given was cordwood. The fire-box in the stove was so small that the wood had to be chopped exceedingly fine in order to be burned in it. Nothing disappears quicker than fine-cut wood in a stove on a cold winter day.

On cold nights, Kay and I took turns staying up late. One of us would stay up till after midnight and get such a roaring fire going that the top of the stove would be red hot. A full kettle of water would be boiling madly when the stove was shut off and the lights put out. By five o'clock the next morning the water in the kettle on the stove would be frozen solid. The walls of the room were decorated with medallions of frost the size of pennies where the moisture had gathered on all the nail-heads. There was one corner where this frost never melted and the medallions grew larger and larger as winter passed.

To keep warm, Kay and Patty and I slept in the same bed. We piled on every blanket and quilt we owned. On top of them we put our overcoats. I put my socks under my pillow when I went to bed and put my hat on a chair within reach. When at last I had screwed up enough courage to get up, I would reach under the pillow, retrieve the socks and put them on. Then I'd slip the bed-clothes expertly aside and get into my overcoat. Towards the end of the winter I could put on my overcoat without getting out of bed and often without waking Kay. In a single motion I would be into my pants and out to the kitchen. Once the match was touched to the paper, I was back into bed again. Sometimes, on a very cold morning, I'd be in and out several times before the house was warm enough to live in.

We had not lived long in the little house on Chalmers Avenue before we began to notice our landlady's wide circle of gentleman friends. We had to be in and out of her kitchen a good deal, and during the first month she must have introduced us to half a dozen old codgers having tea with her. Strangely, we never saw the same one twice. It was not until several months later that she volunteered a rather simple explanation. She had been advertising for a husband, and these were prospective suitors who came in response to her newspaper advertisement:

'Refined English lady, owner of small, comfortable home,
in receipt of old-age pension, would like to meet refined
gentleman, old-age pensioner, object matrimony. Write
particulars to Box 1621, Free Press.'

Her earlier advertisement had not produced a suitable husband, and she was about to try again. She had long since passed the point of surviving on the old-age pension. Our rent helped, but she still couldn't manage and she wasn't going to try any longer. She would insert another advert, she said, if I would take it to the *Free Press* for her. She wanted to assure us, however, that if she was successful it need make no difference to us. She was not going to marry just anybody. She would make sure that the man she got was sober and quiet and would not disturb us. We would just go on living as her tenants, and she hoped as her friends, as long as we cared to stay.

So it was that I took the advertisement to the newspaper and we sat back to await developments. She got perhaps a dozen replies and the winnowing process began. The technique employed was simple. The applicants were asked to call on a given afternoon. The lady made tea, and they sat and talked for an hour or so. If first impressions had been mutually favourable, the old geazer would be invited to return on another afternoon for another cup of tea. If she had drawn a blank, so to speak, he was rejected in the friendliest possible manner. She would invent insuperable differences in taste, temperament, or religion as a bar to union. On the other hand, if she was favourably impressed but the gentleman was not, he would simply not show up for the second date. While this system made courtship much slower than it might have been otherwise, our landlady preferred it that way.

During the next several weeks there was a parade of ancient Romeos to our house. Some of them were spry old fellows who scarcely seemed over sixty. Others looked like lost apostles and came hobbling up on canes. We could have told them that they would not do, for no suitor not sound of wind and limb had a chance of capturing her hand. Often after the suitors left, she would waylay Kay or me and ask for our judgment.

'That was Mr. Armitage,' she would say. "What did you think of *him?*'

With our landlady it was always best to be as vague as possible, so we would mumble something non-commital.

'Yes, he is rather nice in some ways, but he likes bacon and eggs for breakfast. He said his first wife was a wonderful cook and when they lived on the farm he always had bacon and eggs for breakfast, sometimes porridge too. He wanted to know if I liked bacon and eggs, and I can hardly stand tea on my stomach in the morning. Anyway, I'm such a poor cook that I'm afraid he would be disappointed. But he was nice and clean, wasn't he? I always say that if a man is clean that is about all you can ask for. Still, he'd always be thinking of his first wife's cooking. It's too bad, he was quite a nice man.'

If her prospects got over the first hurdle of personality, she went to work on the state of their bodies. She was particularly on the look-out for asthma, which had carried off her last husband. One old fellow got over several hurdles without her discovering that he had a heart condition. He was dropped like a cat in a bag off a bridge.

They came and they went and it seemed for a while that the search was going to go on forever. But one day an aged Lochinvar turned up to sweep her off her feet. His resemblance to cartoonist Bruce Bairnsfather's 'Old Bill' was quite remarkable, for he had the same straggling moustache and round face. He was a bit on the small side and did not look at all like a seventy-year-old. As it turned out, he was not seventy and did not get an old-age pension. His son, with whom he lived, talked him into answering the advertisement and came around to inspect and approve his future stepmother. The son promised his father that he would provide him with $20 a month until he got his pension in a couple of years. He reneged on this promise, and the old lady was to discover to her sorrow that she could have taken almost any one of the other applicants and been ahead of the game.

The old man, however, was a forceful character and swept her off to the altar. The week before the marriage was as hectic as if it was to be her first leap into the matrimonial pool instead of her third, for certain, and perhaps her fourth. She was ecstatically happy and did a thorough house-cleaning job with high enthusiasm. She fixed over her best dress for the wedding and became as flighty as a June-bug. She would make tea and forget to drink it or neglect to put tea in the pot and drink half a cup of hot water before discovering her mistake. She and her intended would hold hands under the table, billing and cooing like a couple of pigeons.

'Don't mind us, Mr. Gray,' she said when I blundered in on them with a kettle of water. 'We are just a couple of silly kids.' In the evening they would walk around the back garden holding hands and laughing, completely oblivious of the amusement they were causing in the neighbourhood.

Love in such riotous bloom in December was amusing indeed. But what were we laughing at? What was so funny about a social order that drove a nice old lady to advertise for a husband in order to stay alive in our community? And not only her. There were dozens of others who sought the same solution for their problems every week. Was this to be our own fate, everybody's fate, fifty years down the same road? It was a melancholy question that was difficult enough to think about without having to live with it. After more than a year on relief, there was no comfort for Kay and me in any of the visible portents. A week after the wedding we went looking for other rooms.

CHAPTER VII

TUXEDOS WERE FOR
DITCH-DIGGING

Everybody on relief had landlord trouble; but not everybody had it at the same time, or with the same frequency. Some tenants could get along with landlords for months at a stretch; other renters moved six or seven times a year. The landlord crisis, therefore, was the reverse of the clothing crisis, which, once it arrived, stayed on as a daily feature of life on relief. The clothing crisis was very much worse for the women than for the men, and for the mothers of small children it often arose half a dozen times a day. It was something, moreover, that came sooner or later to every family on relief.

The clothing policy in 1931–2 was easily stated: no clothes. The authorities were content to leave the clothing of the unemployed to private charity whose time-honoured function it was to distribute cast-off clothing to the poor. The Winnipeg *Tribune*, in the first years, sponsored the Winnipeg Friendship League, which made emergency winter clothing for the unemployed its special project. There were several other charities that also distributed second-hand clothing, but, as we were to discover, their largess was reserved for non-relief families.

Most of the families were well enough supplied with clothing when they went on relief; it was the wearing-out process that did them in. The moment of panic arrived when it was discovered that the trousers to the Sunday suit were the only wearable trousers in the house. What would happen when these wore out? Unless some way was discovered to raise $2 with which to buy a pair of work-pants, the worn-out trousers would be patched and worn, and repatched and worn. It was thus not unusual to see an unemployed musician doing a stint of ditch-digging in the pants to his tuxedo, or an unemployed landscape artist raking leaves in a wind-breaker fashioned out of a painter's old smock.

Our first clothing crisis arrived when my shoes wore out. In fact, the soles had begun to wear through soon after I became unemployed, but, whenever we raised any money, getting shoes repaired was not even on our list of priorities. By the time we got on relief, the soles were worn through and I fashioned insoles out of cardboard before going out. When we ran out of cardboard, and I was ill abed, Kay took a hand and went out to scrounge a pair of shoes for me. In our self-supporting days, we had made the usual contributions towards the Community Chest and other local charities, and in the back of Kay's mind was the idea that perhaps we would get some of our own back. She called on the Community Chest.

A friendly secretary explained that the Chest worked only through institutions, and, while she was sure the unemployed were well looked after, it might do no harm for Kay to call on one of these charities directly. Kay got a couple of names and went off to the Home Welfare Bureau on Main Street. Here she was greeted by a pair of do-gooders who were enjoying a day off from their dishes and housework. They mistook her for a prospective giver when she entered, for she was an attractive girl who knew how to wear clothes, and her clothes were still good. To convince the charity ladies that she had come to get something from them took time. Then they were stumped. No young woman had ever before come in to see about getting shoes for her husband, and they were low on shoes anyway. There were other women sorting clothing in the back of the room and there was much shouting and hallooing back and forth.

'Mrs. Jones,' bawled one of the receptionists, 'do you know where a woman on relief would go to get shoes for her husband?' Several of the ladies left their places at the far end of the room and came up to help solve the problem. One youngish woman quickly took command.

'Tell these people to go to the Relief Department. All they have to do,' she said to Kay, 'is to go to the Relief Department and get the shoes. There is no problem there. My, some of the people on relief!'

The women crowded around Kay, giving advice and arguing with each other. Kay's feelings were badly bruised but she blurted out that the Relief Department did not supply clothes or shoes, and that was why she was there.

Some of the charity ladies were inclined to argue. Others just stared at Kay, and she noticed one of them nudge another and point to her engagement ring. Their exchanged looks said, 'What was a young woman wearing diamonds doing trying to beg a pair of shoes for her husband? What indeed?'

In that winter we had sold everything we owned—car, my watch, fountain pen, cuff links, the radio, and every bit of surplus household equipment we could spare. But the idea of parting with Kay's engagement ring never occurred to either of us, though it had such an attraction for store clerks that Kay stopped wearing it when she went shopping for groceries with relief tickets. The expressions on the faces of the charity ladies that morning was enough for Kay. She fled the place and was still shaking with anger when she got home an hour later.

Strangely enough, I might have saved her this humiliation, if I had made one more inquiry at the Woodyard. I had asked a couple of times about getting my shoes repaired and had been told each time it was out of the question. Soon after Kay's adventure, I was relating the experience while waiting in line.

'Look, friend,' said a relief gang *cognoscente*, 'that's a lot of booshwah about not issuing clothes. Next time you get a work-slip, show the clerk your shoes and he'll send you to the superintendent. You'll get shoes.'

He was right. The superintendent reached into a drawer, extracted a book of forms, and filled one out. It authorized the T. Eaton Company to furnish me with one pair of $3 work-boots. I persuaded the shoe clerk to let me have a pair of dress oxfords, which he readily conceded were work-boots for white-collar workers like us.

The clothing crisis reached its peak for everybody on relief in the late fall of 1931. The Communist Party was still outlawed, but the Communists worked through the Workers Unity League and the Ukrainian Labour-Farmer Temple Association, and were forever trying to get an unemployed association going. The only riot I ever got into was a combined clothing and anti-eviction uprising the Communists staged at the City Hall. Some aldermen got shoved around, some small rocks were thrown, and a few heads were cracked. It was not much of a riot, but it was enough to get some small attention paid to our clothing problem.

By working all the angles, a man on relief could outfit himself with a hip-length work-coat, a pair of heavy work-pants, mitts, heavy socks, and work-boots. In 1932 a shoe-repair depot was set up to service the unemployed. It put most of the shoe-repair shops out of business and their owners on relief. None of these steps were taken, however, until more than 5,000 families had gone without clothing replacements for more than a year, as families were doing all over Canada. Clothing merchants went broke. Clothing factories shut down, clothing workers went on relief, and nobody got any new clothes. When clothing was eventually supplied, the waste was outrageous. Thousands of short-length reefer coats were supplied to people who had very little use for them. The shirts were made of heavy, rough cotton, fitted badly, and looked like a textile designer's bad dream. By 1933 a reliefer in Winnipeg could be identified by his shirt as far as he could be seen. By the mid-summer of 1932, all the clothes I had when we went on relief were worn out. It was, of course, impossible to go looking for the only kind of work I could do in the kind of clothes the city provided. So I didn't go looking for work, and neither did the other white-collar workers who found themselves stranded on relief without clothes. Few of us would have found jobs anyway, and none of us could have taken them in the clothes we owned if a sudden boom had blown up.

During 1932, I was much too busy, trying to get an education and trying to become a writer, to waste time job-hunting. But every few months, a desperate urge to get off relief would set in and I'd stop in at the Grain Exchange to make the rounds of prospective employers. It was like visiting a race-track the week after the races are over—most of the stalls are empty and those waiting to move their horses away are likely to be morose and unpleasant. So it was in the Grain Exchange. Half the building seemed to be empty. The trading floor was silent, minutes would pass between trades in the wheat pit, and the brokers spent most of the day playing dominoes in the smoking-room. The Grain Exchange building, however, was still the Mecca for the former members who had gone broke and the former clerks who were unemployed. They haunted its corridors and soaked up the empty chair-space in the brokerage offices that were still in business.

My visits to the Exchange became highly irregular when the seat wore out of my last pair of pants. I never got over being sensitive about the relief uniform and seldom wore it up town. However, the excuses to go up town seemed to become increasingly compelling after my clothes wore out, and devising a scheme to get a new suit of clothes became something of an obsession.

My problem was solved by a chance meeting with one of my

former employers. Because I was wearing relief clothes, it was easy to explain my clothing predicament and to ask if he could look through his closets and see if he had an old suit I could wear. He outweighed me by forty pounds but readily agreed to see what he could find. A couple of days later he had a suit for me. It was a beautiful cloth and was hardly worn. He explained that it was too small for him, but I always doubted this. I think he simply picked out one of the suits he wore regularly and gave it to me.

When I got home and tried it on, the shine on my trophy clouded somewhat. It fitted like a tent. I had boasted that my wife had acquired a wizardry with a sewing-machine that would enable her to make any alterations the suit required. But the more she looked at it, the less confident Kay became of her ability to remodel it. After spending the better part of a day trying to find the key to the puzzle, she threw up her hands and said the only thing to do was to take the suit to a tailor. There was a tailor shop on Johnson Avenue near Kelvin Street, and the next day we took the suit in for an estimate on the cost of alterations. He was a typical tailor, round-shouldered, near-sighted, and full of pride in his craft.

'People don't buy suits like this any more,' he said sadly as he examined the seams, felt the padding, and looked at the stitching of the lining.

'Beautiful,' he said more to himself than to us. 'A beautiful bit of tailoring! A tailor made this suit, not some ditch-digger running a sewing-machine and ruining a decent trade! You know, friend, I can sit by this window for days and never see a well-made suit go past. The sewing-machine did that. People don't want to pay even for the cost of materials these days, let alone let a man make a living. These cursed department stores! Suits with two pairs of pants for $21! The worst bargain a man can get for his money is one of these ready-made suits. Why, I get them in here to press and it just breaks my heart to look at what passes for tailoring today. I'll tell you it was different when I learned my trade! Why, when I was a boy, you couldn't touch a pair of shears or a needle for the first two years! Today men who have never held a needle are cutters in these factories! Mass production, everything is mass production!'

Eventually he got to the business of considering the alterations. I put on the coat and he stood back and surveyed it for perhaps a minute. Then he stepped up with his marking crayon and marked it along the seams in the back and under the arms. His price for the job was probably reasonable enough—$4—but it gave us quite a shock. I explained that we were on relief and getting that much cash together would take time. He didn't seem to mind when we took the coat away and promised to return when we had raised the money.

'Just bring it in any time and I'll be glad to fix it for you. It'll be a pleasure to work on material like that.'

I was as far from having a wearable suit as ever, for $4 was beyond our ability to pay. Then one day Kay sat looking at the coat and said:

'I wonder.' She wondered some more and took down the coat. The tailor's crayon marks were still on it. 'All I'd have to do would be follow his marks. I'll rip it out along all the seams he marked and then sew it back up along his lines. Why didn't I think of that before?'

The lining was taken out, a razor blade cut the seams, and in a few minutes the coat was reduced to its essential parts. The tailor might have produced a better fit than Kay did, but it would not have been $4 better. When I stepped into the made-over suit and stepped out for a walk, I felt like a million dollars. It was only after the job was completed that we thought of the dirty trick we were playing on the tailor, so we agreed that when we got off relief I would go around and buy a suit from him, but I never did. In the interval I avoided Johnson Avenue in the vicinity of his store.

My made-over suit lasted until we were off relief. The episode only went to prove that a man could usually solve his clothing problem when it reached a crisis stage. But for the women it was ever so much worse, if only by reason of the fact that it never came to the crisis point with the same shattering suddenness. For women it was more a process of erosion, of stockings disappearing into holes, house-dresses disintegrating, party frocks losing their gewgaws to become house-dresses. With us, things were better on this score than in most families. Kay's mother and sisters came to her rescue, and she became so skilful with her sewing-machine that it was possible to keep Patty well enough dressed. Yet even with the generous help she got, Kay's supply of dresses dwindled sadly.

For women without relatives to help, the clothing famine turned life into a near-nightmare. Women were confined more closely to their homes, where eating, sleeping, and living in one room with a couple of children under foot became almost too much to bear. Without the simple diversions and excursions that a good dress could provide, impossible strains were imposed on the marriage ties. Men could put on their hats and walk out, and even the time spent on make-work projects came to have a recreational undertone. Women who put on their hats and went window-shopping in shabby clothes usually returned in worse humour than they had been in when they left. The clothing famine, moreover, was a potent factor in disrupting the whole process of family formation. There was no provision of medical care for the wives of the unemployed who became pregnant, and, more important, there was no provision of the raw materials for the knitting, sewing, and crib-making that is such an ecstatic aspect of child-bearing. It was small wonder that, when sex reared its head in relief-gang conversations, the topic veered around to one of the primary preoccupations of family life on relief—the avoidance of pregnancy.

Yet avoidance of pregnancy was not an inevitable and universal preoccupation. Having babies on relief at least allowed young mothers to reclaim their status as important human beings, if only for a week or two, just as there were young fathers who rose heroically above the relief environment. I met one such prospective father on a relief gang, whose love story was the tenderest I had ever heard. He was approaching fatherhood for the first time and his most recent concern had been to gather together the sum of $3.50. The breakdown was: seventy-five cents for a taxi to take his wife to the hospital, $2 for a dozen roses, and seventy-five cents to get her home again. He had that $3.50, and to remove the temptation to spend it on anything else he had deposited it with a taxi man and a flower shop.

'Maybe it sounds silly,' he said, 'but when we were first married a couple of years ago we used to spend hours arguing about what we would name our first baby. And Betty had everything worked out how she would spot the baby's bed and how she would trim his clothes and everything like that. I used to tell Betty she'd have a private room at the hospital and I'd buy her new roses every day. Well, it was all wonderful then. But when we had dough nothing happened. Then, when everything went sour and we had to go on relief, along comes the baby. Maybe when you've got folks around it ain't so bad. But I got nobody but a couple of sisters out in Vancouver, and Betty's mother died last summer. God, it gets so lonesome at a time like this, especially for Betty.'

He was an unemployed railway brakeman, to whom a watch was as vital as a right hand. But he had pawned his Hamilton for $15 and made an advance payment to a doctor to look after his wife. Then every nickel or dime he could scrounge went for wool and satin with which to make baby things. As the time for the new arrival approached, nickels and dimes became exceedingly scarce. How did he get his essential $3.50 for flowers and taxi fares? By working on relief gangs. Unlike the rest of us, who concentrated on avoiding the boondoggles, he got as many work-slips as possible. The Relief Department provided two car tickets for each day a job lasted. My friend borrowed a bicycle to get to the jobs and at the end of two days had four car tickets, which he could sell for fifteen cents a pair. That gave him thirty cents. Another reliefer, who lined up a couple of odd jobs on the sly, paid him fifty cents a day to do his relief-job stint for him. Two days at fifty cents came to a dollar plus four more car tickets.

I met the man only once on a relief gang and never saw him again. His story stayed with me because of the glow that came into his face when he talked about his roses, and how he knew that Betty would cry when she saw them, but they would make her so very happy.

CHAPTER VIII

INTO THE WONDERFUL
WORLD OF BOOKWORMS

In the life of just about every living thing, there comes a time for a second look, and a momentary halt is called in the struggle with environment. It happens with colts being halter-broken after the third or fourth futile leap for liberty. It happened for most of the unemployed two or three months after going on relief, when they stopped fighting the idea and began to learn how best to live with totally altered circumstances.

It happened for me when Johnny Timchuk wandered into my life in the King Edward Sanatorium. Timchuk was a hollow-eyed, all-skin-and-bones North End Ukrainian for whom time had almost run out. He had quit school in the fifth or sixth grade and had drifted from one unskilled job to another—dish-washer, labourer, waiter, and eventually second cook on a railway dining-car. A routine X-ray had uncovered a tubercular infection and led to hospitalization, which lasted for five years. If he had read anything at all in the pre-hospital years, it was probably trash. He entered the hospital, discovered its library, and picked up a book. He never stopped reading after that. It might almost be said that he read himself to death, for if hospital rules interfered with his reading he broke the rules. He ignored the daytime mandatory sleep periods and read late into the night. A new night supervisor once confiscated his bed-lamp, but he smuggled in a flash-light and read with his book under the bed-sheet. Eventually the hospital let him go his own way, though his condition gradually worsened.

By the time I entered the hospital, he had five years of concentrated study behind him. He could talk knowingly on almost any subject—about Plato and Bruno and Hegel; about Marx and Henry George and Kropotkin. A conversation that started about birds on the hospital lawn could launch him in a flight after the voyage of the *Beagle*. He was the hospital's walking encyclopedia and philosopher-in-residence, who knew about everything and believed in nothing. All this I discovered during my first few days as a patient. Though he was mortally ill, the nurses no longer tried to keep Johnny Timchuk in bed. He visited around from ward to ward during the day, and, perhaps because I was new, he frequently came to see me. He would sit on a chair by my bed for a few minutes and talk. Then he would return to his bed for an hour and come back for another short visit. In the course of the first week, he pieced together his view of the world. It was Spenglerian-*cum*-Marxist— the world was going to hell in a hack. The depression would get worse instead of better and would end in another world war, as had always happened.

But so what? People like us, he said, who had tuberculosis or were on relief, were living in Utopia. For the first time in history people like us could stop worrying about making our own living, because society was keeping us. Think of that! It was giving us a chance only the wealthy once enjoyed—to understand the world in which we lived. Why, he asked, was I so impatient to get well? The depression would still be there when I got out. The depression would have to run its course before there would ever again be jobs for men like me. So why weren't we all using the depression to further our education, to learn about life and what made the world go round? Everything a man needed to know about everything was in a book some place. The only trick was to locate the right books.

He had put his finger on the problem that worried everybody on relief—what were we going to do with the rest of our lives?

Everything we knew about making a living, and most of the skills we had acquired, had become obsolete. What skill could a man acquire that would be in demand when prosperity came back? It was a question that building tradesmen, mechanics, and even professional people were asking, as well as book-keepers, wholesale warehousemen, and retail clerks. Johnny Timchuk said it in a way that made the logic of the situation seem irrefutable. My endless pursuit of non-existent jobs *was* a rat-race to nowhere. The thing to do *was* to stop fighting the depression and start making use of it.

It was indeed.

Whatever thirst-for-knowledge bug it was that bit Johnny Timchuk, he passed the fever on to me, and it was not long before I was almost as hopelessly addicted to reading as he was. He had a small library of good reprints stored under his bed—several dozen books in the 'Modern Library' and the 'Thinkers' Library' that ran the gamut from Hume to Voltaire to Darwin. He had also collected all the writing of that fascinating old American heretic, Bishop William Montgomery Brown. A well-to-do Episcopalian divine, Brown was Bishop of the Arkansas by the time he was forty-five. In 1912, at the age of fifty-seven, he retired to Galion, Ohio, where after the Russian revolution a preoccupation with Darwinism led him to communism. He wrote a book, *Communism and Christianity*, and his fellow bishops charged him with heresy. He was convicted by a court of bishops in 1925 and defrocked. Until his death at eighty-two, Brown waged endless war on Christianity and published a dozen books on science and religion from the Communist viewpoint.

All these Johnny Timchuk pressed upon me with the enthusiasm of a missionary for a new convert. When I left the hospital just before he died, I, too, was afire with determination to make some sense out of the world while I waited for employment to find me, though when I hit the public library I scarcely knew where to begin. I approached the bookshelves almost like a drunk in a liquor store—eager to grab everything in sight. My batting average in selecting readable books was seldom over .500. To set against such palpable failures as Marx and Hegel were discoveries of delight—Thorstein Veblen's *Theory of the Leisure Class* and Alfred Marshall's development of the theory of marginal utility.

In another time and in another context, blundering into Marshall and Veblen together would have been like landing in the middle of a private brawl. But I was able to read both without appreciating the extent to which Veblen's ideas conflicted with those of Marshall, because I was living in the midst of a world collapse in prices, mass unemployment, artificial surpluses of everything man could produce, and *de facto* shortages of everything man wanted to consume.

Marshall's synthesis of the theory of marginal utility at least made our world understandable. Wherever we looked from Winnipeg, marginal surpluses had destroyed the value of whole commodities. A few tons too many potatoes ruined the price of thousands of tons. A comparatively few million surplus bushels of wheat that nobody would buy destroyed the value of a billion bushels that people needed for food. A dozen extra workers might destroy the wage structure of a whole union.

Instead of stagnating while waiting for the law of supply and demand to function, we should be out getting rid of marginal surpluses and managing our forces, to get the economy back on the rails! Like every convert discovering the first traces of a new truth, I was irrepressibly eager to share it and became as hepped on managing surpluses as the Communists were on Russia's five-year plan. I was, moreover, getting so much out of my concentrated assault on the public library's store of knowledge that I was convinced everybody else ought to be similarly engaged, and this led to my only involvement in the do-good field, thirty years ahead of the times.

It was almost impossible to live in polyglot Winnipeg without becoming aware of the handicap the language barrier created for new Canadians, particularly adults. They could neither read nor write English, and thus many avenues of employment were closed to them regardless of their skills or knowledge. They depended on their children to read newspapers for them and to interpret the radio news. It was not long before the children knew more about their country and the affairs of their city than their parents knew; and they knew they did. In such circumstances parental authority was soon challenged. Too many immigrant youngsters got on to crime escalators that moved them from juvenile court to city police court and the penitentiaries.

Several thousand immigrant families were on relief in Winnipeg, all with unlimited time for study. We had scores of vacant buildings in the city, most of them acquired by the city for taxes. We had school teachers on relief. Instead of directing the unemployed to compulsory boondoggles, why not send them to school? The wife could be included and could attend while her husband took care of the children. If they had no children, they could attend together.

I worked out the details of my plan and sent it to the mayor. The mayor replied to my letter but did nothing. I went to the chairman of the Relief Committee and wandered in and out of the City Hall looking for aldermen to buttonhole. Everybody said it was a very good idea, but nobody did anything about it. I took it to the Board of Trade, but the secretary was worried about the effect of the cost on the tax-rate. I wrote letters to labour unions and talked to politicians in all parties. Nothing happened. Nothing ever happened. Eventually I forgot the whole project and concentrated on my own education via the public library.

The library on William Avenue not only did a thriving business lending books, it was a half-way house on the route to the Woodyard, a wonderful place in which to get warm on a cold day. Sometimes there were so many people soaking up heat that half the chairs in the reading-room were occupied by non-readers. It was a special haven for the homeless and ageing single unemployed, some of whom might spend eight hours a day, six days a week, in its warm, friendly quiet. Some of them read, some of them just sat and looked at books and magazines until they fell asleep. The librarians frowned on sleepers and would occasionally clear them out of the reading-rooms. Some of the elderly loafers developed great skill in disguising their slumber, and could fall fast asleep without letting their heads slump or their books fall off their knees to the floor.

All over western Canada, people were reading as never before. They may have fallen asleep over books and magazines that were beyond their understanding, but they were searching for a sign, a light to guide them out of their own personal wilderness. As they searched, the age of dogma came to an end in western Canada. The old ideas over which men had fought so bitterly less than twenty years before gradually disappeared. A new generation of dissenters was about to come into its own, with new heresies, and the leaders of the new radicalism would come from the groups who were once the epitome of orthodoxy and conformity—the teachers and the preachers.

The most avidly read book on the non-fiction shelves of the Winnipeg Public Library in 1932 was *History and Power of Mind* by Robert Ingalese. The author was a California occultist and his thesis went something like this: The universe was permeated by spiritual current into which the human mind could be tuned. By the sheer power of concentration, an individual could achieve any ends he desired by hitch-hiking on the current. Each person's aura—

everybody had one—reflected his personality and the aura in turn was governed by the way the individual related to the cosmic current. Success in life, Ingalese promised, came to those who developed the power of absolute concentration, which raised one materially, spiritually, and morally above his fellows, and led him ultimately to nirvana beyond the stars. The library owned three copies of the book and the end-papers were completely covered by the date stamps. The book was transparent malarky, but its popularity was an indication of the desperate search for an escape from the depression.

As Frederick Lewis Allen pointed out, the depression destroyed the American businessman as folk-hero of the United States. In Canada, it was not so much a matter of reputations being destroyed as of reputations withering away, because after 1929 none of the respectable Canadian leadership cadres produced anything worth listening to. This was true not only of bank presidents, politicians, and labour leaders. It was equally true of professional economists and amateur wiseacres, of newspaper editors and freelance Aristotles of the service-club circuits. The wild improbabilities of *History and Power of Mind* were at least an escape from the dreary platitudes of Prime Minister R. B. Bennett or the Honourable W. L. Mackenzie King.

Canada's coroner's inquest on the capitalist system was complicated by the fascination that the works of Adam Smith held for Canadian deep-thinkers. The Grain Exchange, to a man, fought against the establishment of a minimum price for wheat even as world prices fell to a 400-year low. The idea of a minimum wage was equally anathema to the Canadian business community, and even the hesitant half-steps the Bennett administration took to shore up the sagging economy drew thunderous denunciation from the apostles of *laissez-faire*. In any event, the ideas that were to play any part in the future of Canada had to come from outside the country. Mostly they came from England, and from the Roosevelt New Deal.

The economics shelves at the libraries started to take up more room. Books by Beatrice and Sidney Webb, John Strachey, H. G. Wells, and Aldous Huxley rubbed covers with those of J. M. Keynes, F. A. von Hayek, C. H. Douglas, and Joseph Soddy. They naturally went unread by the overwhelming majority of people on relief, but the ideas sifted down to the unemployed in a veritable blizzard. On any work-gang, in any line-up, name any phase of almost any economic subject, and there would likely be somebody on hand who knew enough about it to talk about it. This was the age of reprints and pamphlets. Tracts circulated in Winnipeg from all over the world, from the Townsend Clubs of California, which were promoting $200-a-month pensions for all unemployed over sixty, to the *Protocols of the Elders of Zion*, which promoted race hatred. There were reprints going around of Pope Pius XI's *Quadragesimo Anno*, tracts from Father Coughlin, British Israel, and the New Thought movement.

It was inevitable, in this worst deflation in our history when a shortage of money affected everybody, that most discussions bore down heavily on the 'money problem'. Monetary cranks materialized out of nowhere. They turned up at church meetings and at union meetings, and the Market Square on Sunday nights was alive with them. Some made speeches, and some heckled other speakers. Even the hell-fire and damnation preachers took occasional time out to direct attention to God's law, which required that all debts be cancelled every seven years.

The Woodyard broke out in a rash of monetary reformers who had been reading up on the Bank Act, or listening to someone who had. The all-pervading lethargy lifted a little, but the more interest was aroused in banking and currency, the less there was in politics and politicians. The inadequacies of politicians were universally assumed and the word became a dirtier epithet than it had ever been before. The process of abasement of politics was accentuated by the new movements, which were essentially anti-political.

Howard Scott, who crossed Thorstein Veblen with Joseph Soddy to produce Technocracy, called for the abolition of political management of the economy. Money must be replaced by a new unit of currency—productive energy. The price system based upon money inevitably got society deeper and deeper into debt, because purchasing power was outstripped by production. For a while the Technocracy theory carried everything before it. Branches with the circular maroon-and-gray emblem sprang up all over western Canada. Yet Technocracy never really got over being the gospel of dilettantes. The best comment I ever heard was on a leaf-raking boondoggle. A recent convert to Technocracy had held the floor for perhaps ten minutes. He paused for breath and a reliefer threw his harpoon:

'Seems to me,' he interjected, 'from what you say, this Technocracy means we should turn everything over to the engineers. It would be sort of like letting the city engineer's department run everything, only on a national scale. Well, we've been working for them guys and you can take it from me, brother—I don't think any goddamn engineer is all that goddamn smart!'

Among the unemployed the tendency at first was to blame the depression on an international big-business conspiracy. Somebody obviously had to be getting rich out of it, or the financial rulers of the world would put an end to the depression. After a while, this argument lost its force, because if anybody was profiting from the depression it was difficult to ferret them out. Even Ivar Kreuger, the Swedish match king, who had corrupted the governments of the world, could not save himself for all his power and wealth; he chose suicide. The president of the New York Stock Exchange went to jail.

All over the United States, the banks were going broke and the richest government in the world was unable to save financiers like the van Sweringens and Insulls. The daily documentation of the disasters that were overtaking the high and the mighty made the selection of scapegoats a frustrating business. However, while the people on relief were threshing around on the surface of things, the agitation that was being stirred up on the other side of the economy was developing deeper and stronger roots.

Those who became most sensitive to the depression were not the politicians but the school teachers and the preachers. Both had their own financial crosses to bear. They were underpaid at the best of times, everywhere in western Canada. School boards advertised for teachers for $500 and $600 a year and were flooded with applicants. In every city, teachers began with submarginal salaries and took all the pay cuts inflicted on everybody else. The urban teachers, however, at least collected their pay. In the country, teachers often ended a school year with nothing but promissory notes to show for a year's work. Yet the shattering blow to the teaching profession was to the heart rather than to the pocket. It was the sight of the vacated seat of the brightest pupil in the room, the seat that most of all should have been occupied.

It did not matter who they were or where they taught, whether they were Martin, Wilkinson, or Salome Halldorson in Winnipeg, Coldwell or Fines in Regina, Scarborough in Edmonton, Aberhart in Calgary, or Low in Cardston. It always seemed to be the gifted pupils who had to leave school to help support a family. It was easier during the depression for a boy to get a job as an office boy than for a father to find work as an office manager.

It became increasingly difficult to maintain interest in class in face of the clamorous unspoken question: What good was an education to anybody? Attention wandered from the decline of the Roman Empire to the holes in the soles of shoes, and to whether there would be any meat to go with the potatoes for supper. The teachers lived with life on relief every day, and they lived it with an intimacy that was deeper even than that of those who were on relief, because their 'families' were so much larger and their experience so much broader.

A pin stuck at random in a map anywhere in western Canada would have hit a school where the experiences of the teacher were typical of those of the others. Gordon Taylor, for example, was teaching at the Church Hill School south of Drumheller in the bitter winter of 1933. On very cold mornings he used to bring the children into the teacherage to keep warm while he was getting the school-house heated. One day two pupils arrived on horseback almost frozen. One of the boys took off his windbreaker and loosened his shirt. His skin was blue with the cold. He had no winter underwear and no overshoes.

'Where is your winter underwear?' Taylor asked the boy, who replied that he didn't have any and that the Relief Office would not give them any.

A very angry Taylor that night went to visit the welfare officer in Drumheller. He was advised he would have to contact Edmonton.

'The father of this boy is a drunkard,' the relief officer told him, 'and I have orders not to issue clothing to him.'

The welfare officer in Edmonton knew all about the case. It was he who had issued the orders that no clothing was to be given to this family, and he was not prepared to make the slightest concession until after a stormy session with Taylor.

'This incident,' said Taylor, 'convinced me that a government that would tolerate such things was just not good enough for the people of Alberta.'

So it was with school teachers everywhere, and the cumulative effect of it all was the drumming and numbing refrain: '*Something has got to be done!*"

But what? Where did one turn? The teaching profession had these advantages: an inclination towards study, an awareness of books, and an interest in what was going on in the world. There was fertile soil in the classrooms of western Canada in which the ideas of Keynes and Webb and Wells and Scott and Douglas might germinate and take root. Why the Douglas-Scott ideas so far outstripped the appeal of the English Socialists among school teachers, I know not. Perhaps the answer is Keynes. The famous author of *The Economic Consequences of the Peace* was at the top of his reputation in 1932. His predictions of disaster from the Treaty of Versailles had all come true. His *Treatise on Money* and *Tract on Monetary Reform* gave the full weight of his great prestige to the criticisms of the monetary system. His appeal to the British government to use public works and budgetary deficits to fight its depression went unheeded in England in 1929.

When anyone with Keynes's reputation called for reform of the 'money system' the spotlight was automatically focused on currency. Monetary policy became the hottest subject for debate wherever western Canadians gathered in the early thirties—at Labour Temple meetings in Winnipeg and Regina, at United Farmers of Alberta conventions in Edmonton, at Wheat Pool conventions in Calgary and Saskatoon, and in school teachers' conventions everywhere. Members of the U.F.A. 'Ginger Group' in Parliament, the vestigial remains of the once great progressive movement, became the country's most vocal critics of the golden standard.

The school teacher who was to start the greatest political prairie fire the West ever knew was Charles M. Scarborough, an Edmonton engineer turned science teacher, who had been converted to the

Social Credit theories of C. H. Douglas in 1925. If there ever was an apostle out of joint with the times, it was Scarborough. He talked Social Credit but nobody listened, not even William Aberhart, who in the 1920s was Canada's most famous lay preacher. Aberhart was a man of boundless energy and physical stamina. His invention of radio evangelism made him a household word wherever station CFCN was heard in 1926. His Sunday sermons to the Alberta Prophetic Bible Institute drew crowds in excess of 1,500. He was the principal of Calgary's newest and largest high school, taught mathematics with Prussian discipline, and ran the Prophetic Bible College the same way. He took his gospel to the deepest Alberta outback in the summers, and found time to get in a stint of marking examination papers every July in Edmonton. It was during the exam-marking period each year that he and Scarborough got together. Year after year, Scarborough talked Social Credit to a stone-deaf Aberhart.

In the winter of 1932, however, the depression came to Calgary with a shattering impact. The city lived largely on its railway shops, agriculture, and cattle-raising. In 1931 the United States closed its border to Canadian cattle. Prices for prime beef at the Calgary stockyards dropped from $7 per 100 pounds to $2. The lower grades of wheat and coarse grain shipped out of Alberta returned barely enough to the grower to cover the freight costs. The C.P.R. closed down its shops and Calgary business was in a state of collapse. Wherever he turned, Aberhart met economic problems that were distracting the attention of his flock from the Kingdom of Heaven. Aberhart, in fact, had economic problems of his own, for his salary was cut along with those of all the other teachers, and the collections dropped sharply from his religious services. That summer, when he went to Edmonton to mark examination papers, he listened to Scarborough and was converted to Social Credit. From that moment in July 1932, western Canada was never to be the same again.

Scarborough gave Aberhart precisely what he needed—a simple, easy-to-understand, do-it-yourself solution to all the economic problems of mankind. Within a matter of weeks, he was retreading his vast store of biblical allegories to make them applicable to Social Credit. He shifted the emphasis of his missionary activities from Ecclesiastes to economics. He began distributing Sunday-school-paper summaries of Maurice Colbourne's summary of C. H. Douglas. Wherever he went, he carried the Douglas gospel with him and he reinforced his personal selling job with a flood of material to his mailing list of teachers and preachers in Alberta.

For the teachers and preachers, Social Credit was the bolt-from-the-blue answer to the money problem. For them, the truth of the Douglas thesis was apparent on every hand: in the drastically reduced salaries they were unable to collect, in the travail of the once-prosperous ranchers who could not sell their cattle in a starving world, in the troubles of the merchants going bankrupt with stocks of clothes they could not sell. By custom, politics had been something teachers left to the school trustees and preachers stayed out of. But Social Credit was something above and beyond politics, something that could be studied in groups with U.F.A. grain-growers, Liberal merchants, and Conservative ranchers. It was not long before Douglas had been percolated through Colbourne and strained through Aberhart, and was being savoured by the school-teachers of Alberta, Saskatchewan, and Manitoba.

A roll-call of the Alberta teachers who fell under Aberhart's influence reads like the 'Who's Who' of Social Credit. Nathan Tanner in Cardston, Alf Hooke in Red Deer, Solon Low in Sterling, J. A. Marshall in Canmore, W. F. Kuhl in Spruce Grove, John Blackmore in Raymond, Earle Ansley in Blackfalds. In the years to come, a dozen teachers would be elected to the Alberta legislature in the first Social Credit landslide, and a third of the first batch of federal members of Parliament would be teachers.

The impact of the Aberhart 'Social Credit Sunday School Papers' was felt in western Manitoba, though it took longer for it to reach Winnipeg. As in Alberta, it was in rural Manitoba where the influence was greatest, and again it was the school-teachers who turned Social Credit into a political movement.

But for the teachers and preachers who had been digging deeper, who had gone from Keynes to the Webbs, Cole, and H. G. Wells in their flight from both capitalism and Marxism, Social Credit was not enough. Or perhaps it was only that, in their disgust with the Liberals and Conservatives, they turned to the handiest alternative.

In Saskatchewan the handy alternative was the newly organized Co-operative Commonwealth Federation, and the teachers rushed from classrooms to get into it. The C.C.F., with M. J. Coldwell at its head, was both nurtured and energized by such ornaments to the teaching profession as Clarence Fines, Woodrow Lloyd, John Sturdy, and George Castledon. If something had to be done, they were prepared to make the sacrifices that were needed to make it happen. In the process the crowning paradox of the depression developed. Those who threw themselves into the struggle to remake the world were those who lived above the storm. Those who were most concerned, the unemployed on relief, backed away from the combat to become arguing spectators on the sidelines. Nowhere was this more apparent than in Winnipeg, the stone-cold hotbed of Canadian radicalism.

In the provincial election campaign of 1932, when there were more than 20,000 men and women on relief in Winnipeg, campaign material piled up in the offices of the Independent Labour Party, because we could not recruit sufficient volunteers to deliver it for us. Having been freed of compulsion to provide for their own basic needs, the unemployed could afford to take a second look at their environment. It contained no Bastille that cried out to be stormed, and, if we argued Socialism *versus* Communism at the Woodyard and on Market Square, only rarely did the argument generate sufficient heat to lead to bloodied noses. When the first flushes of idealistic enthusiasm passed, we returned our patronage quietly to the graven images of the Liberal Party.

CHAPTER IX

THE COMPLETE SCOUNDREL
AND THE HONEST JUDGE

To be a newspaper reader anywhere in western Canada during the depression required a masochistic streak a foot wide. It is doubtful if there was ever a time when the attention of the whole world was held for so long by such an avalanche of bad news. Disaster beat upon disaster, day after day, for months on end, stretching into year after year. Misery might love company, but enough was enough, and most of us on relief gradually let our subscriptions lapse and our interest in the world shrink to the Woodyard, the stores, and our own front stoop. Local, national, and international calamities beat such a rat-a-plan on everybody's consciousness that the insulating numbness of the unemployed gradually extended a protective coating to everyone else. They escaped the horrors on the front pages by turning quickly to the comic strips and amusement features. Occasionally, however, the thread that ran from one worsening crisis to another was lightened a little by the pompous pronunciamentos of the graveyard whistlers.

On January 8, 1931, Sir Herbert Holt, president of the Royal Bank, propelled this opinion on an inattentive world: 'The present interruption in the normal trading relationships of the world is not going to persist. There are a sufficient number of reasonably favourable factors in the Canadian situation, so that the resumption of the expansion of Canada cannot be long delayed.'

His opposite number at the Bank of Montreal, Sir Charles Gordon, went on record that 'The return to prosperity will probably be slow, but there is ground for believing that the bottom of the depression is near at hand.'

Any Canadian who took business risks based upon the judgment of these greatest of Canadian bankers would have been bankrupt within the year. With but minor flurries and ephemeral recoveries, those faithful mirrors of the times—the stock markets of Canada and the United States—continued to decline. From a high in October 1929 of $64.75, Canadian Pacific Railway common stock dropped to $25 in June 1931 and to $8.50 a year later. International Nickel reached $72.50 before the crash, touched $9.50 in 1931, and then went to $4.50. Winnipeg Electric Company sold at $109.50 in 1929, at $10 in 1931, and at $2 in 1932. Abitibi had a high of $57.75 and sold for $1 in 1932. In 1929, the fifty most important Canadian stocks had an aggregate value of $6,265 million. By 1932 the value had shrunk to $880 million, a drop of 85.9 per cent.

Not since the South Sea Bubble had the investors in a country's future taken such a shellacking. Moreover, no one was ever permitted to forget that the depression was not just Canadian, but that the world was in turmoil. In May of 1931 the greatest bank in Austria—Credit Austalt—closed its doors with liabilities of £76 million. A few weeks later a huge wool co-operative in Bremen went broke and brought down the great Darmstadt National Bank. The German government closed all German banks for three weeks, and the Hungarian government followed suit. In August, Ramsay MacDonald formed his National Government to save the British pound and the gold standard. It managed to save the gold standard for thirty days. British abandonment of the gold standard, Prime Minister R. B. Bennett lamented, shattered the economies of every country in the world except two.

By Labour Day 1931, southern Saskatchewan had become a Sahara and the Red Cross launched an appeal for clothing and food for 125,000 persons who would be destitute in the winter of 1931–2. Things were much worse south of the border where 1,000,000 acres of crop land in Minnesota, Kansas, and Iowa had been stripped bare of vegetation by the worst grasshopper invasion in memory. In China, things were worst of all, for 30,000 had died and 30,000,000, were homeless as the result of floods. On the heels of China's greatest natural disaster came the invasion of Manchuria by the Japanese war-lords. The world got a preview of horrors to come when the Japanese air force began its experimental terror-bombings of Chinese cities.

Then everything got worse—everywhere in the world. The Nazis began to fasten their grip upon Germany, hunger-marchers clogged the streets of British cities, a bonus army of 12,000 marched on Washington to be routed by the American army. The collapse of the Swedish match monopoly in 1932 sent violent tremors through the financial world, toppled governments, and started panic selling of foreign securities. Food riots rocked the American cities and the worst drouth in history devastated the American great-plains states.

In Winnipeg we had a whole series of local convulsions to occupy our attention. The head of the city's most respected brokerage house was caught with his hand in the till and went to jail for eighteen months for stealing $275,000. Rumours of insolvency forced the government to close the Provincial Savings Bank, and there was a succession of relatively minor defalcations by provincial government employees. All only served as a prelude to the great Machray scandal.

Unlike the Kreuger scandal, the Machray affair broke no banks, but it broke the hearts of many hundreds of Canadians when it erupted in the summer of 1932. John A. Machray, K.C., was Winnipeg's most revered churchman and lawyer, the sort of person who could easily have been elected 'Anglican Layman of the Year' any year. The nephew and protégé of Archbishop Robert Machray, one of the West's most beloved and respected clergymen, he had lived a life of seemingly impeccable respectability and affluence. When the news of the Machray embezzlements first broke, there was a wave of sympathy for him on the assumption that he was just another victim of the depression who had got into trouble as a result of the Wall Street crash. In fact, he was a common thief and embezzler and had been for at least twenty-five years. As the story unfolded, after Machray went to the penitentiary, the provincial government appointed a Royal Commission to investigate. The commission dug out a record of crime, duplicity, negligence, and incompetence unmatched in western Canadian memory.

For months after the story broke, Winnipeg talked of little else. Each week brought new revelations of negligence, new evidence of incompetency and guile. Archbishop Machray of Rupert's Land, the first Church of England primate of all Canada, brought John Machray to Canada from Scotland in 1875, as a boy of ten. The senior Machray sent his nephew to the University of Manitoba, and then to his own college at Cambridge University. Machray came back to Winnipeg to the practice of law. He was appointed honorary bursar of the University of Manitoba in 1903, Councillor of the University in 1906, Chancellor of the Diocese of Rupert's Land of the Church of England, honorary bursar of the Anglican St. John's College, and financial agent of the University of Manitoba in 1907. As a result of these appointments, he was not only placed in charge of the trust funds and endowments of both institutions, he managed the investments of both.

In a conspiracy with one R. H. Shanks, the accountant in his office, he immediately began to loot the trust funds and he kept looting them until the death of Shanks in the spring of 1932. The double function that Machray performed for the church and the

THE COMPLETE SCOUNDREL AND THE HONEST JUDGE

university enabled him to switch the assets of one to the other to hide his defalcations from gullible government auditors. The capacity of the auditors for being taken in by Machray was seemingly without limit. He was permitted to switch into bearer form the blocks of bonds that were registered in the name of the university. All the trust securities were tossed together into one box and were identified only by scribbled notations pinned to them.

The auditors for the Royal Commission eventually got everything totalled up. Machray had looted the university trusts of more than $900,000 and the church lost over $800,000. Included in the church losses was one small item that spelled out the nature of the defalcation better than any other. It was: 'Clergymen's widows-and-orphans fund, $34,000'.

Over many years, through bequests and windfalls of one kind and another, the Anglican clergy had built up a modest fund of $34,000 out of which their widows and orphans might draw succour in times of emergency. Whether Machray hesitated before he made off with the widows-and-orphans fund was never discovered, but make off with it he did, as he made off with almost $300,000 in private trust funds.

Clients who left real-estate titles with him for safe-keeping found their titles encumbered by mortgages. An Elmwood greenhouse owner, who had worked a lifetime to pay for his home and his flower business, discovered at sixty that one lifetime would not be long enough. Machray had remortgaged the property and consumed the proceeds. Everyone who had entrusted anything to Machray lost it.

As the Machray scandal began to pall, another circus was brought in for public consumption. It was the famous judicial fitness trial of Judge Lewis St. George Stubbs, who had blown up a one-man hurricane in the law courts of Manitoba. Stubbs had been a Laurier Liberal in the election of 1917 and was soundly beaten on the conscription issue in the Lisgar constituency of Manitoba. His reward from Mackenzie King was a county court and surrogate judgeship in Winnipeg.

Stubbs brought to his job even less judicial impartiality than the Winnipeg police magistrates, who were invariably recruited from the ranks of the Crown prosecutors. The magistrates accepted without question any testimony given by a policeman. Stubbs publicly proclaimed that he would not believe a policeman, even if he swore on a stack of Bibles. He had other deviations in personality that failed to endear him to constituted authority. His politics had veered somewhat to the left of the C.C.F., and he was a belligerent agnostic and boisterous pacifist. Once in an address to a meeting of the Canadian Legion in St. James, he described soldiers and preachers as the twin scourges of mankind. He had an unshakeable conviction that there was one law for the rich and another for the poor in Canada and never lost a chance to call attention to the fact. Lewis St. George Stubbs was a maverick to start with, and there is little doubt that the Macdonald will case turned him into a crusader.

Alexander 'Sandy' Macdonald was Winnipeg's proverbial 'millionaire with a heart of gold'. He had built a substantial fortune in the grocery business, had personally supported a number of private charities, and was particularly interested in homes for wayward girls. Macdonald, as he grew older, worried a lot about the disposal of his fortune. In 1923 he instructed his solicitor to draw a will, making ample provision for his charities. The will was duly drawn, signed, and sealed, but it was attested to by only one witness. Manitoba law required two witnesses. In 1928 a second will was drawn up and presented to the eighty-four-year-old Macdonald on his death-bed. In it the charities were completely left out, and the entire estate was left to Macdonald's daughter and son-in-law. The story of the second will had all the dark trappings of an Agatha

Christie thriller, including mysterious witnesses, midnight visitors, and an angry nurse with a bilious eye for the Macdonald heirs.

The second will was presented for probate to Stubbs as surrogate judge in January 1929. He granted the probate. The disinherited charities immediately raised some doubts about the will, so Judge Stubbs revoked the probate and ordered the will proved in solemn form. That started proceedings that kept the Macdonald will case before the courts for the next year. Stubbs, after a lengthy trial, refused to probate the will and in his judgment said: 'The circumstances connected with its preparation, its execution, and the proofs of its execution show unmistakeable signs of stealth, deception, falsity, and fraud. Nothing appears to be open and above-board, everything seems to be devious and underhand.'

In addition to everything else, Judge Stubbs found that Mr. Macdonald's advancing senility had robbed him of his testamentary capacity, and declared the will void on that ground as well as the others.

Stubbs sought to have the estate, which approached $2 million, placed in the hands of a trust company until the Manitoba legislature could validate the first will. However, the heirs carried the case to the Manitoba Court of Appeal, which leaped over Stubbs's head and hurriedly granted probate without having seen either the trial transcript or Stubbs's formal judgment in which his reasons for his action were set out!

Assuming the role as the champion of Macdonald's charities, Stubbs then sought to rouse public opinion so that the Manitoba legislature could take action. When the newspapers refused to report his judgment, he got S. J. Farmer, the C.C.F. leader in the Legislative Assembly, to read the judgment to the legislature. The newspapers, still professing to fear the libel laws, refused to report the Farmer speech—an act of journalistic pusillanimity wholly and inexplicably out of character for both the *Free Press* and the *Tribune*.

Stubbs thereupon wrote scathing letters to both newspapers, which they printed in expurgated form. His next step was to publish a thirty-six-page pamphlet in which he set forth the salient passages from court testimony and severely criticized the Manitoba Court of Appeal. Then he went on a year-long public-speaking campaign, beginning with a mass meeting that filled the Walker Theatre.

Somewhere down the line, he collided head-on with the Honourable W. J. Major, the attorney-general, and a bitter feud developed between them. It was not long before Stubbs carried his war against the attorney-general and constituted authority into his own court. Strikers accused of picket-line violence, who would have been automatically convicted in city police court, were acquitted by Stubbs. Merchants seeking judgments against delinquent debtors lost their suits in front of Stubbs, and were roundly abused in the process. Lawyers began to manoeuvre to get their criminal cases before Stubbs where, if their clients were convicted at all, they could expect a light sentence.

The Stubbs performance reached its peak with his comment on the sentence of an accused embezzler. The man had been held in jail for four months awaiting trial on a charge of stealing $4,500 from the provincial government. In acquitting him of the charge, Stubbs made a sarcastic reference to the case of William Martin, Jr., who stole $275,000 from his brokerage office clients and got eighteen months in jail. Stubbs mentioned that the man before him had already served more time in jail than would have been called for under the Martin formula of eighteen months for $275,000.

Unhappily for Stubbs, these comments were reported in a distorted form in the newspapers, and that did it. Constituted authority swung into action and Mr. Justice Frank Ford of the Supreme Court of Alberta was appointed to determine whether Stubbs's conduct was prejudicial to the administration of justice in Manitoba.

The Honourable E. J. McMurray, K.C., himself a maverick Liberal and the best criminal lawyer in the province, volunteered to act as Stubbs's counsel. Marshall Gauvin, the Rationalist Society lecturer, organized a Stubbs defence committee to circulate petitions in support of Stubbs. I was one of the first volunteers on that committee. All of us discovered that working for a professional martyr could be painfully frustrating. Stubbs never seemed satisfied with our efforts, and after we had collected thousands of signatures the committee quietly expired.

That Stubbs himself was bent on martyrdom can hardly be doubted. His trial began to 'standing room only', and standing was in fact permitted. Physically, Stubbs was built like a cross between a bantam prizefighter and a bantam rooster. Instead of letting McMurray make his case, and McMurray might well have won the day, Stubbs seemed to do everything imaginable to make sure that he lost. He stomped around the court like a pint-sized Darrow, posturing and pointing like a caricature of a freshman law student. He turned his back to the judge and harangued the assembled spectators in purple phrases that would have embarrassed William Jennings Bryan himself.

An abomination to constituted authority, Stubbs became the hero of the downtrodden and destitute. After his removal from the Bench, he returned to the practice of law and, if he could have afforded to do so, he might have spent the rest of his life doing nothing but fighting lost causes. He got the sweetest revenge any martyr could have experienced: in 1936, when he ran for the legislature, he polled more votes than the next ten candidates combined. His was the greatest personal electoral victory in Manitoba history, possibly in Canadian history.

Winnipeg elected, by the single transferable-vote system, ten members to the fifty-five-seat legislature. Each elector was handed a ballot a foot and a half long containing upwards of twenty-five or thirty names. He was required to go through the list and vote for his choices in numerical order. As the low candidates were eliminated, the second, then third, choices on the eliminated ballots were transferred to the candidates still in the running. At the other end, when a candidate reached a certain quota of votes he was declared elected, and the surplus he had polled above the quota were shuffled to other candidates. This cumbersome, complicated, and pointless system often resulted in the ballots being counted fifteen or sixteen times before all the results were sorted out. In the 1936 election, it was Stubbs first and the rest nowhere. Of the 75,000 votes cast, he received almost 25,000 first choices. The second candidate was the Communist, Jim Litterick, who polled 5,864. Stubbs got more votes than all the Conservative Party candidates combined and almost double the total of all the Bracken candidates. He outdrew his arch-enemy, the Honourable W. J. Major, by five votes to one. Though he became something of a common scold in the legislature, Winnipeg never tired of Stubbs, and he sat in the legislature until he retired in 1948. He died full of honour in 1958 at the age of eighty-one, as honest and courageous a judge as ever sat on a Canadian Bench.

CHAPTER X

THE GOLD-STOCK SWINDLERS
GAVE CANADA A BOOST

Whether we were employed or unemployed, and whether we lived on farms, in towns, or in cities, the people of western Canada made their peace with the depression environment. But while we had to accustom ourselves to the economic fog, we did not have to like it, and searching the skies for a ray of hope became a major preoccupation.

We emerged from each winter with renewed faith that the worst was over. Spring floods along the Portage plains of Manitoba augered well, always, for a bumper crop. All during the late spring and early summer, the best gloss possible was put on the crop reports. Any improvement in retail trade was widely heralded. If one economic conference after another broke up in a welter of confusion, others were confidently called.

Our spirits in the West got temporary lifts periodically, and two of the greatest lifters were the Roosevelt New Deal and the boom in phoney gold-stocks. One, in fact, led to the other. Though the best brains of our country viewed the Roosevelt experiment of 1933 with suspicion and even dread, the rest of us watched with envious enthusiasm. For the first time in three years, the government of some country was undertaking positive measures to combat the depression. That the action came at the very bottom of the depression made it doubly welcome.

The Canadian gold boom, which President Roosevelt's revaluation of the price of gold set off, did violence to all the copy-book standards of moral behaviour. It was a boom in the great tradition of the South Sea Bubble, of the Grand Trunk Railway, and of Charles

Ponzi, the outrageously improper Bostonian. None the less, it was one of the good things of the depression, for it built thriving new towns in the wilderness and provided life-long jobs for thousands of Canadians. Investors flocked back into the brokerage offices in 1934 as they had not done since 1929. The board-room chairs filled up quickly, and spectators were soon standing three and four deep in front of the stock-quotation boards. Those who stood and watched had something new and exciting to talk about, something to take a man's mind off his business problems, his financial problems, his family problems. It was indeed an antidote to despair, the first real antidote of the Thirties.

It all began with the American banking crisis, which forced President Franklin D. Roosevelt, in March 1933, to shut down the whole banking system the day after his inauguration, to place an embargo on gold exports, and completely recast the U.S. Bank Act. After the smoke cleared, the price of gold rose steadily until, in January 1934, Congress stabilized the price permanently at $35 an ounce.

The boom came on so quickly that it caught completely by surprise the brokerage office where, by now, I had a $15-a-week job marking a quotation board. Nobody on the staff knew anything much about mining stocks or the mining industry. The long-neglected statistical files contained little but out-dated clippings from the *Financial Post* and the *Northern Miner*. Thus, when potential customers came in to inquire about the new mining strikes, we had nothing to tell them. If it occurred to the management to hire a real expert, nothing came of it. They settled for a rank amateur, namely me. I was assigned to reorganize the files, watch the stocks that were becoming active, and prepare brochures for the customers. In short, I was to become an expert on gold-mining promotion as quickly as possible, preferably overnight.

The 1933 boom was even more fraudulent than the one in 1929 because the native Canadian swindlers were reinforced by emigrants being driven out of the United States. Over the years, the ancient art of separating the gullible greedy from their money had been honed to a much finer edge in the United States than it had been in Canada. Competition among swindlers was far keener, and opportunities were also much greater because the United States never seemed to run out of new products for fraudulent promotion. It was only a short crooked step from Florida swamps to California desert to Texas oil to Colorado gold. The American financial system, however, had been so thoroughly investigated, exposed, and discredited by generations of writers, from Ida Tarbell, Lincoln Steffens, and Gustavus Myers to John T. Flynn and Stuart Chase, and by government investigations of long successions of bank scandals, railway scandals, and utility scandals, that something ultimately had to give. That something was the Federal Securities and Exchange Commission, which in 1933 took rigid control over American financial institutions and securities salesmen.

Driven out of New York, Michigan, and Ohio by the S.E.C., the swindlers moved their boiler-rooms to Toronto, where, in offices equipped with batteries of long-distance telephones, they fixed the Canadian public in their sights. They first sought to convince holders of bonds or good mining stocks to switch into shares of the near worthless companies they had acquired. Their next step was to get the public into the mining market with new mining promotions.

While the canyons of Bay Street filled up with displaced American swindlers, the north woods filled with prospectors. They found gold outcrops all over the Precambrian Shield, staked their claims, and went back to Toronto searching for brokers to transmute their claims into gold-mining companies, and get them enough cash for a month on the town.

It was no part of my job to separate the legitimate sheep from the illegitimate goats, but it was a function I could hardly avoid as the flow of new issues reached flood stage. The inquiries usually followed telephone calls from the high-pressure Toronto boiler-rooms. One customer became provoked with us when he brought in some stock to sell and the best offer we could get for it was two cents a share. He had been assured by the telephone caller that this company had been reactivated, that its shares were now selling for twenty-five cents and would be going to fifty cents the following week. The telephone salesman was under the impression our customer still owned ten shares of International Nickel which were worth around $200, and was trying to switch the customer out of the Nickel into 1,000 shares of his promotion. Our customer no longer owned the International Nickel, but by coincidence still owned 5,000 shares of the dormant company the salesman was trying to peddle. He was naturally overjoyed with the news that his holdings were worth $1,250 and quickly offered to sell his shares to the telephone salesman, who promptly hung up. He brought his certificate to us, and then angrily took his business elsewhere when we got him the two cents quotation.

Compared with the impact of the gold boom on Ontario, the effect on Manitoba was superficial. Yet more than fifty gold-mining companies were organized in Manitoba and some of them actually got mines into operation. In any event, the smell of profits from gold-mining shares drifted all the way from Bay Street to the brokerage offices of the West. Those who had saved any of their mining investments from the crash saw the nearly worthless paper of 1932 miraculously restored to life. San Antonio Mines rose from twenty-five cents a share in 1932 to $6.30 in 1934. Central Manitoba which had sunk to four cents a share rose to twenty cents. Central Patricia went as low as two cents a share in 1932 and touched $1.25 in 1934.

The established mines which had been making profits all along were the bellwethers of the boom. Dome rose from $9 to $32; Hudson Bay from ninety cents to $15; Hollinger from $4.25 to $21.25; Teck Hughes from $3 to $8; International Nickel from $4 to $29; McIntyre Porcupine from $14 to $50. But the real frenzy was in the penny dreadfuls of the mining market. Bagamac went up and down like a yo-yo, from two cents a share in 1932 to sixty cents in 1934; B.R.X. jumped from twenty-two cents to $1.41; Wiltsey Coghlan from one cent to eighteen cents; Sudbury Contact from half a cent to sixteen cents; Lamaque Contact from three cents to forty-eight cents. Scores of such issues delighted the common man, and in 1934 many hundreds of Winnipeggers whiled away the long cold nights calculating their paper profits on God's Lake, Island Lake, Gunnar, Gold Lake, Howey, and Towagamac.

For many Winnipeggers mining was more than a mere stock-market fever, however. They saw it as the economic panacea—the diversifier that would at last rescue western Canada from the tyranny of King Wheat and the one-crop economy. The Manitoba discoveries could not match the big finds in Northern Ontario, but nobody on Portage Avenue would concede any such thing in 1934. Sherritt Gordon and Hudson Bay were in production, San Antonio, Central Manitoba, Gunnar, and God's Lake were on their way. When the price of gold reached $35 an ounce, the board-rooms buzzed with talk that the price would ultimately go to $50. This would make hundreds of marginal properties profitable to develop, and double and treble the profits of all the other producers. It was heady stuff and this was surely no place nor time for doubters.

In our brokerage office, the customers did not appreciate being warned away from the disasters being fashioned for them by the Toronto boiler-rooms. The get-rich-quick salesmen had stoked up their depression-jaded imagination and they wanted confirmation, not disillusionment. Often they would only come to seek advice after they had fallen for the wiles of the telephone salesmen.

How do you protect such people from the consequences of such enchanting lunacy? There was no way. Although the structure of mining-stock promotion could be cleaned up and tidied up, fundamental changes were impossible. With all its fraudulent overtones, it was the sort of system that suited the investors because it was the only one they had ever known. The gold-mining industry was one in which the risks were so high that extraordinary profits had to be promised or money could not be attracted into it. It was useless to shout about the under-capitalization of mining companies, which arose from issuance of penny shares, when the public demanded penny shares. It was far easier to sell 10,000 shares of ten-cent stock than ten shares of $100 stock because the romancing the investors could do over 10,000 shares far exceeded anything possible with ten shares.

Expectation of dividend income was never a factor in the purchase of mining stock. Who cared if Porcupine-Moose ever earned a profit or paid a dividend? Mining stocks were not bought for dividends, but in the hope they could be sold for double or treble what they had cost. This was not investing capital, it was an out-and-out long-shot gamble. Yet it was a gamble where there was usually a chance, at some point, for the gamblers to get out with a profit. It was the sort of gamble, moreover, in which a four-fold or five-fold return was anticipated. There was scarcely a listed stock on the Toronto Mining Exchange which did not show at least that range between the low of 1932 and the high of 1934.

Few of the purchasers of new shares in the marginal successes that were spawned in the 1933-4 boom ever got their money back with much more than bank interest. Most of them would have been further ahead leaving their money stuffed in a mattress. But the country would not have been further ahead. The money supplied by the long-shot gamblers in penny shares got a tremendous development going. All across the north country from Bridge River to Flin Flon, to Rice Lake, to Red Lake, to Pickle Lake, to Little Long Lac, to Larder Lake, new communities bloomed around mines in the bush, and jobs were created in Vancouver, Winnipeg, Fort William, Sudbury, and Toronto. Some of the communities and many of the jobs would last for thirty years. There would be no dividend income for the shareholders, but the gold that was extracted was a vital asset to the Canadian economy. Within a short space of three years, between 1933 and 1936, Canada's annual gold production rose by almost one-third, from 2,949,000 ounces worth $84 million to 3,748,000 ounces worth $131 million. The marginal gold mines produced hundreds of millions of dollars worth of gold over the next twenty-five years, and became so important that in the end the federal government subsidized many of them to keep them in operation.

Meanwhile, out in Calgary, a group of imaginative oil promoters had come up with a radical new scheme to finance the drilling of oil-wells. They called it the net royalty system, and it was set in motion in the spring of 1934 at a time when the economy of Alberta had ground to a dead halt. It would have been impossible then to have sold shares in the Canadian mint to Albertans, never mind shares in an oil company. Oil shares had been so discredited that many bitter Calgarians used worthless certificates as wallpaper to remind them of their folly. The last thing any Calgarian was prepared to do with a dollar in 1934 was put it back into the oil market.

It was in this climate that George Bell and R. A. Brown decided to revolutionize oil financing. That alone points up the fact that the bite of the oil bug has the same effect as the bite of the gold bug. An oilman could no more give up searching for oil than a gold-hunter could give up the hunt for gold. Bell and Brown were the Gilbert LaBine and Jack Hammell of the oil business. They prompted one of the first honest oil companies in Alberta, and they did it with two fetching arguments. If oil was discovered, every barrel produced would be apportioned through a trust company to those who put up the capital. If oil was discovered, every shareholder would be repaid several times over for his investment. It was all in a trust deed, and no trust company was going to permit the operator to siphon off any of the income through fanciful expenses. And, to cap the pitch, income from oil royalties was return of capital and hence not subject to income tax.

Bell was the publisher of the near-bankrupt Calgary *Albertan*. Brown was the superintendent of the City of Calgary Electric Light Department. Brown, with several other Calgarians, had developed a theory that a pool of oil lay below the gas cap of the limestone in Turner Valley. Huge quantities of natural gas soaked with natural gasoline or naphtha were being produced from this formation. At first the liquid was completely colourless. Then, after the wells had been in production for some time, it began to turn brown. Black oil, they concluded, was mixing in with the natural gas so there had to be crude oil below the gas.

Most professional geologists, with some notable exceptions, scoffed at this theory and held that the only thing under the gas was water. Bell, Brown, and the other oil-bitten Calgarians got their minds off their troubles by arguing about the geology of Turner Valley. The more they argued, the more determined they became to drill a well and test their theory. They picked up a sixty-acre lease in January 1934 and incorporated Turner Valley Royalties. They turned in some drilling equipment they owned plus the lease acreage for about twenty-five per cent of the net royalty. They set out to sell the rest at $1,500 a point, which meant that anybody who put up $1,500 would be guaranteed one per cent of the net production from the well.

Unhappily for Brown and Bell, most Calgarians who still had money were quite content to hold on to it. They did, however, locate a few small companies that had survived the crash with money in the till. They successfully tapped these companies for $10,000, which was enough to build a rig and get drilling started. Drilling stopped when the well ran out of money and the rig stood idle for almost two years. Then British American Oil and Imperial Oil put up some cash and equipment, three or four other small oil companies put up smaller sums, and the well blew into production in June 1936.

For all the excitement it caused in Calgary, it was a lead balloon in Winnipeg. Too many people had been swindled on oil stocks in the 1920s for news of a new oil strike to generate any enthusiasm. However, as understanding of the complexities of the net royalty system spread, greater interest was created. Death had taken Bell from the picture, but Brown quickly organized two more royalty companies to drill two more wells. They, too, were successful, and it was the quick six-to-one pay-out of the original investments in these wells that got the new, and uniquely honest Turner Valley boom off the ground.

Until the glut of oil developed, and it came all too quickly, the oil royalty system seemed to be the answer to financing oil exploration. Certainly the public thought it was. Then the surplus of oil drove the prices down and forced drastic reduction in production. The income from oil royalties declined sadly and the *coup de grâce* was administered by the federal income-tax authorities. They ruled that oil royalties were not a return of capital after all, but ordinary income, and subject to income tax.

Thus ended a noble experiment in honest financing. An instrument that, in later years, might have saved the oil industry from complete appropriation to foreign capital became lost in the shuffle. But, while it lasted, the oil boom did for Alberta what the gold boom did for Manitoba. It broke the spell of the depression and permitted the warming flow of optimism to course through the economic blood stream.

CHAPTER XI

THE WEATHER THAT MADE
THE THIRTIES DIRTY

Nothing was dirtier in the Dirty Thirties than the weather. Indeed, it was the exceptional 'dirtiness' of the western weather that gave the label a particular prairie flavour. In many ways, in many areas, and for many reasons, the weather, the dirty weather, was even more difficult to abide than the depression itself. It was never wholly bad everywhere at once. However, within the Palliser Triangle—from Lethbridge to Battleford to Melita—it was bad all the time. Outside the Triangle the weather ranged from the intolerable to the occasionally delightful. Alberta came off best; except for the disaster years of 1933 and 1936, its central and northern areas escaped most of the drouth. The worst weather in Alberta generally was in 1933, when drouth, hail, wind, grasshoppers, rust, and frost all combined to produce the lowest crop yield of modern times.

Northern Saskatchewan shared the frightful cold of the depression winters, but good rains, when precipitation was needed most, gave that part of the country average crops, even if the crops were worth little or nothing to the producers. Over the 30,000 square miles of the Great Plains, outside the Palliser Triangle, there were the usual local variations that were to be expected. But on the average, over the whole area, 'dirty' was the word for the weather for the whole of the 1930s.

It began bitterly in January 1930, when the thermometers dropped to thirty below between Winnipeg and the Rockies and a series of blizzards drifted the country roads into impassable condition. Then the climate moderated, and for most of the rest of the year the weather gods were on their best behaviour. The fall of 1930 was beautifully warm and dry. The cold spells of the winter of 1931 were short and sharp, but from Winnipeg to Calgary and beyond the temperatures for the winter months reached the highest point in twenty years. But there was no snow anywhere on the southern prairies during the winter of 1931, and the first of the great black blizzards whipped up as the strong westerly winds blew the topsoil of Saskatchewan into Manitoba and North Dakota. From then on, the weather in both winter and summer went steadily down-hill.

The hot, dry summer of 1931 brought a complete crop failure to the south country, but good crops were the rule in the north, setting the pattern for the next five years. The rains fell where they were needed least, in the Red River Valley, on the Portage Plains, in the northern half of Saskatchewan and Alberta.

In 1932 the worst plague of grasshoppers in fifty years hit the Red River Valley. Sometimes the infestation built up slowly. In other places, a sudden invasion out of nowhere of clouds of hoppers would devour every scrap of garden greenness, strip every leaf from Caragana hedges, and whirl on to devour the heads of a ripening grain crop in a strip a mile wide. In Winnipeg the hoppers even made the golf courses unplayable.

Jack Thompson, the greens-keeper at Kildonan Park, gained a fleeting fame by inventing a grasshopper trap, the world's first mechanical grasshopper-harvester. He mounted a ten-foot screen across the front of a tractor and attached a vat to the bottom of the screen. He filled the vat with oil, into which the hoppers fell after hitting the screen. In one day's operation, he garnered a pile of drowned grasshoppers, ten feet long and three feet high, but made scarcely a dent in the numbers of insects on the course. As the drouth worsened, so did the grasshoppers. Abandoned farms became hatching grounds for the insects. They came and they went.

From 1932 onward, the winters got steadily colder and the summers grew steadily hotter until 1936. By then clouds from the Dust Bowl had given Moose Jaw and Regina a steady overcast, gritty sidewalks, and perennially dusty furniture in homes and offices. Brandon, too, became obscured by the high, blowing clouds of dust, and occasionally the hot wind was felt and the dust haze experienced in Winnipeg.

Then came 1936.

Never before and never since has western Canada lived through such a year! Beginning in the first week of January and continuing for two solid months without even the semblance of a break, an unbelievable cold spell held the West in its grip. It was the year Winnipeg earned its reputation as the coldest city of its size in the world, though it wasn't even as cold as Edmonton that February.

The cold settled in during the first week in January: on the seventh of the month, it was -35° in Winnipeg, -39° in Brandon, -35° at Regina, and -39° at Saskatoon. Then it snowed, and the wind blew, and the temperature moved up a little, but the respite was only temporary. When the wind and snow stopped, the temperature dropped. By mid-month the thermometer was back down to -32° and it dropped to -30° or colder in Winnipeg every day for the next week.

A howling blizzard on January 23 halted railways and buried rural Manitoba, but it at least brought the temperatures up a few degrees. Between the first and the fifteenth of February, there were only four days in Winnipeg when it was not at least thirty below. Day after day it got well below -40°; and on February 6 a malfunctioning of the official thermometer set the whole town on its ear.

Weary residents of St. James and Fort Garry and North Kildonan broke the encrusted hoar-frost from their instruments to see temperatures recorded well under fifty below. The general belief was that an all-time record of -52° was established. Unhappily for the weather-proud people of Winnipeg, the official thermometer got stuck at a relatively balmy -43° and the record was never officially registered.

Yet Winnipeg, that February, was not even the coldest place in the West. Brandon, during the first half of the month, recorded a temperature of below -40° on nine days, of which five were -45° or colder, and the coldest was -49°. The week of February 11 to 17 was probably the coldest week ever experienced by large groups of civilized people anywhere. On February 16 it was -51° at Edmonton, -54° at Regina, -43° at Saskatoon, -36° at Calgary, and -40° everywhere in between.

Mostly the city schools stayed open, but the country schools closed and stayed closed. The West took on the characteristics of a deserted village. Only those who had to go out ventured out. The squeaking wheels of the streetcars could be heard for blocks as the frost in the wheels and rails made traction difficult. Railway schedules became completely disorganized. Railway crews fought hot boxes and flat wheels on almost every train.

Automobiles disappeared from the streets. In the mid-thirties many motorists still laid up their cars in winter. Block-heaters were not in common use, winter-weight oil was unknown, and a common expense of winter motoring was the replacement of anti-freeze. The odour of alcohol permeated the cars and those who used ethylene glycol found their cooling systems tragically leak-prone. They were confronted, at the shank end of an evening, with a round pink stain on the snow under their radiator to show where their anti-freeze had gone.

In the rural west, motor transportation was completely immobilized. Most cars and trucks used outside the cities were still crank-equipped. But cranks could not spin frozen engines, and many a desperate farmer seeking to heat his truck engine with a blowtorch succeeded only in setting it afire. For most farmers, there was little point in starting a truck or tractor, for there was no place to go. The sideroads from Winnipeg to the Rockies became blocked by snow drifts. However, in 1936 most farms still had a team or two of work horses and a Bennett buggy—a car with its engine removed, pulled by a team of horses. As long as air could be kept in tires, Bennett buggies were easier to pull than farm wagons.

For two months, half a million farm people huddled around stoves and thought only of keeping warm. If food supplies ran low, they ate less. Only when fuel reached the vanishing point would they venture to town for a load of relief coal. By 1936 there was relief coal and relief food for anybody who needed it, and it was available for the asking, but it was available in town, and for many farmers town was eight or ten miles away.

The wait for moderation seemed interminable. Thousands of farm families lived permanently in their kitchens, bringing in their mattresses at night to be near the heat from the cook-stove. To augment their coal supplies, they gathered the celebrated buffalo chips—cow dung that had dried in the sun and hardened to a burnable consistency. Bags of weed seeds from straw stacks were mixed in with soft coal, as another way of stretching fuel supplies.

The farmers could stay home by the stove. But in the cities anybody with a job had to get out and get to work. Much of the work done that winter consisted of tabulating business losses. The prime status-symbol in Winnipeg was the beaver coat, and next to it was the raccoon coat. The Winnipeg policemen, with their huge buffalo coats, were the envy of every other citizen with an outdoor job and particularly of the mail-carriers, who had the worst jobs in Canada. This was a winter in which everybody dressed for the weather. The Winnipeg fur hat, which could be pulled well down to cover ears,

neck, and forehead, was the most prized of all headgear. It established a male fashion in the West that still survives. Around our
necks we wore heavy woollen scarves and a Winnipeg-style overcoat with its high collar that could be lifted well over the ears.
Anybody who had to be out much replaced gloves with double
mitts—leather outside and wool inside. Long underwear and lined
overshoes were universal attire for both sexes. The younger women
wore knee-length knitted overpants under their skirts, while their
elder sisters put on ankle-length drawers.

In most prairie cities, it was a lot easier to walk than wait for the
streetcars. Even at forty below, a half-mile walk was made possible
by stopping en route in stores, office-building lobbies, brokerage
offices, and banks. That was everybody's standard procedure for
getting around all the cities of the West. Each city is built around a
core of retail establishments, and far more people used the aisles of
Simpson's in Regina and Hudson's Bay in Calgary and Edmonton
than walked the sidewalks outside. None of the department stores
did enough business to pay for their heating costs.

Some of the small neighbourhood stores, curiously enough, did
better with the bad weather. Housewives stopped lugging armloads
of groceries home from the chain stores and lived from hand to
mouth with carryable purchases they could take home at a jog-trot
from the corner store. While country schools were closed by
blocked roads, city schools stayed open and attendance hardly suffered at all. Even Winnipeg's famous outdoor skating rinks stayed
open and, though the numbers dropped sharply, the kids still
skated, forty below or no forty below. But they didn't skate for long,
or very often.

As January closed in 1936, Winnipeg and the other cities looked
hopefully to the traditional 'bonspiel thaw', which occasionally
mitigated the prairie winter. It never came that year. The cold deep-

ened instead of moderating. Over the whole of Saskatchewan, the temperature was a full twenty-five degrees below normal. Regina's mean temperature of -20° for the month of February had never been equalled before, and has never been equalled since. Edmonton with a mean of -17° was almost twenty-five degrees colder than normal, and Calgary's mean of -12° was twenty-seven degrees under normal.

Ironically, for a large area of southern Alberta, it would have been better for everybody if everything had been worse in January. A chinook wind had blown in from the Pacific in early January, melting the snow on the cattle ranges. The balmy breezes brought rain; then the wind switched abruptly to the north, and the cattle ranges were tragically coated with ice from Wild Horse to Pincher Creek and Brooks. It was then that the winter settled over southern Alberta in all its fury, with blizzards that drifted the roads and immobilized the ranches. There was nothing for the cattle to eat and no way of getting food to them. They perished, by twos and fives and tens, and when the spring came, the farmers and ranchers were too busy getting rid of the carcasses to bother with the count.

For the ranchers of Alberta, 1936 was the dying end, and there was scarcely a cattleman in the south country who wouldn't have called it quits if he could have got out. The drouth of 1933 had driven 500 farm families out of southern and eastern Alberta to the bush country north-west of Red Deer. More hundreds would have gone in 1936, but there was no way out. Those who had any money went as far north as Edmonton and brought in feed by the carload. Those who had no money got relief feed that the government shipped in.

The severe winter of 1933 and the plague of grasshoppers in the summer had forced a vast flood of unfinished cattle onto the market and the price for the best beef Canada could produce fell to $2.48 a hundredweight on the Winnipeg market. But there was no good beef to be had from Alberta in the liquidation of the herds of half-starved cattle. It happened again in 1935, and the climax was reached in 1936 when the Dominion government stepped in and bought 15,000 head of half-starved cattle for a cent a pound and slaughtered them to get them off the market.

Winter ended with a thaw at the end of February 1936, and presently we were into summer, which was to be much worse.

One could get away from the cold in the winter by retreating inside and staying there. There was no escape from the heat and wind and dust of the summer of 1936. There were good rains that spring outside the Palliser Triangle, but the big heat-wave began to build in Kansas in late May and reached the Prairies in June. The crop outgrew its moisture reserves and was beginning to wilt by Dominion Day. Two weeks later it was gone.

High temperatures and hot winds out of the south-west gave Saskatchewan and Manitoba a perpetual overcast. The soil blowing across the roads and railway tracks was caught and held by Russian thistle until it drifted to the tops of fences and snow-fences, and all that could be seen was the tops of the posts. In southern Alberta, the C.P.R. used snowplows to clear the tracks of soil drifts ten feet high. From Calgary to Winnipeg there was almost nothing but dust, in a bowl that extended clear down to Texas. Within the bowl was stifling heat, as if someone had left all the furnace doors open and the blowers on. By Dominion Day, ninety-degree temperatures were the rule between Winnipeg and Lethbridge. At Foremost, it reached into the nineties every day but three for the next six weeks. At Willow Creek, in south-western Saskatchewan, it went above 100° on thirteen days in July. The heat not only covered the Great Plains, it fastened a deathly grip on Ontario and the Great Lakes as well.

No one who lived in southern Ontario that summer could have failed to understand what life was like on the Prairies. From Windsor to Belleville, for a solid week in July, it was 100° above or hotter every day, and in Toronto it reached 105° on three successive days. During that awful ten days, 500 died in Ontario alone from heat prostration. The Associated Press in New York developed a ghoulish passion for statistics, and issued daily reports of the mounting death-toll from heat prostration in the United States. The total touched 1,160 on July 13 and passed the 3,000 mark a week later. On July 14, a hundred died in southern Ontario. In the West, nobody bothered to keep track of the toll. The newspapers might report a dozen deaths in Winnipeg, half a dozen in Regina and Calgary, but the story of the 1936 heat wave was too big to cover and too dreary to tell.

What made the heat intolerable was the way the wave built. Every day was hotter than the previous day, with heavier haze and more dust. At the end of the first week in July, people were taking pillows into the down-town parks in Winnipeg and Regina in an effort to get some rest. In the down-town tenements, beds were deserted as the inhabitants stretched out on floors, on verandahs, and on lawns. But there was no escape. Swarms of mosquitoes and crickets made sleeping out of doors almost impossible in Winnipeg. In Regina even mosquitoes would have been welcome, for their presence would have meant there was water some place. The only visible sign of water in Regina was the circles of moisture around the trees on Victoria Street; the city saved the trees by hauling water in fire trucks.

The Manitoba peak was reached on July 11 when the temperature reached 108° in Winnipeg, 110° in Brandon, and 110° at Morden. During the third week in July, it went over 100° every day everywhere in the south country of Saskatchewan and Alberta. In Winnipeg, the weather story was bigger even than the provincial election. A dozen people died daily from heat prostration, and soon we were reporting the deaths of dogs, cats, and canary-birds.

After the temperature reached 108° on Saturday, the heat wave in Winnipeg and eastern Manitoba ended in a wild electrical storm that blew down the usual quota of trees and power-lines and de-roofed barns and outbuildings. But the worst was far from over for the rest of the Palliser west. The extreme heat persisted in southern Saskatchewan and southern Alberta until well into August. Not since records had been kept had the country seen the like of it. In the last week of July, the new Social Credit government of Alberta stopped trying to revolutionize the banking system long enough to send its Minister of Agriculture to Ottawa to plead for help to move 400,000 starving cattle out of southern Alberta to available pastures in the north.

Then in the midst of it all, at the very height of the heat wave, a new terror struck—infantile paralysis. That was the summer the word 'polio' first became a part of the common language of Canada. There had been outbreaks before, but never on a scale sufficient to cause a general alarm. At most, there would be a few dozen cases a year in Manitoba. In 1936 the first of the great polio epidemics hit Winnipeg, and then spread to rural Manitoba. Before the epidemic ran its course, 558 cases of polio were recorded with thirty-seven deaths in Manitoba.

As a general-assignment reporter on the *Free Press* that summer, I wrote the weather stories and helped to cover the polio epidemic. I learned about public panic from polio. Both the provincial and city health departments maintained maps on which the new cases of polio were marked each day with coloured pins. In Winnipeg the primary concern was with polio, but the provincial authorities gradually became alarmed over an outbreak of equine sleeping sickness, which in early August began to spread to human beings. A second coloured-pin map was set up in the provincial health department, and, as the maps filled in, the question arose more frequently: Was there some relationship between sleeping sickness and polio?

The polio stories that summer were the first ones read by every newspaper subscriber with a young family. Few ever suspected how we wrestled with our consciences in the Winnipeg newspaper offices over how much to write about polio. In the beginning, we treated it as we might have treated any other story, by writing everything. We reported the number of new cases in the last twenty-four hours, where they were located, the age of the afflicted, whether there was paralysis present, and whether there were other members afflicted in the family.

Our telephones rang steadily. Frantic mothers called the *Free Press* and *Tribune* instead of their doctors. They would describe the symptoms their children had and ask us if it was polio, searching obviously for the reassurance they were afraid they would not get by calling their doctor. We published the best advice we could get from the medical profession, but it was sketchy at best because so little was known about how the disease spread or how to treat it.

Those who could get their children out of town did so. Gradually our telephone calls changed. Instead of reeling off symptoms, the callers wanted to know about Grand Beach, or Winnipeg Beach, or Clear Lake, or Kenora, or Bemidji, or even Banff. Was there any polio there? Was there any sleeping sickness there? Did it look as if there was going to be any polio at Winnipeg Beach? Was it true that there was polio at Gimli and that it was being kept secret? The flight from Winnipeg was on.

Then the nature of the phone calls changed again to calls from doctors or nurses. Couldn't we just, for one day, forget about polio, they pleaded, couldn't we stop writing about it, and let them get a little rest? The more we wrote about it, the worse flap Winnipeg motherhood got into. The more carefully we described the symptoms in our effort to dampen down public concern, the worse we made everything. One of my former book-keeping clients went to the extreme of buying me a lunch to plead the case of the medical profession.

'If you ask a little girl with the colic whether she's got a pain in her neck she'll probably say "yes",' he said. 'On any given day in Winnipeg 5,000 kids will come down with belly-aches for one reason or another. Usually 4,995 pains will go away and the others may turn out to be scarlet fever or an angry appendix. But they don't get time to go away any more.'

Hysterical mothers were watching over children as they had never watched before. At the first sign of a belly-ache, they would pop the children into bed, stick thermometers into them, and start manipulating their necks in search of polio symptoms. In such circumstances, any child would find symptoms he otherwise would never have thought of. As things then stood, the mathematical odds against any Winnipeg child getting polio were at least 500 to one. Polio, real polio, was hard enough to contend with without the panic that was sweeping the city. Polio wouldn't go away if we ignored it, but perhaps the hysterical mothers would quieten down. Eventually public concern did subside, though polio was with us all that summer. It returned in milder form the next year and then subsided to the pre-1936 level. Sleeping sickness returned in 1937 and 1938 and then it, too, subsided.

Around the edges of the Palliser Triangle, everything improved in 1937. But inside the weather got worse, and 1937 became the year all Saskatchewan went through the wringer. The winter of 1936-7 was a black one in Saskatchewan, black physically because of lack of snowfall, and black spiritually because the people knew that without snow to heal the scars of the 1936 drouth they had a date with an even greater disaster in 1937. A near rainless fall was followed by an almost snowless winter. Minor flurries brought a few inches of snow in December, a few inches in January, a few inches in February.

Over the years, Saskatchewan counts on at least forty-four inches of winter snow to get its crop away to a good start. It got half that in 1937, and most of it wound up in drifts along fence lines and railways. Winter came early in the autumn of 1936 and stayed late. October and November were punctuated by a series of brief but bitter cold spells, with temperatures down to -8° in October, -20° in November, and -40° in December.

Over the whole province of Saskatchewan, January of 1937 was probably the coldest month on record, and not so much because of extremely low temperatures but because it never warmed up. Thermometers dropped to -30° or -40° during the night and even in the bright sunshine of midday would still be down around -20°. Regina was typical of the province and there, over the entire month, it only got as high as zero five times. Light showers in May got some of the crop started, but that was the end. Little rain fell in June, almost none fell in July, and everything that grew over the whole of Saskatchewan was written off as failure. And the write-off took place earlier than ever before.

The worst dust storm ever recorded hit in the first week of June, sweeping the whole of the southern third of the province. At Shaunavon in the south-west, visibility was reduced to inches and so great was the wind force that the dust was driven three feet into the straw stacks in the area. The soil that was stirred up by the near hurricanes in June was blown back and forth across the province for the rest of the summer. By mid June the Prairie Farm Rehabilitation Administration set the disaster area at over 60 million acres, of which 45 million were once prosperous and occupied farm land.

All governments, provincial and federal and what was left of municipal administrations, moved in on the disaster. Cattle that had been living off the leaves they could strip from bushes and trees were shipped to available feed supplies in Manitoba and northern Alberta. Moving out with the cattle were the people of the small towns, to drift aimlessly into Regina, Saskatoon, and Moose Jaw. Or they jumped freight trains and headed for Alberta and Ontario in such numbers that both governments warned indigent Saskatchewanites to stay out of their provinces.

And still the dust blew. On June 24, it blew with such fury that it forced the Moose Jaw fair to cancel its horse races and shut down. The force of the storms blowing across southern Saskatchewan was felt as far east as Winnipeg, where once again a dust haze obscured the sun.

Highways became so drifted with dust as to be impassable. South of Moose Jaw, the blowing alkali from dried-up Johnstone Lake coated the countryside a dirty white and drove everybody indoors. Sixty miles to the south, near the town of Rockglen, Fife Lake, which had once been thirty-five miles long, dried up completely. Far to the east in the Oxbow area, the Lake of the Rivers went dry and in the process a great mass of prehistoric buffalo bones was uncovered. The farmers of the area lived that year on the returns they got from the fertilizer plants for the carloads of bones they managed to harvest. Near Arcola, the trains were delayed by the myriads of grasshoppers that lit on the rails and were ground to grease.

The Saskatchewan crop was destroyed by the fourth week of June. Then the heat got worse. At the end of June, 100-degree temperatures were common everywhere and the areas as far north as Prince Albert got a bitter taste of what Regina and Moose Jaw had experienced in 1936. The peak came on July 5, when it touched 110 degrees at Regina, Moose Jaw, and a dozen other southern communities. For the rest of the summer ninety-degree heat was the rule, for the hot weather extended well into August, and records were established all over on August 23, when it went well over the 100-degree mark again. There had been hotter Junes than 1937, hotter Julys, and hotter Augusts, but taken together there had never been a longer and hotter summer.

Neither Alberta nor Manitoba suffered as Saskatchewan did that year. The near crop-failure in southern Alberta was more than balanced by a comparatively good crop in the north. Manitoba, with the exception of the dust-bowl corner, had a good average crop that went eighteen bushels to the acre.

Almost as soon as the Saskatchewan crop was destroyed, the perverse gods of the weather seemed to relent. Widespread thunder showers and late summer and fall rains were reinforced by heavy winter snows. The Saskatchewan government went in hock in the spring of 1938 for $20 million worth of seed grain that it dispensed to its destitute farming communities. The melting snows of winter got the crop started. Abundant rains in May and June kept it going. For the first time in years, a cautious note of optimism crept into the Wheat Pool's crop forecast. It began to look, on Dominion Day, as if Saskatchewan might harvest 225 million bushels of wheat compared with the 33 million it had scraped up the year before. Manitoba and Alberta were also hopeful, so there was every indication of a crop well over 425 million bushels, the best since 1925. Then came hail, rust, and grasshoppers to Saskatchewan and western Manitoba. Within a single week, hail alone cause the Saskatchewan Wheat Pool to drop its estimate from 218 million to 190 million bushels. Rust and grasshoppers forced even this figure down by a third. The grasshoppers came in clouds, curiously from the north, in concentrations never before experienced in Canada. Huge swarms appeared over Saskatoon and Regina in late July. They devoured everything in their path as they ate their way out of sight. They travelled in narrow paths, but only the broken straw of what had promised to be a bumper crop was left behind. Then, seemingly out of nowhere, came a second and even greater invasion.

The worst grasshopper blizzard within the memory of man hit Regina on August 11. The grasshoppers covered everything—the walls of buildings, sidewalks, streets, telephone lines. Then it rained and the downpour washed grasshoppers into storm sewers in such numbers that the intakes were clogged and the streets were flooded. Anybody who lived in Regina that summer and could not get over being squeamish about walking on wall-to-wall grasshoppers stayed indoors. Clouds of the insects obscured the sun, and a Regina man almost choked to death in a dentist's chair when a hopper flew in the window and lodged in his throat while he was having a tooth extracted.

This was the summer in which all the Saskatchewan legends about grasshoppers were created, about grasshoppers that chewed holes in stenographers' stockings as they rushed from buses to offices, about grasshoppers stalling trains and streetcars, getting into safety deposit boxes, and devouring florists' stocks. Above all, it was the year of the gulls. On August 22, the Franklin gulls arrived by tens of thousands to the Wascana Lake in Regina. There they fell upon the hoppers and gorged themselves to a point where they could barely get into the air.

It was indeed a historic day, for, with the coming of the gulls to Regina, the dirtiness of the 1930s came to an end. The weather turned salubrious, autumn passed pleasantly, the winter brought snow, and the rains came back the next June as they had in 1915. Saskatchewan, in 1939, raised 250 million bushels of wheat, the best crop anyone had seen since 1928. But it was not a crop that would be long remembered. There was little room for remembering in the minds of those who grew it—not at the end of a decade they would spend the rest of their lives trying to forget

CHAPTER XII

'THAT YE HELP ONE ANOTHER'

The word 'fellowship' has been so thoroughly debased by forty years of claptrap at service-club orgies that I hesitate to try to reclaim its simple virtues. But of all the things that were good about the depression, by far the best was the deep sense of fellowship that took root and flourished. It took many forms. There was the spontaneous generosity of eastern Canadians for the dried-out farmers of Saskatchewan in 1933 and 1934. There had been the 'Friendship League' promotion in Winnipeg, which eventually petered out, but it began in the hearts of kindly people as a gesture of fellowship. There were the people who supported the Goodwill Industries, who joined the man-a-block scheme because they wanted to do something for somebody, who, in another hackneyed phrase, helped the Salvation Army out of 'the goodness of their hearts'. But there was another and a better side to it, a personal relationship between two human beings, of people 'looking out' for their friends and neighbours. On relief, everybody was everybody else's neighbour.

By 1933, the urban society of western Canada had shaken itself down into the employed and the unemployed. People stopped thinking of unemployment as an ephemeral phenomenon that would be gone next month, and society began to live with mass unemployment as a fact of life. The cities were still living economic organisms and if hundreds of jobs were being closed out, other hundreds of new jobs were opening up. As openings occurred, there was a lot of frantic scrambling to get them for neighbours or friends.

Early in the depression, everybody scrambled after every rumour of a job, whether it was for an assistant janitor or a mechanical draftsman. The 1931 impression that the unemployed were mainly idlers or goldbricks probably arose from the desperate lies we told in trying to fight our way into jobs. Many an employer discovered that the new auto-parts clerk he had hired actually knew nothing of auto parts. He might run through half a dozen phoneys before he got the job filled properly. Once the frenzy of job-hunting passed, it was conceded to be simple stupidity for a file clerk to try to pass himself off as a journeyman plumber.

In the new world in which the unemployed circulated, passing friendships were loosely formed on work-gangs and in Woodyard line-ups. Two boondogglers on a dandelion gang might hit it off well together to the extent of sharing their problems and their hopes and ambitions. They would stop and visit wherever their paths crossed. If one of them ever heard of a job the other could fill, he'd go to endless trouble to try to find even a casual friend and tell him about the job.

Once, on my walk to the Woodyard from Chalmers Avenue, I stopped into the Glenwood garage to get warm. Business wasn't good, and the boss was wondering out loud if he might not improve it by hiring a part-time mechanic to work nights on cars of people in the neighbourhood. When I left, the garage operator had about convinced himself he had a workable idea. All the way to the Woodyard I bounced the job around, trying to recall who among my acquaintances had ever mentioned being a mechanic. At last I recalled a pleasant fellow I had met months before. His name eluded me, and I hung around the Woodyard until late afternoon in the hope that he would turn up for his tickets. Just before closing time I remembered his name, and one of the clerks supplied his address. Next day I hiked out and told him about the possibility of the job. We walked back to the garage together, and I was almost as happy as he was when they made the deal and he got the job.

There was more than a touch of this sort of thing in most of the jobs that were filled during those years. It was a succession of helping hands that enabled me to make the long leap from a participant in the depression to a chronicler of it. It began with the wildest sort of *deus ex machina*. In one of our many moves, we rented a room in which the closet was half filled with cardboard cartons. The cartons were full of magazines, and the landlord said that with his weak back he had not been able to lug them to the trash pile. If I wanted to use the closet, I could dispose of the books.

The cartons contained a complete collection of the *American Mercury* from 1925 until 1930. I read the entire collection from cover to cover, over and over. Whenever the heavy diet I was getting from the public library palled, I turned to Mencken and Nathan and the sparkling prose of Asbury, Beer, Goldberg, Idwall Jones, James Cain, Ernest Boyd, James Stevens, James T. Farrell, Benjamin deCassiers. I used to carry a *Mercury* with me to read in relief line-ups and on work-gangs. On one occasion I slipped away from the gang and found a soft spot and settled down for the afternoon with my magazine. The foreman found me and was about to bounce me off the gang until he bought my excuse that there was a story in the magazine he should read. It was 'Hatrack', Herbert Asbury's classic yarn about the small-town prostitute that got the *Mercury* banned and H. L. Mencken jailed in Boston. I urged the foreman to sit down and read it.

'Oh boy,' he said afterwards, 'if you've got any more books like that, bring them with you and we'll take turns reading them.' Unhappily, there was only one 'Hatrack'.

It was no accident that, when I launched my own writing career, the prose style that evolved had a decided *American Mercury* tinge. My career began with a notice, somewhere, that the *Mercury* was scheduling a series of critical articles on sports and sports promotion. The list of the subjects wanted included horse-racing, and I asked myself why didn't I write an article for the *Mercury* on the art of doping race horses.

Indeed, why not? If I was completely without any qualifications for a writing career, I would be in good company. The libraries were full of books by the unqualified—Joseph Conrad, Mark Twain, Robert Service, Thomas Paine, Charles Dickens, Ernest Hemingway, and a hundred others. Besides, the *American Mercury* was noted for the breaks it had given to new and unknown writers.

We had been on relief for over a year when I decided to become a writer. In the next year I was to discover the meaning of fellowship. I had only to mention that I was writing an article on doping horses for the *American Mercury*, and people seemed to want to do favours for me. To write requires paper and pencils, lots of paper and lots of pencils. I went down to the Grain Exchange with the idea of scrounging some old insurance forms or clearing-house pads. I emerged with a pocketful of pencils, a dozen books of ruled foolscap, and enough envelopes to last a year.

Yet, with all the needed equipment, my article-writing bogged down for a very simple reason—lack of facts. Horse-racing in the 1920s in western Canada attracted the dregs of both humanity and horse flesh. Hop-headed jockeys, thieving swipes, and swindling owners and trainers dominated the 'sport' and the medicine chests that hung along the shedrows were cluttered with syringes, hypodermics, and stimulants that were used on most of the horses before they went to the paddock. Saliva tests were unknown, and half the trainers on the track fancied themselves as masters of the art of doping or 'sending' horses. When our own horse, Dick, had shown some speed in one race and then faltered, I was besieged with offers by friendly trainers to 'let me send him for you and we'll win a bet'.

Most of the horses went to the paddock loaded not only with heroin or morphine but concoctions of nux vomica, strychnine, nitroglycerine, brandy, aspirin, and anything else that was handy. Nor was it only the trainers and owners of the horses who did the doping. Sharpshooters around the track were forever on the alert for a horse that they might 'send' and bet on, without even telling the owner or trainer. Doping somebody else's horse was a common lark. Indeed it was regarded as common sense for drug experimenters to try out their prescriptions on somebody else's horse before they risked it on their own. Somebody tried out something on Dick one day that didn't start to work until after the race was over and he was back at the barn. I was still walking around and around the barn cooling him out long after dark that night.

So I knew all *about* doping race horses, but when I sat down to write I discovered I did not know with any precise accuracy *when, how, why,* and *how much* of the drugs to administer. Without this and other information, I was lost. I wrote some letters to horse-training friends at winter tracks and these letters were long delayed in delivery. Weeks passed before I got any replies, and then the answers were incomplete. I received a dozen different dope prescriptions but none of the trainers could give any explanation for the use of any ingredient except that it was included in the charge to make horses run faster. They didn't know what they were doing; they only knew results, which were all that ever counted on race-tracks.

I decided to consult some of the doctors I had encountered in the previous winter in my book-keeping promotion. Without exception, they were delighted to help me. While patients nursed their aches and pains in their waiting-rooms, they pored over long-neglected medical books to pin-point the organic reaction of combinations of nitroglycerine and nux vomica. When some of the prescriptions were analysed, the result was more bafflement than enlightenment, for the concoctions seemed to be composed of anti-pathic ingredients. One of the doctors telephoned the head of the veterinary department at the University of Manitoba and made a date for me on the theory that the mixtures might work differently on horses than on people. Together we went over the prescriptions and made sense out of some of them, but he could find little scien-tific basis for many others.

While awaiting replies to my letters to the trainers, I had filled several books with anecdotes about the race-tracks, dealing with the use of drugs and misuse of horses. With the scientific data I went back to the books and tried to put the whole article together. In ten days I had the job done. I went off in a corner and read it aloud to myself.

It was awful!

I decided to try again. This took about a week. Another reading aloud indicated that the thing still did not hang together. In all, I rewrote the piece six times, which at 5,000 words per writing made 30,000 words that had gone through the pencil. I had read some-where that Sinclair Lewis wrote a million words before he had a sin-gle acceptance, and it began to look as if his record would be broken.

The article eventually took shape, but by the time it did a good many issues of the *American Mercury* had come and gone. The arti-cle went off and Kay and I could hardly contain ourselves for the next two weeks wondering if the *Mercury* was going to take it or not.

Eventually the article came back and we died a little at the sight of the big brown envelope in the postman's hand as he came up the walk. Instead of the printed rejection slip I was to get to know so well, there was a three-line note from Charles Angoff, the managing editor. He had liked the article and was sorry he had not received it sooner. They had bought a piece on horse-racing, which was then in type. Good luck. That was all. But it was enough to convince me I was on the rails at last. And it was enough to sustain me for almost a year as the rejection slips poured in, and my wordage on paper soared far beyond the 100,000 mark and headed for 200,000. Six months after I started writing, I had three or four pieces en route to different editors all the time. I never found a customer. I knew almost to the day when each publication would return my article. If it failed to show up, Kay and I would live with new hope until it did. But the big brown envelope never contained anything but a rejection slip.

My writing career created many new problems. One was for money for postage and pencils and paper. I needed at least $1 a week to keep my stuff in circulation. This ran our weekly budget of needs up to $2.50 and getting that kind of money was almost impossible. It cost eight or ten cents to ship a manuscript to New York or Toronto and return postage had to be included. Once, when I was completely out of cash, I sent a manuscript off without return postage. It came back as quickly as the others. Thereafter, I never enclosed postage and never lost a manuscript. When the manuscripts became frayed from their rounds of the magazines, they went into a bureau drawer.

Tidying up the drawer in the early spring of 1933, I came across my first article. It was readable enough to be saleable to somebody, and I thought about the Winnipeg *Free Press* magazine section. It could make a timely article in a few weeks when the horse-racing season would reopen in Winnipeg. I took it down to Frank Williams, the features editor, and he bought it on the spot. I knew that day how Irish Sweepstake winners felt, and the feeling lasted for a week. Kay and I started making small plans for all the things we would buy with the cheque for the article, the first real money we would have seen in thirty months. We speculated endlessly on what it would bring. The *American Mercury* would have paid $250. The *Free Press*, we reasoned, could hardly pay less than $50. We hoped for and counted on $50. The article was published, and we got a cheque for $10.

An anti-climax? It was cataclysmic, but Kay and I both recovered, largely helped by another act of fellowship that came belting out of a clear sky. A casual acquaintance from the old days in the Grain Exchange came looking for me with a job—marking the quotation board in a new brokerage office that was opening on Fort Street. It paid $10 a week and I leaped at it, although our net income after car-fare would be less than we would have received on relief. The pressure was eased somewhat by months with five pay days and by the steady sale of previously rejected articles to the *Free Press*. In addition, I got an afternoon job as an accounting clerk in the stock department of the company. This yielded an extra $3 a week and a steady job in the stock department when the Fort Street office was closed that fall.

The big bull-market in wheat that was expected with the collapse of world currencies failed to materialize. But as President Roosevelt hatched his famous Blue Eagle in June 1933, launched the National Industrial Recovery Administration, and began to revalue the price of gold upward to $35 an ounce, other things happened. The New York stock market came back to life, and I was shifted to marking the New York stock quotation board in the morning and to functioning as the company security analyst and statistician in the afternoon. By then, in the spring of 1934, I was earning $15 a week, and was on the receiving end of so much fellowship that I began to feel like the anointed of God. Frank Williams not only bought everything I wrote, he loaned me books on writing and journalism from the *Free Press* library and introduced me to the news editor, who was then George V. Ferguson.

Ferguson had begun his career on the financial desk, and we talked about the booming gold-mining stock market and the boiler-room swindles in Toronto. He asked me to write a couple of articles for the *Free Press* on the mining-stock rackets. When they were published, he suggested I expand them into magazine articles for the *Canadian Forum*. He wrote a glowing note to Steven Cartwright, then the editor of the *Forum*, and I was soon a regular unpaid contributor to the magazine. The *Forum*, Ferguson explained, was Canada's most influential magazine, after *Saturday Night*, and some surprising things had happened to people who had written for it. How right he was!

I wrote a history of the Winnipeg cenotaph for the *Forum*, which brought me a fan letter from H. L. Mencken himself.

The cenotaph in Winnipeg was the only demonstrably fourth-rate war monument in the whole world. The first design contest was won by the famous Toronto sculptor, Emanuel Hahn. The committee was so appalled at the idea of a memorial to Canadian war-dead designed by a person with so German a name that they paid Hahn the prize money and threw out his design. A new contest was held, and it was won by Elizabeth Wyn-Wood of Toronto. The committee breathed a sigh of relief with a so thoroughly Anglo-Saxon winner. Unhappily it turned out that Miss Wood was the wife of Emanuel Hahn. She too was paid off, and her design was also thrown out. In desperation, the committee leaped over the second-prize winner and accepted the design that it had placed third. It was the work of a local architect who was unrelated to anybody named Hahn. So outlandish, even outrageous, a story wrote itself, yet I cherished the Mencken letter and it still hangs framed over my desk.

My articles for the *Forum* on the mining-stock swindles came to the attention of John M. Godfrey, who had been appointed

Ontario Securities Commissioner by Premier Mitchell F. Hepburn when the Liberals took office in 1933 and Hepburn fired George Drew. Godfrey wrote applauding my insight and suggesting that I call on him for further ammunition. We quickly established a rapport, and I so wrote my way into his confidence that he obtained a job for me in Toronto with another young friend he had helped into the brokerage business. The friend was George McCullagh and through Godfrey's efforts McCullagh had become broker-manager for William H. Wright. As McCullagh's statistician, I would be paid $50 a week to start, with prospects of lots more to come. To get me and my family to Toronto, Godfrey wrote his old friend John Dafoe, the editor of the Winnipeg *Free Press*. If Dafoe would pay the expenses to Toronto, of my wife and me, Godfrey suggested, he would open his files to me so that I could write a whole series of articles on the mining-stock rackets for the *Free Press* in repayment.

Ferguson telephoned me at work and asked me to come and see him. He said Dafoe's reaction to the letter hand been: 'If this fellow can write well enough to get a tough old criminal lawyer like John Godfrey so excited, what are we doing letting him get out of Winnipeg?'

'I'm going to take you in to meet the Chief,' he said, 'and then we'll go and see Victor Sifton. If they are impressed, we will offer you a job.'

How, I wondered out loud, did I go about impressing Dafoe and Sifton?

'God damned if I know,' said Ferguson. 'Dafoe hired me by mail-order from Oxford.'

Nobody asked me anything about my education race, religion, or even my age. There were no scientific aptitude tests or even application forms to be filled out. I must have impressed them, however, because they offered me a job as a reporter at $20 a week. I accepted on the spot; and the Dirty Thirties were well over before my salary reached the level George McCullagh had offered in 1934. But the choice was one I never regretted. I never got over being amazed at the helping hands that were suddenly being reached out to me from all directions. If the Dirty Thirties brought out the worst in our economic system, it also brought out a lot of the best in human beings and created an atmosphere of genuine fellowship that has hardly been surpassed in any other age.

CHAPTER XIII

A GOY AMONG JEWS

In my search for employment I was free to range over the whole of commercial Winnipeg and nobody denied me a job from any ulterior motive. This did not hold true for the Ukrainians, Poles, and Jews. For them, Winnipeg was far from being a city of 250,000 in which they too were free to search for work. As much as two-thirds of it was barred and bolted against them.

None of the city's chartered banks, trust companies, or insurance companies would knowingly hire a Jew, and anyone with a Ukrainian or Polish name had almost no chance of employment except rough manual labour. The oil companies, banks, mortgage companies, financial and stock brokers, and most retail and mercantile companies except the Hudson's Bay Company discriminated against all non-Anglo-Saxons. For the young Ukrainians and Poles, there was a possible solution if they could beat the accent handicap. They could change their names. So they changed their names, sometimes formally and legally, but mostly informally and casually. Caroline Czarnecki overnight became Connie Kingston, Mike Drazenovick became Martin Drake, and Steve Dziatkewich became Edward Dawson. But, for the Jews, a name change was not enough. It was not even enough to leave the synagogue, as did many of the young Jews who became Communist converts. In the minds of anti-Semitic Winnipeggers, there was no way in which a Jew could escape from Judaism. In plain truth, the unhappiest Jew in town would have been one who managed to sneak into a job in any of the Anglo-Saxon companies.

All this I discovered as a by-product of an act of kindness by a Jewish lawyer, who introduced me into the Jewish community after my bout with tuberculosis. During my last two weeks in the King Edward Hospital I thought I might be able to get a job in the Grain Exchange if I offered to start again as an office boy. I wrote to seven or eight people I knew, told them that I was being discharged soon, and asked for help. I offered to work for $10 a week just so we would not have to go back on relief. No one answered, and it was all terribly discouraging. One day, however, I got a note from Sam Drache, asking how I was getting along and saying that he had an idea that might develop into a job for me when I came out. Drache was a young lawyer who had had the bad luck to be starting in practice the summer after the Wall Street crash. My only contact with him was as lawyer for some of my miniature golf-course creditors, and when we sold the course, he did the negotiating for me. Getting that note from him was the nicest thing that happened that year.

As soon as I got out of the hospital I went to see him, and he outlined his plan. He said doctors were having a hard time making ends meet. Few of them had paid enough attention to their courses in medical economics, and keeping books was a distasteful chore anyway. Some of them forgot to send out bills, others forgot calls they had made and forgot who had paid them and how much. So, reasoned Drache, there was an opportunity for someone to bring some system into the lives of the medicos. He nominated me. He had plenty of office space, so we could start a book-keeping company right there. We would charge each doctor $10 a month for keeping books and sending out bills and we thought that it would be possible to get at least ten or fifteen clients. The financial arrangements were that I was to keep all the money above expenses until we got on our feet, and then we would make some kind of a deal to split the profits.

I accepted the proposition, cleared it with the Woodyard, and was eager to be off on my rounds of selling the doctors. Unfortunately, we were in the dandelion and dead-leaf offensives on relief work-gangs, so action had to be postponed until relief work became less regular. In the meantime, Drache undertook to give me a concentrated short course in salesmanship, and wrote a set sales pitch that I committed to memory.

Doctors, as a breed, turned out to be the world's worst appointment-breakers. They had a perfect system for giving salesmen the brush-off.

'Oh, I'm sorry I can't see you now, old chap—just got a hurried call for a maternity case, come back next week, will you?' Before I knew it, I was out in the corridor, again and again. I chased after some of them for weeks and never did get in to try my sales talk.

When we discovered our first obstacle, we took measures to overcome it. On the day before the fifteenth of the month, pay-day, we inserted a small, one-column display advertisement in the newspapers, with Drache putting up the money:

Just a Gentle Reminder!
MAKE TODAY
Your
Doctor's
PAY-DAY
TOO
The Accounting & Office
Management Company
601 Boyd Bldg.
Doctors' Book-keepers

This, we reasoned, would at least notify the medical profession of our existence. It did. The next day I got a request to call on a prominent doctor in the Medical Arts Building. I gave my sales talk a special rehearsal, for I knew that if I could land him others would follow. It quickly developed, as I entered his office, that he had no need of our service. He had a nurse and a girl book-keeper on duty. He wanted to see me only as a member of the executive of the doctors' union and his first words were:

'Well, what kind of a racket is this?'

By this time I had lost most of my awe of the medical profession. I matched his tone of voice.

'What do you mean by "racket"?' I demanded angrily.

The bedside manner appeared. The medical association, he said, was interested in our advertisement, and he had been instructed to find out what it was all about. Perhaps I should first of all tell him how I hoped to gain any profit from an advertisement of this kind?

I would indeed. I pointed out that many doctors could not even afford an office nurse or a book-keeper. Some of them neglected to send out their bills, or to keep track of their income. These were the men we were trying to reach and to help. For $10 a month I would keep the books, make out the bills, and send them out. If I could get twenty doctors, which was all I could handle at the moment, I would have an income of $200 a month, less expenses. He was not impressed. Yes, he said it ought to be worth $10 a month to a doctor to have his books kept in shape and get his bills made out, but he didn't like the advertisement. It smelled too much like some kind of racket.

The interview with the official of the doctors' union was inconclusive, but the advertisement did open a few doors for me and I got three or four clients. During the interviews with the doctors, I discovered one of my arguments alarmed rather than comforted them. With our system in operation, it would make the filing of income tax returns ever so much simpler. The cash income, with adequate records, would be brought forward each month so that at the end of the year it would be a simple matter to compute the doctor's income and make out his income-tax forms.

'My friend,' said one of the early interviewees, 'you couldn't have given me a better argument for not having you keep my books!'

He regarded the payment of income tax as akin to robbery. He was always having trouble with income-tax inspectors because his books were not in order. But, if he strictly accounted for all his income, he would have had to pay $300 or $400 a year in income tax.

'And can you tell me why in hell a doctor who donates so much of his time to this community should have to pay income tax? No, you bet you can't! The less I have on the books, the better I like it, and when a patient is cured and the account is paid it comes out of the book, I can tell you. Why, I do more work for nothing every day than I get paid for. The hell with the income tax, what they don't know won't hurt them, or me either.'

Getting clients was like pulling stumps with string, but getting paid for my work was harder. One doctor wound up owing me about $30 I never collected. He had an excellent practice, or at least I thought so. Having done my work, and it took about four days a month to take care of him, I wanted my money. It was, however, only after he was a good deal in arrears that I started to press, sometimes twice a day. At noon he would stick his head out the door, smile, and ask me to come back later in the afternoon as several good-paying patients would be coming in. I'd drop back at five and he would be full of apologies, because he hadn't taken in a dollar.

This game went on day after day. At the end of the week I would go in and make up the accounts. It was a simple matter to arrive at his cash income for that week. He marked his payments and charges on a daily calendar-pad, from which I transcribed them into the account book. He never took in less than $150 a week, not counting the cash he might have collected from furtive patients to his *sub-rosa* venereal-disease clinic. His endurance was greater than mine, and eventually I simply gave up and quit calling on him.

Another client turned out to be a brilliant surgeon who went wrong. His private life was a shambles, and his practice was gradually disappearing in an alcoholic fog. He owed money everywhere and would call me up frequently to help him search his books for someone who might be dunned into paying something on account. Before the wet rot attacked him, he was well on his way to the top in his field. When I caught up with him he was about at the bottom. Yet with all his weaknesses, he was my favourite client, even if he never paid me either.

Eventually Drache and I had to admit that our brain-child was not worth trying to save. If he felt that I was a bust, he never said so, and after we dissolved the Accounting & Office Management Company, he often found ways of helping me in my search for the eternal $1.50.

When I was trying to become a writer, Drache was the one who gave me solid encouragement and help. He provided me with paper and allowed me to use his office for typing my manuscripts. Without Drache's help I would never have been able to make the grade, so when my Gentile friends start denouncing Jews, I can only think about Sam Drache, who could give any Gentile I ever knew lessons in kindness and generosity. What was true of Drache was true in varying degrees of most Jews I encountered in my struggle to get off relief. It was particularly true of the Jewish doctors and dentists who adopted us.

It was through Drache and the other Jews that I came to appreciate for the first time the tremendous advantage it was to be a Canadian Anglo-Saxon in Winnipeg. And as time passed, the advantage widened when, as if racial intolerance was not enough, a new terror for the New Canadians began to stalk the land in the form of Immigration Officers with deportation orders in their hands. In 1931 the Communist Party was outlawed and the party leaders were arrested and sent to jail under the notorious Section 98 of the Criminal Code. Other aliens who were suspected of Communist activity were arrested at night and rushed secretly to Halifax for deportation. But deportations did not start or end with Communists, or even with the foreign-born. Many hundreds of British subjects were also seized and returned to the United Kingdom. Deportation became a useful and popular instrument for cutting down municipal relief costs. In Edmonton, the superintendent of relief announced that deportation proceedings were being started against all aliens on relief and that he had asked for 400 such orders.

Once public attention focused antagonistically on the aliens, it stayed there. The Canadian Legion clamoured for employers to fire aliens and give their jobs to war veterans. During the next two years, more than 10,000 New Canadians were deported, and twice as many, mainly those of British birth, left voluntarily.

The threat of deportation, which suddenly became terribly real for every alien on relief in western Canada, cast a pall over the Woodyard. The foreign-born, who had once chattered amiably while waiting in lines, sought more and more to melt into the background, say nothing, hear nothing, and escape to the protective coloration of their own communities. Those of radical persuasion would have faced prison or death in Poland, Germany, or Italy. For all of them, it would have meant taking their families back to an environment they had tried to leave behind. From 1931 onward, the deportations kept the subject in the newspapers, and the relief lines in a turmoil. A family might be seized in Winnipeg and spirited away to Halifax. Then there would be habeas corpus proceedings, Immigration Department hearings, questions in Parliament, and sometimes they would regain their freedom. In the intervals between alarms, the super-patriotic groups kept things stirred up with inflammatory resolutions at conventions.

For those with citizenship papers, which exempted them from the threat of deportation, discrimination served as a prod that intensified their urge to 'catch up' with the Anglo-Saxons. As the opportunities for employment shrank in commerce and industry, all ethnic segments tried to direct their brightest young people into the professions. They ran head-on into the barricades of prejudice all over again. The self-perpetuating control bodies of the professions established quotas to keep medicine, law, and accounting from 'being overrun with Jews and Hunkies'.

Certainly life was much less tolerable for everybody else than it was for the Anglo-Saxon Herrenvolk, and racial prejudice made it so. Racism, however, was not something that covered the community evenly like a paint. It was more like a laminate. Or, to switch the metaphor, ours was a society with a well-defined pecking order of prejudice. On the top were the race-proud Anglo-Saxons, who were prejudiced against everybody else. On the bottom were the Jews, against whom everybody discriminated. In between were the Slavs and Germans. By the mid thirties the Germans had become deeply infected with Hitler's poison and discriminated against Ukrainians, Poles, and Jews. The Poles hated the Russians, Ukrainians, and Jews, and both the Ukrainians and Jews subdivided again into 'Reds' and 'Whites' who endlessly refought the Russian revolution.

In all groups there were naturally many exceptions to the ruling prejudices. Nevertheless, racial discrimination was so much a fact of life that it drove the minorities into economic ghettoes. Jews tried to live off the trade of other Jews; and Ukrainians, Poles, and

Germans tried to live off other Ukrainians, Poles, and Germans. This drive to survive in a prejudice-ridden community produced the rash of small industry and of bootstrap manufacturing that developed in Winnipeg.

The ingenuity of the Jews and Ukrainians in finding things to get into was almost without limit. A garment-district janitor gathered up and took home all the chamois scraps from the cutting-table. He made dies with which to cut the scraps into rectangular 1"x 2" pieces. He tediously sewed hundreds of pieces together until he had a huge patch-work blanket that he sold back to his employer, who re-cut it into chamois linings for cheap coats. As long as he got his raw material for nothing and could hire neighbourhood women to sew for fifteen cents per hour, he was in business.

Small-scale garment factories, glove factories, shoe factories, printing plants, and dress plants proliferated. Long, empty ware-house space in the old wholesale district began to fill up with Jews trying to scratch a living in manufacturing. The North End filled up with home-based contractors. When a Ukrainian went into the construction business, he trailed a small army of other Ukrainians behind him—a Ukrainian excavator, a Ukrainian concrete-mixer, a Ukrainian plumber, a Ukrainian carpenter, a Ukrainian painter, a Ukrainian plasterer. It was the same with the Germans. The Jews tended more towards commercial enterprises and manufacturing.

Despite what amounted to a mass crusade of group self-help, with each racial group trading within the group, there was no passage to prosperity by that route. The groups were too small to provide a market of sufficient size to make for an efficient or profitable operation. The great Jewish drive to catch up had produced five times as many doctors and lawyers as the Jewish community itself could support. Racial discrimination drove the businessmen and professionals in among themselves, but economic necessity drove them out into the larger community again to batter at the citadels of prejudice. Because of the greater compulsion upon them, the Jews worked harder for smaller rewards than anybody else, and the paradox was created of anti-Semitic businesses doing an increasing volume of business with Jewish enterprises. I once asked a Jewish friend who was prospering by making clothing for a huge retail outlet how he managed to do so much business with people who were so notoriously anti-Semitic.

'They keep me in business,' he said. 'I make more money from them than any other customer I have. Why? Because they are anti-Semitic. Anti-Semitism distorts their judgment. In the back of their minds on every deal is the idea that they have got to beat down a Jew till he loses money on the trade. This business of having to grind down the Jew is a trap they keep making for themselves! And they don't even know when they are caught in their own trap. They have one absolute rule—to pay less than last year. They have to be able to brag to the other managers what they did to the Jews.

'Let me tell you about last year! Last year they cut the price so much I have to walk away and they go to Herzog Cloak. It happens he's got a government contract, so he is half-busy and they have to pay him $4 more a garment than they offered me. They can't come back to me; but Herzog comes to me and I do half the order for him in my plant at the price he gets!

'And let me tell you about the year before last! Maybe you know they buy coats on a staggered delivery—one-third by October 1 and the balance by November 1. They forget to fill in the first date on the order, so when it turns cold they start screaming for coats. "Work overtime," they say. "Do anything, but get us the coats!" I knew this had to happen, so I planned for it. I made up the garments to meet the usual schedule and waited. They pay me a big fat bonus for overtime I never had to work! And not only a bonus for me! I tack on a dollar a coat for my wife's Hadassah! When she gives me the receipt, I tell her better she should send it to the buyer, or better still she should send it to his boss and thank him for the donation his company has made to Jewish relief! What a joke that would be!'

From his laughter, he had told that joke over and over to everybody in the Jewish community.

There were few Jewish businessmen in Winnipeg who had my friend's shrewdness and mastery of the business he was in. But most of his co-religionists made up for anything lacking in natural instinct by a capacity for concentration on what they were doing. They also had the physical stamina needed to work an eighteen-hour day, if necessary, and behind them was a driving force far greater than any to be found in the 'white' community.

All this is recalled not to exacerbate old wounds that time is healing, or even maliciously to recall the sins of the fathers of that day for their sons and daughters of the third generation. It helps, however, to set the crowning paradox of the depression in its proper perspective: The best thing that ever happened to Winnipeg was a Jew, and he happened in the first week of June 1935.

His name was Sam Herbst, and, far from recognizing his potentiality for good, I had great difficulty convincing myself he was real. I was covering the labour beat and the relief-camp strike at the time, and when I returned to the *Free Press* newsroom there was a note in my box. Somebody by the name of Oiybst had phoned to say he was opening a new labour union office and wanted a story in the paper. His office was 305 Donalda Block. I wandered over.

Three or four people were moving desks around and hanging pictures in the throes of moving in. I introduced myself and when I said *Free Press*, a head popped around the corner of the private office. At first glance, he looked like a youngish Leopold Stokowski. He was a tiny little fellow with very long curly hair, happy blue eyes, and a broad smile. He was the unlikeliest looking labour organizer I had ever met.

He held out his hand, and when he spoke his accent was so straight off Union Square that I understood him only with difficulty. Getting his name down right was the first hurdle. While it was spelled 'Herbst', it was pronounced 'Oiybst', with the 'b' sound tending to get lost in the shuffle. Sam Herbst's message was more incredible than his accent. He was the personal representative of David Dubinsky, he said, and he had been sent to Winnipeg to organize the garment industry for the International Ladies Garment Workers Union. The first shop with which he proposed to negotiate a contract was Jacob and Crowley, and he expected to sign that contract within a week. Otherwise there would be a strike. Winnipeg, he said, was the dirtiest blot on the ladies'-garment map. The I.L.G.W.U. had organized the Toronto sweat-shops, and the Winnipeg sweat-shops were a threat to the standard of living of the garment workers in Toronto. David Dubinsky had assured the employers of eastern Canada that the unfair competition of the Winnipeg sweat-shops would be ended. David Dubinsky had sent him to Winnipeg to carry out this promise. He, Herbst, would now do so.

Never have I misread the character of a man as badly as I misread Sam Herbst. The note of reverence that came into his voice when he mentioned David Dubinsky's name and the emotion that almost choked him when he strung I.L.G.W.U. together were unnerving. I immediately wrote him off as a bumptious, ignorant New Yorker, who ought to be wisened up to the facts of labour-union life in Winnipeg. I had only recently written a 20,000-word history of the Winnipeg labour movement, fancied myself as an authority, and still carried a great store of factual information in my head that I was eager to show off. I undertook to enlighten Sam Herbst.

He had come, I told him proudly, to the city that had made labour warfare famous. This was where Canadian labour militancy reached its fullest growth in 1919, and was destroyed in the general strike that held and crippled western Canada. As for the garment industry, the Communists had been trying to organize it for five years. Strikes at Jacob and Crowley were as predictable as the seasons and the results as inevitable. Organizing the Toronto sweat-shops would be child's play compared with Winnipeg, even though its cut-throat garment industry employed less than 300.

Herbst listened politely, and that in itself set him off from all other labour organizers. He never lost his poise or his smile.

'Okay,' he said. 'So okay. So you know about Winnipeg. I take your word for Winnipeg. But I know about garment workers. I know about the I.L.G.W.U. I know about David Dubinsky. I know about President Roosevelt, who calls David Dubinsky to Washington when he wants advice about organized labour. David Dubinsky gives him advice, and President Roosevelt takes his advice, because David Dubinsky is the biggest man in organized labour in the world. And when David Dubinsky sends me to Winnipeg as his representative to organize the ladies' garment industry, then the garment industry will be organized, and by me, Sam Herbst!'

He caught his breath and went on: 'So, Gray, I don't want you should do me no favours. Don't even put my name in your newspaper. Who cares about Sam Herbst? All I want is that the garment workers of Winnipeg should know that David Dubinsky has sent his personal representative to organize Winnipeg for the I.L.G.W.U. What's past is past. What is important is what comes next and what is coming next is organization of the needle trades in Winnipeg.' (In his more than twenty years in the city, Sam Herbst never learned to pronounce the city's name—which made everything even. Nobody in 'Vee-ee-nee-peeg' ever learned to pronounce his name the way he did either.)

I wrote two paragraphs about the arrival of Mr. Herbst in Winnipeg. The story found a hole on the inside pages of the *Free Press*. A week later, Herbst phoned again for me to call on him. By now the moving-in process was over, and his office was well ordered and clean. He wanted to announce, he said, that he had signed a one-year closed-shop contract with Jacob and Crowley that called for a substantial increase in pay and a forty-four-hour week. From that moment on, I sat up and paid attention whenever Sam Herbst had anything to say. I was all questions, and the biggest one was how he had managed to sign up the Jacob and Crowley employees after their disastrous experience in previous strikes. It was simple, Sam explained. He had not gone after the employees. He had gone after Ben Jacob.

The Jacob and Crowley firm had pioneered in making ladies' garments in Winnipeg, and had been caught in the middle in the depression deflation. To stay in business, it cut prices and wages and protected itself as best it could. Low wages led to desperation strikes by poorly organized unions under Communist leadership. When the workers lost, as they always did, the company recruited new workers. The old workers went into business on their own and undercut prices to Jacob and Crowley's customers.

'You know', Sam Herbst said, 'that half the one-man shop operators in Winnipeg got their start working for Jacob and Crowley. I showed Ben Jacob what he has been doing. He's busier making competition for himself than in making money for himself. And I ask him how does he hope to make money when his workers can't even earn enough to buy food, let alone buy the clothes they make? And I show him what David Dubinsky advises President Roosevelt. The workers have to get paid a living wage, but the employers have to live too, and the I.L.G.W.U. wants the bosses to make a fair profit.

'I show him the bank account the I.L.G.W.U. has opened for me in Winnipeg. I got more money in the bank, he says, than he has. Anyway, I give him a good choice because we want him first. Simple. I offer a good agreement and I promise him that if the other employers don't sign a better agreement I will strike their plants. If he won't sign, I'll get some others, then he will have to sign a better agreement than his competitors or have a strike. Ben Jacob thinks about it, and he is convinced he can't lose. So he signs. And the employees sign up with the I.L.G.W.U. 100 per cent next day!'

Sam Herbst, that morning, could hardly contain himself. He had done what he had set out to do, and what else he and Ben Jacob had agreed upon I had no way of knowing. He was unwilling to discuss any of the terms of the Jacob and Crowley contract because, as he said, there were other contracts to be negotiated.

I liked Sam Herbst less on the second meeting than I had on the first. It was a sleazy way to organize a trade union, though he was not the first who had organized a shop by first dealing with the employer. According to legend, it was used by John L. Lewis's United Mine Workers of America in Alberta after the collapse of the One Big Union. The miners in Drumheller and in the Crow's Nest Pass, in 1920, were required to tear up their O.B.U. cards in the mine offices and take out U.M.W. cards before they could get back to the pits. The use of such odious tactics endeared Herbst to nobody, least of all to the leaders of the established union.

Sam Herbst did what he had to do with whatever tools came to hand. There was probably no other way in which the garment industry could have been organized. The Communists had failed. The Trades and Labour Council unions had done little organizing since 1920. Many of them were little more than paper unions that functioned only on government construction jobs, and infrequently even on those. The organizational drive of the Committee for Industrial Organization was only barely started in the United States and had made no impact in Canada. And in Winnipeg the effects of the 1919 General Strike were still tormenting the working population.

That strike had been the product of post-war turmoil, militant Marxian socialism, and a revolt of Canadian trade unionists of British origin against American craft unionism. The fight for the eight-hour day and the right to collective bargaining had become deeply submerged in ideological warfare, and ideological differences were magnified by the defeat. Bob Russell struggled on alone to keep the One Big Union alive; George Armstrong preached the pure socialist word in Market Square; Woodsworth and Heaps went into federal politics, Queen and Ivens went into provincial politics, Blumberg and Flye were elected to the city council; the foreign-born workers drifted into the Communist party under John Navis.

Not only was the trade-union movement leadership splintered, unionism itself was in a state of sorry disrepute. The railway workers who had gone on strike in 1919 lost their pension rights. Those who had played any major part in the strike lost their jobs. It was only in the most desperate circumstances that anybody with a job would listen to a union organizer, and only the foreign-born would listen to the Communists who preached class hatred and practised physical violence. A Communist strike without inflammatory speeches and a picket-line riot was rare.

With the arrival of Sam Herbst, the era of the class struggle ended on the picket lines of Winnipeg. He took the business of organizing unions back to the days of Sam Gompers, stripped away all the ideological trappings, and concentrated upon improving wages and working conditions for the workers and on co-operation with the employers. He selected his lieutenants shrewdly, welcomed

Communists and anti-Communists into the union with equal warmth. The Communists went along with Herbst in the hope of taking over his unions. They never came close to success, because he was too well schooled in the Communist techniques of boring from within.

The building of the union, however, was the least important thing Herbst did. His greatest achievement was in his single-handed transformation of labour-management relations in the garment industry. To get his union organized, he played one employer against another. Once the contracts were safely in the vault, Herbst turned to his main purpose, to create in miniature in Winnipeg what David Dubinsky had created in New York—a prosperous garment industry in which management and labour co-operated through an industry council to abolish sweat-shop conditions and cut-throat competition, and to increase the efficiency and crafts-manship of the industry.

He accomplished this mainly with soft soap and testimonial dinners. He would organize a testimonial dinner at the drop of a contract. It was not enough just to sign a contract. Ceremonial flourishes were required and Herbst provided these with his dinners. Though he loved these occasions, he let others have most of the spotlight, while, beaming happily upon everybody, he sat down near the end of the head table, and accepted with becoming modesty whatever verbal tributes or gifts came his way. In his career as an organizer of testimonial dinners, Herbst tried never to overlook anybody who had done his union a service. He once organized such a dinner for the entire Mall Medical Clinic, whose doctors had helped the union organize its own medical insurance program.

'And so what's wrong with testimonial dinners?' he demanded once, when I chided him about the cost to the union treasury. 'The cost is nothing. And nobody can refuse to attend a dinner in his honour. Have you ever heard of anybody saying no to such an invitation? They love it. But you know what? The dinners ain't really for them as much as for my members. These are little people who don't get around hardly ever. They spend their lives in crummy garment-shops, but they never get to wear nice clothes themselves. We get them out to live it up and see the other side of the world. You notice at these dinners it is the union officers who do everything. They all have to get up and make little speeches. They become very important people, important to themselves and to their wives, even.

'Look, nobody on the whole street where they live ever ate in the same room with the Chief Justice, or with the Premier, or with three of the richest employers in Winnipeg! Just being there with these prominent citizens is something, and at the head table, yet! It gives our officers confidence, which they need in dealing with employers, and it lets them see how nice things are when people are polite to other people. Let me tell you something. The first time I ever make a speech at a dinner I'm tongue-tied. But I will never forget that night. So these things give my boys and girls a night to remember for the rest of their lives. So why not?'

Herbst himself lived modestly on what, for a union official from New York, was a small salary. It was, however, enough so that he could afford to discourage admiring members from raising his pay.

'When Herbst needs a raise in pay, I'll let you be the organizer,' he'd tell his officials. 'Let Herbst first earn a raise in pay by negotiating bigger and better contracts for the members of the I.L.G.W.U.!'

So the members would compromise and send him on an expense-paid junket to New York and back.

After Herbst, the garment industry grew to become Winnipeg's most important single employer and wealth-producer, next to food and drink. Freed from the grip of the wage-cut, price-cut spiral, the Winnipeg employers became models of industry and enterprise.

Not only did Winnipeg become a garment centre under Herbst's prodding, it became a design centre able to produce clothing that sold profitably in eastern Canada and in the United States. From the few hundred workers when Herbst arrived, the Winnipeg garment industry grew into a $50,000,000-a-year business that employed 6,000 workers. The ratio of jobs to capital dollars invested is probably as high in this industry as it is in any other in Canada. So there are probably 15,000 or 20,000 auxiliary jobs being filled in Winnipeg that would not exist if Sam Herbst had not brought peace, quiet, and goodwill to labour-management relationships in Winnipeg.

In the end, something big had to be done for Sam Herbst, and it was the Winnipeg employers who came up with the idea of a tribute suitable for the occasion. Morris Neaman, whose factory had been the prime target of the 1937 fur strike, and Mr. Justice Sam Freedman, Chancellor of the University of Manitoba, became joint chairmen of a campaign to raise $200,000 to build a centre for delinquent youth in Rehovah, Israel. The money rolled in from the Winnipeg garment industry, whose employers had waxed fat and whose skilled employees now took home pay envelopes that more than matched those of the snootiest secretaries in town. The Winnipeg economy had come a long way on the back of Sam Herbst.

CHAPTER XIV

TWO NINE-CENT MEALS A DAY
AND THE RELIEF-CAMP TREK

On a January morning in 1932, the city hall reporter for the Calgary *Herald* trudged up to the third floor of the police station for his usual call on the city relief office. Half-way between the second and third floor, his progress was arrested by a solid mass of men waiting to register for relief. There were usually lots of applicants on hand, but this morning they were unusual—they were all Chinese and were applying for single-men's relief. For the first time, the Chinese community of Calgary could not look after its own and eighty of its destitute unemployed were applying for help. The reporter had a three-paragraph story for the local news page.

The Calgary Chinese were single for the same reason most other Canadian Chinese were single: the rigid exclusion of Chinese women by Canadian immigration regulations, coupled with Chinese reluctance to marry Occidentals, kept them that way. Thus, while the Chinese lived together, often three or four to a room, they had no family life and the only relief they could qualify for was as single men. The Chinese were not single men in the ordinary relief sense. The latter were housed by the Salvation Army or at the city hostel and fed at a soup-kitchen. There was no surplus sleeping accommodation available for the Chinese, and the strictly Occidental food of the soup-kitchen didn't seem much to offer them. So that morning the City of Calgary Relief Department had a rare rush of common sense to the head. It made an exception in the case of the Chinese and meted out some preferred treatment to them. The Chinese were permitted to go on living in Chinatown, provided they lived cost-free to the city, and the city would provide them with tickets for two nine-cent meals per day.

Here was an unusual step, taken by a kindly city official to bend the rules to accommodate deserving people. But it was taken with the mean, niggling, penny-pinching manner that was characteristic of the prevailing attitude toward the single unemployed. Whether the unmarried women had it worse or better than the unmarried men depends upon the viewpoint. Women were not chivvied about and driven from town to town as the teen-agers and young men were. Nor were they fed in soup-kitchens. In some communities, like Winnipeg, they were given room rent and grocery allowances, if they lived by themselves. In Calgary, the Sunshine Society maintained a hostel for single women, and the city, in the beginning, subsidized the hostel to the extent of $5 a week per person for room and board. Then it put the auditors in and cut the subsidy down to $3.50 a week.

In the main, the number of single women on relief was small compared with the rising tide of male unemployed. For one thing, women worked for a lot less than men, and employers who could fill a vacancy with a woman seldom thought of hiring a man. As Canadian merchandising became addicted to part-time employment, thousands of women subsisted on two or three days' work a week. Yet there quickly developed a hard core of single women on relief that became a sort of obsession with the authorities. The existence of a permanent body of destitute women sat badly on everybody's conscience, so every government at one time or other took a run at solving the problem. Usually, matters were made worse— much worse in the case of the great crusade to put them all into domestic service.

The essentials of the scheme were that the unemployed girls would be put into housework by the carrot-and-stick technique.

Those who would take the girls in and provide bed and board would be paid $5 a month by the government, which would also pay the girls $5 a month for themselves. The system did nothing for the waitresses, stenographers, retail clerks, and nurses who were unemployed, and it destroyed the wage structure of the housemaids who still had jobs. There were, of course, good employers and bad employers. Many kindly housewives turned their subsidies over to the girls, helped them with clothes, and tried to find better jobs for them. Others put the girls on seven-day, sixteen-hour shifts and ran bleating to their aldermen when the girls wouldn't work for them.

Periodically, the well-heeled aldermen in Winnipeg, Calgary, and Edmonton rose in their places to ask why it was that the city was keeping 130 women on relief while their neighbours were unable to get housemaids? Was there no rule that women who refused to take housework could be cut off relief? There were such rules every-where, but they were rarely enforced. Sooner or later, the welfare officials got to know the names of most of the local termagants and dealt with them imaginatively. When they got a particularly trou-blesome girl, and they had troublesome girls, they would match her off with a troublesome employer.

For the single men, the relief office was a sort of Bridge of Sighs where hope was abandoned. Under the urban relief regulations, teen-agers reached adulthood on their eighteenth birthday. They were then cut off from their families as far as eligibility for relief was concerned and transferred to single relief—which meant eating at the soup-kitchens and sleeping in slum-area rooming houses. It was not long before they joined the restless young men from the farms and small towns in a 'search for work', which took them back and forth across the country on an endless chain of railway box-cars in such thousands that the railways stopped trying to keep them off their freight trains.

All the large cities took care of their own single unemployed with $1.25-a-week room tickets and two meals a day at the soup-kitchens. These were men qualified with twelve months' permanent residence. They were legitimate Winnipeggers or Edmontonians, or Calgarians like the Chinese. For those who came of age during the depression and went on the fruitless search for work, there was no home town to go back to if they stayed away too long. They lost their residence eligibility and became permanently classified as the 'transient unemployed' who could demand soup-kitchen sustenance for two days in Vancouver or Winnipeg or Toronto, and thereafter they were on their own. Being on their own meant that they could catch the next freight out of town and check into a soup-kitchen in Montreal, London, Brandon, Calgary, or Saskatoon. If they missed the freight, they could beg the price of meals and beds for a few days, then check back into the soup-kitchen.

Until the full flood of the single unemployed hit the country in 1933, 'riding the rods' had been partly a way of life, partly a pleasant summer pastime. In the fall the railway police tended to look the other way as harvesters moved around the country. Coming west, they rode in empty box-cars and could get into very little mischief. Going back east, they rode the grain trains on which there was nothing to steal.

The Canadian railway police kept a sharp eye on their merchandise trains at other seasons. Their trains were looted periodically by skilful railway burglars, who could break a seal on a box-car door while a train was rattling along at sixty miles an hour, open the door from the roof, scramble in, and strip the car of its high-value merchandise in a matter of minutes. Anybody riding a merchandise train was a natural enemy of railway policemen. As the depression deepened, there were fewer trains of all kinds and more transients riding them. Catching and jailing transients had such little effect in discouraging the travellers that the police chased them only for exercise.

Most of the time, the transients weren't really going anywhere. At first they moved out of the West in great numbers looking for work in the factory towns of Ontario, and found a welcome as cold as a Manitoba winter. One excursion into the country between Hamilton and Sarnia was enough to discourage a second visit. They learned, too, to take enough food to get them through northern Ontario and such unfriendly places as Kenora, Schreiber, Chapleau, and Kapuskasing. By 1933, the idea of getting a job had been abandoned and the legions of single unemployed moved back and forth across the country because they had nothing else to do. The railway towns of the West were overrun in the summers by young transients, who dropped off freight trains to try to exchange a day's work in a garden for a square meal or two. There was nothing cheaper than food, and few would have begrudged the odd transient a meal, particularly if he were young and clean. But one transient always led to another, and another, and another. The young unemployed exchanged addresses where meals were obtained like soldiers in war-time exchanged telephone numbers. We never turned anybody away if we had any food we could spare, even after watching them walk clear down the block, past house after house, and turn unerringly into our gate.

I had no garden to weed, but I liked to sit with them while they ate and try to get them to talk, but it was rarely we fed a talkative type. Mostly they were so very young, and they just wanted to sit for a while, eat, and get on their way again. Besides, there was little of interest in their lives to talk about. They had left home in Glace Bay or Kitchener or Nelson to look for work because their families were on relief. They were often homesick but were resolutely heading in the opposite direction. They had been on the road long enough to have lost any hesitancy about asking for a meal, but few of them had ever been arrested, or chased by police, or had their shoes stolen while they slept, or encountered a girl on the bum, or mixed with any criminal types, or had any box-car brawls, or broken into a box-car full of booze.

Conversation was almost without interest to them, and when they did talk it was mostly about the relief camps they had been in, about the food and isolation and military discipline. Those who had never been in bush camps before thought the camps were awful. Those who had worked in the bush, or on construction jobs, thought they were not so bad.

Conversationally, the legitimate unemployed were the antithesis of the professional bums of the hobo jungles—the winos, rubby-dubs, sneak thieves, hopheads, and perverts who were all accomplished and enthusiastic liars. Their whole lives were lies; lies they told to themselves, to each other, to the police, or to outsiders like me who occasionally horned into their conversations. For them, the depression was one long clam-bake. Panhandling was easy, the cops were tolerant, and, if they could still eat after a canned-heat cocktail, there was always the soup-kitchen. How much of their conversation was the reflected hallucination of deranged minds, and how much was simple hogwash, I never could decide. A simple, direct question would get them started. Like:

'You ever been in Dawson Creek?'

'Kee-ryst, yes, I been in Dawson Creek. Five, six years ago I was drivin' a lumber truck in a tie camp. I come out of that camp with $640 that spring, and I hit Edmonton and I'm going to buy me a filling station and settle down. Then this broad picks me up on Jasper Avenue and I wind up in a hook joint and before I know it I'm locked in an empty box-car being sicker'n a dog. Every time the train stops, I take off my boot and bang on the door. You know where somebody opens the door? Yer right, Dawson Creek! The guy who opens the door is a railway bull and I do fourteen in the Dawson Creek jail.'

The Higgins Avenue hobo jungle was on a detour to the Woodyard from our rooms in Elmwood, and in the summer I wandered through it regularly in search of excitement. Here were men who had been everywhere, had done everything, experienced every experience, and gave a damn about nothing. It didn't take long to discover their tall tales were untrue because they all told the same lies. Their stories invariably began with a big bank-roll that had been lost, or stolen, or given away, and how they had had to start all over again. It didn't matter what the question was, the answer usually followed that Dawson Creek pattern. Unlike the young people who knocked on our door, they started talking easily; it was stopping them that was difficult.

With the first fall of snow, the jungle was deserted for the winter and the trickle of transients to our door dried up. The transient unemployed went where the weather fitted their clothes, which wasn't Winnipeg or Regina. Special problems were created for Calgary by the fall influx, and the worst problems of all were for Vancouver, where transients from all over Canada gathered every winter. Though the worst of the food riots were in Vancouver, the prairie cities all had outbreaks at one time or another. Mostly the trouble centred around the soup-kitchens and complaints about food. In Saskatoon a policeman was beaten to death, a score were injured in Edmonton, and there was some enthusiastic head-whacking in Winnipeg from time to time.

The plain truth was that soup-kitchen food was usually good. Eggs were available everywhere at ten cents a dozen. The best roast beef cost, at most, twenty-five cents a pound, sausage retailed for six or seven cents per pound, butter was ten cents a pound, and pota-toes were usually available for thirty or forty cents per 100-pound bag. At the wholesale level, where the soup-kitchens bought, the food itself cost less than it cost to move it, so there was no point in buying poor food. The soup-kitchens, however, were always foul-smelling, and that the food was unappetizing cannot be denied. The soup-kitchens always seemed to be located in unsuitable premises that some politically favoured landlord had rented to the govern-ment. The odours of the food cooked last year were mixed with the odours of last month and last week. To serve such masses, heavy reliance was placed upon boiled dinners, hash, and cereals. Everything was overcooked and usually served on metal plates with twisted forks and knives. Nothing about the soup-kitchens was conducive to enjoyment of food, least of all the company of an ill-clad, unkempt, unhappy, and unwashed legion.

After serious riots in 1931, the British Columbia government itself set up some winter bush camps to take the single unemployed out of Vancouver. The next year the Dominion government spon-sored the camps and the province ran them. In 1933 the Dominion assumed responsibility and opened scores of camps across the coun-try under the administration of the Department of National Defence. In its five-year hassle over unemployment, nothing the federal government did caused it more vexation than the relief camps. They were investigated and Royal Commissioned, griped about, rioted about, and in the end played a not inconsiderable part in the destruction of the Bennett government. The fault lay not in the conception of the camps, but in the administration; the idea was first-rate, but the execution was disastrous.

Whenever any government tried to find work for the unem-ployed, it collided head on with some vested interest. The single unemployed, with the aid of modern machinery, could have cut enough lumber in winter to rehouse the entire farm population of western Canada, who desperately needed rehousing. Or they could have built highways on which the whole country might have rolled. But they were unable to do either because of the opposition of the lumber business, the contracting business, and the employees of both. The work camps, hence, had to subsist on the sort of work nobody else would do. This meant gigantic projects, with a dozen widely separated camps: clearing trees from the shores of Lac Seul in eastern Manitoba for a future hydro development, and building minor roads through national parks, and landing-fields in the forests. At the peak in 1934 more than 25,000 young Canadians were hived away in the bush camps, and during the four years the camps were in operation more than 115,000 were run in and out of them.

The fatal error of the government was in placing the camps under the Department of National Defence and making the *King's Rules and Orders*—K.R. & O.—the procedural Bible. This step guaranteed that whatever grievance did develop in the camps would be bottled up until it reached explosive proportions. No organization of any kind was permitted in any camp, and no petition could be circulated, and no committee could be formed to complain about anything. Anyone with a grievance could take it to the foreman of his gang, then appeal to the foreman of the sub-camp or the supervisor of the project. But he could do it only by himself without the vocal or moral support of a comrade. Anyone who tried to organize a protest in a camp faced expulsion and in some camps that meant being expelled in midwinter at the camp gates a hundred miles from the nearest habitation. Perhaps few of the men in the camps would have joined a Relief Camp Workers' Union if it could have been organized. But the fact that no organization was permitted became a rankling grievance.

Equally to blame for morale trouble in the camps was the pay of twenty cents per day. There was something about that twenty cents per day that came to symbolize everything that was wrong with the lives of everybody on relief. It affronted human dignity as little else could have done. It was just the right size to be insulting.

Underlying these main defects of the camp system was a host of picayune grievances. In addition to the twenty cents per day, the men also got a tobacco allowance—based on 1.45 cents per day for each day in camp. Thus, before a new-comer was able to get a ten-cent package of tobacco, he had to get seven days of camp life behind him. Because the camps were established as a temporary measure to meet a condition that was expected to pass away next year, many were devoid of recreational facilities. There was no place for a hockey rink or baseball diamond and no equipment for either game. In many remote camps, outside communication ceased when a rickety radio went dead. There was little reading material and no means of pursuing an education or a hobby. Nobody was allowed to have a camera in camp.

So they griped about the food, the clothing, the bed bugs, the over-crowding in the dormitories, the martinetish regime, the latrines, and any other grievance they could conjure up. But to the inspectors, who were not condemned to live in them, the relief camps were first-class bush camps. None of the investigators realized that the lives of the ordinary bush workers were made tolerable by visions of making a stake and getting out to spend it. The sub-marginal quality of camp life could be tolerated for wages that could be saved or sent home. Here and there, a camp supervisor understood this fact, and took steps to provide substitute motivation. In such camps there would be provision for correspondence courses, recreational facilities—as many amenities as could be scrounged. But, in the main, the single unemployed got only the worst of the bush camps. They got the boredom, the loneliness, the unhappiness, without the compensating vision of a binge at the end. The worst thing was the hopelessness. All the investigators who roamed the camp—social workers, preachers, Members of Parliament, and Royal Commissioners—were unanimous on this point: the single unemployed regarded themselves as Canada's forgotten men. They had been filed and forgotten and nobody cared if they lived or died.

But the Communists cared. In British Columbia, they were forever sending organizers into the camps to stir up whatever trouble they could find. The strict military security resulted in agitators being quickly unmasked and expelled. Regular bulletins were circulated warning officials to be on the alert for certain organizers for the Workers Unity League who were travelling under assumed names. In the bush camps, the Communists built a reputation for initiative and courage simply by not being afraid of expulsion, and by standing up to the spit-and-polish sergeant-major-type straw-bosses.

The inevitable collisions of the Communist organizers with the authorities were always a tonic for inmate morale. That one man was willing to stick his neck out on their behalf was at least passing proof that they were worth fighting for. To many of them, the Communists were the sort of men they wished they could be. But they had been through the wringer of hunger and loneliness so often that they could scarcely face expulsion from the camps.

Despite insuperable obstacles, the Communists worked overtime organizing the relief camps, and they had the field completely to themselves. And for them, stirring up trouble in the camps was almost a labour of love. It was the one way in which they could hit back at the Bennett régime for its persecution of their movement. To them, R. B. Bennett was the Robespierre of Canadian Fascism who was trying to fasten a personal dictatorship on the country. The outlawing of their party and the jailing of its leader too closely paralleled what had happened in Germany for them to harbour any serious doubts on that score. The Communist Party's organization of the 'Relief-Camp Strike' and the 'On-to-Ottawa Trek' in 1935 was the party's belated reprisal for the imprisonment of Tim Buck and the other Communist leaders. Mr. Bennett had set out to destroy the Communist Party and, if the Communists did not alone destroy Mr. Bennett, they had a hand in his destruction, and this was their revenge.

The On-to-Ottawa Trek was a lot of different things to a lot of different people. To those of us who covered the story as it unfolded, as I did for the Winnipeg *Free Press*, it was tense journalism at its best, a lifetime's chance to record history in the making. To the Conservative government of Prime Minister Bennett, it was an incipient Communist revolution. To the Liberals in the West, it was a heaven-sent chance to let Mr. Bennett stew in his own juice and to heat up the juice by unsubtle acts of omission and commission. For the still-toddling C.C.F., it was a chance to participate in a great mass protest movement.

In Vancouver, Mayor Gerry McGeer, a famous Liberal monetary reformer, helped launch the trek by sponsoring a civic tag-day that raised $6,000. In Regina, the Reverend S. B. East, a C.C.F. alderman, was arrested trying to lead a truck convoy out of town. In Manitoba, S. J. Farmer, M.L.A., the C.C.F provincial leader, was elected chairman of the 'Anti-Slave-Camp Conference'. The Communists, in this era of the United Front, welcomed everyone of liberal leaning into the Front organizations. At the same time, they were infiltrating everything from the Y.M.C.A. to the Institute for Pacific Relations. When the western leaders of the C.C.F. elbowed their way into the support organizations of the relief-camp strike, the Communists were delighted. It was not only the C.C.F. that co-operated; young Liberals and dissident young Conservatives also nudged their way into the act.

Though they welcomed all the support they could get from all sides, the Communists kept tight control over the march itself. For them, it was a deadly serious war game. If there should one day be a march to the seat of power, as most Communists believed, those who made the revolution would have to know what they were about. A l ot could be learned about the logistics of moving a revolutionary army by moving a couple of battalions of unemployed across hostile territory.

Western Canada, apathetic though it might be in 1935, was far from hostile territory for either the Communist Party or the single unemployed who followed it. Though the On-to-Ottawa Trek was a Communist inspiration, it was very far from being only a Communist conspiracy. The times were out of joint for Mr. Bennett. His great New Deal Program had become bogged down in the courts. He was reaching the end of his tenure, and, with an election coming up, the times were ripe for constructive trouble-making.

The bulk of the camps for the single unemployed were in the interior of British Columbia. When spring came, the camps emptied quickly as the young men succumbed to the urge to wander and headed for Vancouver to catch the trans-continental freights. It therefore appeared in 1935, when the western Communists called upon the relief-camp workers to down their tools and join the On-to-Ottawa Trek, that the unemployed were responding by the thousands. The truth was that the first time many of them heard of the strike was when they landed in Vancouver. Then they joined the trek for many reasons. Some were planning to grab a freight for the east anyway, so why not join the trek? The Communist Party members or sympathizers naturally went along. The uncommitted followed the Communist leadership because, for five years, nobody else in Canada had lifted a finger on their behalf.

Whatever reason men may have had for joining it or supporting it, the trek captured the imagination of western Canada. For one thing, the demands the strikers wanted to present to the government impressed most people as being eminently reasonable. The demands included: payment of fifty cents an hour for their work; the right to the protection of workmen's compensation; the right to belong to a union and have grievance committees; abolition of military control of the camps.

The plea of the single unemployed for a program of work and wages attracted support everywhere. The Honourable H. H. Stevens, a former Conservative cabinet minister, made an eloquent appeal in the House of Commons that spring for a vast plan of reforestation, highway-building, and road-building in national parks that would have rivalled the scope of the famous Civilian Conservation Corps projects in the United States.

Arthur Evans, who led the march out of Vancouver, was a dedicated Communist veteran of a dozen picket-line brawls who once went to jail for using United Mine Workers' funds to buy food for striking miners in Drumheller. On June 4, an army of 600 followed him onto a C.P.R. freight train while another 400 followed the next day. The relief army was well organized and disciplined, and those in charge stood for no nonsense.

The army was divided into companies and sections, and each group elected a chairman and marshal. As it moved from city to city, the discipline that was maintained would have done an *élite* corps proud. Rigid rules of public conduct were maintained. Panhandling was forbidden and cleanliness was a prime requirement. Expulsion from the trek was the penalty imposed for any serious offence. The latter might include theft of any kind, drunkenness, or even refusal to attend meetings.

Establishment of a record for exemplary conduct was a stroke of public-relations genius. To the general public, these boys were not hoodlums looking for trouble. They were clean-cut young Canadians who were tired of being pushed around and wanted something better than relief-camp life. This was the impression they left everywhere, on the people of the cities and towns as they passed, even on the reporters who joined their trek from time to time—able reporters like Fred Griffin, Charles Woodsworth, and Fred Johnson. None of us who wrote about the trek was completely dispassionate. There was a lot of built-in bias on the side of the strikers, even though we tried to keep it from showing.

After the itinerary of the trek was announced, committees sprang to life in all the centres where the tour would stop. These semi-official groups arranged for billeting the trekkers in rinks or exhibition grounds, pressured authorities to open soup-kitchens or provide meal tickets, arranged for tag-days and donations of clothes and tobacco. It was a leisurely schedule the organizers had worked out. There would be one-day stops at Kamloops and Golden, three days in Calgary, a day each in Medicine Hat, Moose Jaw, Regina, and Brandon, four days in Winnipeg, two in Fort William, two in Port Arthur, one in Sudbury, and two in Toronto.

The organizers of the trek made one fatal mistake: they assumed that the C.P.R. would be content to let the men ride their trains all the way from Vancouver to Ottawa. Instead, the railway demanded that the federal government enforce the Railway Act, which specifically excluded trespassing on freight trains. The day after the trek started, the Royal Canadian Mounted Police announced in Winnipeg that the trek would be halted. But when it moved unmolested into Calgary and out again three days later, the conviction grew that the authorities were bluffing. However, the government had been quietly concentrating the Mounties at Regina, and when enough strength was built up to stop the trek the government announced that Regina was the end of the line.

The fourteenth of June was a dismal day for the trekkers. They arrived in Regina chilled and wet, after a long ride through the night in a near-freezing rain, to be greeted with the news that their adventure was over. At a series of meetings at the Exhibition Grounds, where they were quartered, they shouted defiance at the government and voted to go on with the trek. By now the 1,000 that left Vancouver were well over 2,000, as strikers from the camps en route and city unemployed joined the relief army.

A tag-day was arranged in Regina and $1,500 was raised, in addition to which merchants donated clothing by the cartons to the strikers. In an effort to persuade the men to return home, the Prime Minister sent the Honourable Robert Weir and the Honourable R. J. Manion to Regina to confer with the leaders. They arranged for the leaders to travel by train to Ottawa to present the demands of the single unemployed to the Cabinet.

It was at this point that the situation in Winnipeg began to heat up. I had been assigned to cover the strike from the outside and Ben Malkin got the unpleasant task of covering the story from the inside. Journalistic fiction is replete with stories of reporters acting as undercover agents to ferret out corruption and cupidity. The fictional reporters may relish these assignments but real-life reporters seldom do. Malkin reluctantly got on a suit of old clothes, queued up at a soup-kitchen, and was quickly caught up in the machinery set up to handle the strike when it reached Winnipeg. He was registered as Ben Levi, an unemployed printer from Montreal, and was supplied with a food card and a ticket entitling him to use half a double bed in a rooming-house on Spence Street for a week.

In Regina, the *Tribune* had Charles Woodsworth travelling on the freight trains with the strikers and writing exciting copy every day. For Malkin, there was only boredom and frustration with nothing to write about. Instead of brutal bureaucracy, he encountered unfailing courtesy and kindness at the soup-kitchens. There were no wild-eyed revolutionaries to write about, only bewildered young men who were in Winnipeg en route elsewhere. Some of them were impatient with the trek, because it had put an end to riding the rods and they were stuck in Winnipeg.

From my place on the outside, it was quickly apparent that a lot of other phoneys besides Malkin were also getting into the act. On one afternoon, a call came into the office over the police radio about a disturbance on Water Street near the old C.N.R. immigration hall. Ten minutes later, when I got there, the disturbance was over and there was a group of forty or fifty unemployed gathered in the vacant lot across the street. One of them was standing on a mound of dirt making a speech. What the trouble had been about was not clear from his speech. He was urging the crowd to set up an organization to send a delegation to the Parliament Buildings to protest against the treatment they had received in the hall. He was urging them to elect a chairman and an executive. Somebody in the crowd shouted:

'You got a good gift of the gab, I nominate you.'

By this time I had edged in close enough to recognize the speaker on the mound. It was Mitchi Sago, a recent graduate from the Young Communist League, whom I knew quite well. He declined to stand with a modest disclaimer:

'No, comrade, I think not. I suggest your chairman should be someone who has had a longer experience with these slave camps than I've had. Someone, for example, who had come in from Lac Seul or Shilo recently. Anybody here from Lac Seul?'

'How about Johnny McCarthy?' another voice in the crowd suggested. 'He started that row in there and that looks like a Shilo sweater he's got on.' Everybody applauded. McCarthy stood up—a shortish, dark fellow in his early twenties—and agreed to stand. He was elected unanimously. Then somebody nominated Fred Mowbray as secretary, Mitchi Sago nominated Harry Binder, another Y.C.L. alumnus, as vice-chairman, and Mowbray nominated Sago as organizer. It was all a classic example of a Communist organized take-over.

As the concentration of single unemployed in Winnipeg mushroomed in the next couple of weeks, the organization's strength zoomed into the hundreds, of whom perhaps a third were legitimate unemployed single men from the camps. The others were mainly Communist Party liners from the North End who habitually turned out *en bloc* to every Communist demonstration. From that day forward, Binder, Sago, McCarthy, and Mowbray directed the affairs of the trekkers, though only Binder and Sago were full-time Communist Party functionaries. McCarthy's role was rapidly de-emphasized as Binder and Sago took control. Mowbray was a maverick Red whom I got to know very well. A tall, raw-boned, fun-loving miner's son from Glace Bay, Mowbray never took the trek any more than two-thirds seriously. After the trek, Mowbray used to turn up at our place regularly for a meal as he went back and forth across the country. The last time I saw him, he was *en route* to Toronto in the fall of 1936 to enlist in the Mackenzie-Papineau Battalion to fight in Spain. He died there.

Unlike the others, who liked to cloak even the time of day in conspiratorial silence, Mowbray maintained a completely candid relationship with reporters. He saved us many weary hours by letting us know the meeting schedules and, in a useful if vague way, what the general program was.

The government action in stopping the marchers in Regina stirred up a whirlwind of activity in Winnipeg. There were mass meetings on Market Square, parades to the Legislature, parades to the Ukrainian Labour Temple on McGregor Avenue, meetings of the Anti-Slave-Camp Conference in the Chamber of Commerce Building on Princess Street. An electric current of anticipation crackled around Winnipeg.

Winnipeggers were always great strollers, and during the depression it almost seemed as if the whole city's favourite pastime was to parade up and down Main Street and Portage Avenue. Those who owned automobiles would drive down town in the evenings, head their cars into the curbs, and sit for hours munching peanuts and sunflower seeds and watching the walkers.

In late June of 1935, the sidewalks were crowded as never before. The waves of pedestrians would veer off at Carlton Street to gather in front of the *Free Press* to see what was on the late-news bulletin boards. Then the strollers would continue down Portage Avenue to the *Tribune* and the Water Street soup-kitchen, down the other way to Market Square, Winnipeg's Hyde Park. It was a common occurrence for scores to gather around the square on an evening just on the chance a meeting might be held. Usually, that last week in June, they were not disappointed.

The Ottawa conference on June 22 between the Regina strikers' delegation and Mr. Bennett and his Cabinet degenerated into a shouting match between the Prime Minister and Arthur Evans, the strike leader. Mr. Bennett called Evans a thief, and Evans called the Prime Minister a liar. At that moment public opinion began to turn against the strikers. Evans's behaviour was a sobering shock to thousands of unaligned Canadians, who had been more than sympathetic to the strikers, and even disenchanted many of the dedicated Bennett-haters. Nobody could call a Canadian Prime Minister a liar with impunity.

The Ottawa conference was such a failure that it left everybody baffled as to why it had been held. Mr. Bennett rejected all the demands of the strikers with less than a shred of consideration.

Evans took off from Ottawa for Toronto to address a mass rally there. Then he stopped over in Winnipeg to speak to between 4,000 and 5,000 at Market Square on June 25. The following night, one of the biggest rallies in Winnipeg history was held on the Legislature Building grounds at which Mayor John Queen, S. J. Farmer, M.L.A., Fred Lawrence, M.L.A., the Honourable E. J. McMurray, L. St.G. Stubbs, the Reverend Stanley Knowles, Alderman Jacob Penner, Alderman M. J. Forkin, and Jim Litterick spoke. We reported the speeches briefly, for everything that could be said was being said over and over. But the impression that something was building up to a climax was strong enough to taste.

Back in Regina, on the same night, Arthur Evans told 4,000 at the Regina Stadium that the trek would go on, by truck if necessary, but it would go on. Earlier that day, the federal government passed an order in council authorizing the taking of all necessary measures to halt the trek at Regina. The government's will was tested almost at once, when the Reverend S. B. East headed out of Regina on June 27 with a five-truck convoy of strikers that was stopped by the Mounties, who arrested all the occupants.

Among the people of Regina, tempers were now beginning to rub thin. The city had had an army of 2,000 camped on it for two weeks, and the army had just about worn out its welcome. The members of the army, for their part, had been sleeping on straw in the stadium and waiting with growing impatience for something to happen. Towards the end of the week, the men began to straggle into the transportation office that had been set up for those who wanted to go home.

In Winnipeg, the main agitation centred upon the demand for mass billeting of the strikers. Under the Winnipeg system, the strikers were scattered in rooming-houses all over the city. The strike leaders argued that they had great difficulty keeping order and discipline because they were never sure where their followers were. Neither the provincial nor the federal authorities, who were paying the cost of maintaining the strikers, were prepared to yield on the billeting issue. One night the strikers got hold of half a dozen large tents and set up a camp on the Midland Railway yard in the centre of town. Orders came that the camp had to be broken up, and the tents were moved out to the North End Exhibition Grounds.

On Sunday, June 30, I got a message from Fred Mowbray. Today was the day, he said, and if I was going to cover the meeting that night on Market Square I should come prepared to travel, because everybody else would be. The same message went to the *Tribune* and the radio stations, so the Market Square was knee-deep in reporters that night. The trekkers had certainly come to travel, for each man carried a bundle of clothes and a blanket. They formed up at the Ukrainian Labour Temple, marched to Market Square, and were harangued by their leaders for a full hour.

By this time, I had taken about all the relief-camp oratory I could absorb. My feet were sore from following relief-camp paraders all over Winnipeg, and my behind was sore from sitting around in conference rooms as I listened to endless arguments. I sought the sheltering coolness of a Market Street drug-store and drank a milkshake while the oratory raged outside, and thus I missed the start of the parade to the C.P.R. station. I caught up with it just as the leaders turned it off the street at the corner of Martha and Henry and stormed into an old abandoned brick warehouse. The point of this action remained a mystery. The wildest story circulated that night was that the strikers were tipped off that the R.C.M.P. had secreted a machine-gun crew in the building. After a ten-minute halt, the parade formed up again and marched to the C.P.R. station, a couple of blocks away. Again it came to a halt while the leaders held a long conference.

At this stage there were perhaps 600 to 700 strikers, with packs on their backs, and 2,500 citizens waiting for something to happen. At last, in the gathering dusk of a stifling humid evening, the parade again moved off. This time it crossed Main Street and headed south on Princess Street. At the corner of Ross Avenue, the leaders suddenly led the parade in through the front door of the provincial government's soup-kitchen, a huge three-storey converted warehouse. Within a matter of minutes the entire body was inside the building with the doors barricaded.

Winnipeg had the makings of a first-class riot on its hands. The news of the seizure of the dining-hall went out over the radio, and in a matter of minutes more than 5,000 spectators were jammed into Princess Street in front of the building. The curiosity-seekers could hardly have been any more baffled by developments than the marchers themselves. To try to find out what was going on inside, I fought my way through the crowd to the back door, climbed up a wall, and poked my head through a window. Eventually a couple of the marchers opened the door for me. They must have thought I was one of them—an easy mistake because I had been around the trek longer than most of them.

I went hunting for Sago, Binder, and Mowbray, and it dawned on me that my enterprise in getting into the building was sadly misspent. The heat was insufferable, the air was almost unbreatheable, and the trekkers were stripping down to the waist. By the time I located Sago, I had absorbed more than enough atmosphere for the night. He and Binder were both angry to find me inside, and for a while they talked about keeping me as a hostage along with six city policemen they were holding. The policemen had been on duty when the parade marched into the hall and, being without instruction, had assumed a passive role. When the men were due to go off duty, the strikers wouldn't let them leave until their places were taken by six other policemen. As Sago told the crowd outside, they were holding the police because the Mounties would not storm the hall with city police inside. In the hiatus, the policemen sweated off the poundage in the dining-hall office. I hung around while the parade leaders argued about what they would do next, and, when they eventually opened the front door to let Binder and Sago out to speak to the crowd, I slipped out behind them.

The seizure of the dining-hall had every indication of being a spur-of-the-moment decision, for it was well on towards midnight before anybody came up with an explanation that made sense. Harry Binder first said that their departure for Ottawa had been called off, because they had learned that a troop of 200 Mounties were armed with machine-guns at Rennie, sixty miles east of Winnipeg, waiting to trap the trekkers and herd them into concentration camps. Later it was explained that the hall was seized in order to force the city to take the Mounted Police out of Winnipeg. Finally, it was decided that the seizure was made to obtain central billeting for all the marchers at the old Exhibition Grounds.

The seizure of the soup-kitchen was a completely lawless act, so the question that ran back and forth through the crowd was: 'What is Bracken going to do now?' Both Premier Bracken and Mayor John Queen were out of the city that week-end. Alderman Jack Blumberg, the acting mayor, and the Honourable W. J. Major, the Attorney-General, shared the top responsibility. From a legal point of view, either could have cited a list of reasons a foot long for moving in the police to evict the strikers. A dozen times that night, the rumour flashed through the crowd that the police were on the way. Once, when the wail of a police siren was heard heading towards the soup-kitchen, a minor stampede developed on Princess Street. It was only the paddy-wagon *en route* to pick up a couple of drunks in near-by Chinatown. A little later, the crowd was electrified again when a fire engine roared away on a false alarm.

While we were sweating it out at the soup-kitchen, the authorities were concentrating all the police they could find at the Rupert Street police station, three blocks away. Word of the concentration reached the strikers, and Sago appealed to the crowd outside to jam the streets and lanes and in effect make the strikers their prisoners, so the police could not turn the seizure into a blood-bath. The crowd was noticeably frightened by that idea and thinned quickly. However, instead of acting, the authorities talked, and, while they talked, time and the weather were softening up the relief-camp strikers.

The Attorney-General, who had been several times at the point of ordering the police into action, eventually settled for conciliation. Arthur Macnamara, the Deputy-Minister of Labour, went down to the soup-kitchen for a personal meeting with the strikers. With the acting mayor, he quickly worked out a deal. The city agreed to provide enough tents to billet the strikers on the old Exhibition Grounds, and an appointment was made for Mowbray and Binder to discuss other grievances with Premier Bracken. By noon on Dominion Day, everything was back to normal in Winnipeg. The debris left from the all-night occupancy was being cleared out of the dining-hall, and the staff was getting ready to serve the regular customers.

In Regina, however, everything was irrevocably set on a collision course. The strikers were getting ready for a mass meeting later in the afternoon on the Market Square. The Mounted Police had received orders from Ottawa to arrest the strike leaders when they turned up for the meeting. The arrests set off the bloodiest riot in almost twenty years.

The old Market Square in Regina was only a block from the police station and there were between 3,500 and 4,500 strikers and spectators on the square when, on a whistled signal, the city police moved towards the speakers' platform from one side of the square while the R.C.M.P. marched in from the other. In a moment, panic seized the crowd, the air was filled with stones and clubs, and the riot was on. Where self-defence broke off and frenzy began became blurred. Spectators fled in terror, or joined strikers in beating back the attacks from the police. Policemen who were wrestled to the ground were beaten and kicked. Bystanders who chose to run at the wrong time, or in the wrong direction, were clubbed down by the police. Cars were overturned and barricades erected.

From the Market Square, the riot surged back and forth onto Eleventh Avenue for three hours. Every store-window between Scarth and Cornwall was shattered. Tear-gas filled Tenth and Eleventh avenues and the Mounties rode up and down on horseback to break up the rioters. At the end of the riot, a city detective, Charles Miller, was dead, a dozen policemen had been seriously injured, half a dozen civilians had been shot, and more than 100 had been injured by police clubs or rocks thrown by strikers. In addition to the eight trek leaders, the Mounties took thirty-six people into custody and the city police arrested forty.

With the leaders in jail in Regina, the great On-to-Ottawa Trek of the relief-camp strikers was over, and all that was left was to sort out the trekkers and send them back to where they came from. But the Winnipeg group turned a blind eye to the facts of life. They held rallies, made speeches vowing to carry on the struggle on behalf of the martyred strikers of Regina, held tag-days and raised enough money to charter nine buses to take 250 of them to Kenora, Ontario, where they hoped to board a freight train for Ottawa.

The Kenora junket, two weeks after the Regina riot, was an anti-climax, almost a fiasco. The Ontario provincial police stopped the Manitoba buses at the Ontario border and the strikers were forced to walk the thirty-five miles of mosquito-infested highway from the border to Kenora. The police were instructed to seize the car of anybody who picked up the strikers on the highway. The local police chief laid in a supply of sawed-off axe-handles and there was a concentration of provincial and railway police sufficient to keep the strikers off the railway.

The strikers obtained temporary billeting in the basement of a church, and local citizens fed them for a couple of days. Sago and Binder were still vocally defiant, but even they recognized there was no way out of Kenora and they were never going to get to Ottawa. Moreover, the trekkers were bitterly resented in Kenora where their presence was disrupting the tourist season on which the community depended. At the end of three days, the frustrated trekkers were happy to surrender and accept a government offer of transportation back to Winnipeg.

The relief-camp trek was the most exciting story I ever covered in my career in Canadian journalism. A hundred assignments may have been more important, but none was more exciting. Coming back on the train with the strikers, it dawned on me that most of the authentic relief-camp strikers had left the trek before the journey to Kenora. The relief-camp-issue khaki sweaters and army pants and shoes, which had been so obvious around the soup-kitchens in Winnipeg a month before, were notably absent. A count of relief-camp uniforms led to the conclusion that the part of the story I had been covering was the phoney part, made up mainly of young Communists from North Winnipeg playing at making a revolution.

By mid July, Parliament had been prorogued, and the country was embroiled in a general election that would destroy the Bennett government, but nothing much changed for the single unemployed. They went back to the bush camps the next fall, and the winter was over before the Liberal government got around to their problem. Then it raised their allowances to $15 a month, made a deal with the railways to put 15,000 of them to work on track maintenance, and closed the camps.

CHAPTER XV

ONCE ACROSS THE DUST BOWL

There were worse things than being on relief in Winnipeg, and worst of all was being a farmer in the Dust Bowl. I first stumbled onto this fact in a chance encounter with a drouth refugee at the Woodyard and I confirmed it at first hand five years later in a trip across the Dust Bowl. The farmer at the Woodyard was one of the very first who had abandoned his farm in south-western Manitoba and moved into Winnipeg to go on relief. The exodus from the Dust Bowl was a mere trickle in 1931, but by 1935 the trickle had become a flood. The destitute farmers came in such numbers to Winnipeg and to the other urban communities that efforts were made to extend residence qualifications for relief to two years to dam the flow.

The first refugee farmer I encountered was a man of perhaps fifty. He had been handsome once, but the lines in his face were then so deep that they seemed to go right through his cheeks. He was a big man, over six feet, and had a frame that could have carried 220 pounds. But his clothes now hung so loosely on him that they looked several sizes too large. He stood behind me in the line, and I tried to pass the time in conversation. Sometimes he would answer with mono-syllables. Other remarks would elicit no response at all. He just stood and stared and edged along with the line. I turned elsewhere and forgot all about him. A few weeks later, I recognized him again on a work-gang. Which of the many boondoggles it was, I have forgotten, but there was digging being done, and the soil interested him. He said:

'If you ever think of going farming, son, watch out for spruce trees. Soil that grows spruce trees is good soil to leave growing spruce trees. Took me ten years to find that out.'

When I tried to pursue the subject, he lost interest and didn't seem to be listening to anything I said. Then, apropos of nothing, he would give out with little snatches of unrelated subjects.

'Everybody talks about the wonderful prosperity of 1929,' he said, 'but 1929 was one of the worst years we ever had. I didn't get five bushels of wheat to the acre. What good is $1.60 for wheat when you don't have any to sell?'

Or, an hour later:

'One time I was readin' about the law of supply and demand in *The Prairie Farmer*. Said if the prices went down, farmers planted less wheat, and if the prices went up, they planted more. Any damn fool knows that if a farmer's got a mortgage he sure has to plant *more* wheat when the price is low. A farmer has to plant *more* wheat!'

Or, that afternoon:

'The mortgage company sent a man all the way out from Brandon to try to get me to stay on the place 'cause they didn't want to foreclose on me. Talked real friendly for an hour. I figured if the mortgage company didn't want my farm, it was time for me to get off it.'

Or, at lunch time:

'My wife was brought up in a city, you know. She was always sayin' mebbe the year after next we would get a crop when the price was high and buy a Delco plant and maybe put a pump in the house. We got electric lights and inside plumbing now, but I don't know.'

He was the first, and the others I met were more communicative, but there was a melancholy sameness to their stories. When drouth, debt, and prices drove them off their farms, they held the usual auction sales. Farm machinery that was covered with liens could not be sold, so the sale would consist of surplus household equipment, farm animals, and the usual array of spare machinery-parts, spare harness,

and assorted junk that had accumulated through the years. When
the local debts were paid, the dispossessed farm family might wind
up with $200, $300, or $400 in cash. With that money they would
move into Winnipeg, rent a room, and try to maintain themselves
for a year to become residents of the city and therefore eligible
for relief.

Except for the south-west corner, Manitoba's agricultural distress
never even approached that of Saskatchewan. The crop failure of
1929, followed by the disaster of 1931, forced Saskatchewan to get a
system organized that took care of its people before the worst years
descended upon it. In that province, moreover, the exodus from the
dry belt ultimately became more a slow migration from the bad-
lands of the south to the good farm lands of the north than a flight to
the cities. The government paid the freight on livestock and household effects, but the farmers usually made it from Climax to
Battleford, or from Minton to the Parkland, on their own with their
families in their farm wagons. En route, they kept mainly to themselves, camped along the roads or in the yards of friendly farmers,
always stopping to let their horses graze when they came to patches
of grass. Occasionally, when health or equipment broke down, they
would be stranded.

How many people were involved in the migrations in
Saskatchewan is unknown, for no records were kept. It must have
run into the thousands, however, for W. A. Mackintosh encountered them on the road in 1931 and there were still families on the
move at the time of the Munich crisis in 1938.

As a prelude to take-off, the migrants naturally tried to get cash
for everything they could not carry. That of course included their
farms, and the classified columns of the farm publications were full
of farms for sale. Occasionally, as in the advertisement below, a final
note of defiant humour crept into the want ads.

FOR SALE: 800 acres highly improved
stock farm, located on Pelletier
Creek. Would sell on cash instalment basis. If interested write Fred
Hearsey, Duncairn, Sask. N.B.: I
might be tempted to trade this farm
for something really useful, say some
white mice or goldfish, or even a
playful little monkey. F.H.

The distress in Saskatchewan was at first confined largely to the
Palliser Triangle in the south. There the system for distributing
relief became through experience much more humane than in the
north, where the first total failure of the crop came abruptly in
1937. When the refugees from the south became stranded in the
north, they got a very frosty welcome.

In Prince Albert, for example, relief could only be obtained in
return for a stint of manual labour. The family of an ailing farmer
could get relief only if his wife would sign a complaint charging her
husband with non-support. Once, in 1936, a relief recipient turned
up to do his wood-cutting with his wife to help because he had an
injured arm. The foreman fired the man on the spot. He was
charged with non-support, convicted, and sent to jail for sixty days.
In the south country, where even the councillors who dispensed the
relief were themselves on relief, such harsh conditions never existed.
There was, however, endless correspondence between municipalities all over the west as they billed each other for relief to migrant
families from outside their borders.

Most of us in the cities were only vaguely acquainted with the
extent of the disaster in the country. The story was simply too big,
and too slowly developing, to be reportable in the city newspapers

as hot news. In every city there were, of course, islands of awareness of certain side effects of the disaster. The employees of Eaton's and Simpson's mail order departments in Winnipeg and Regina knew that there was something amiss when orders stopped coming in from the country and their jobs wasted away. Travelling salesmen understood what had happened to their jobs when their once-productive territory evaporated in searing heat and dust. The running crews on the railways knew there were crop failures when there was no work for them in the fall. Every credit manager in every wholesale office in Canada knew there was something wrong in the south country when hundreds of country merchants disappeared into thin air. They stopped paying bills, stopped answering dunning letters, stopped ordering goods. They simply lived off their inventories, and when they had eaten or traded the last of their supplies, they went on relief.

Nevertheless, the national attention was rudely and sharply focused on the disaster area periodically, and, when it was, the reaction was one of the very best things that happened in the Dirty Thirties. It happened first on August 1, 1931, when the Canadian Red Cross sent out a nation-wide appeal for help for 125,000 destitute farm people in Saskatchewan. The response, particularly from Ontario, was magnificent, and contributions came from every province in Canada. The churches across the country became the gathering-points for the donations of clothing and blankets, sheets, etc. In 1931 the United Church sent 135 carloads of food, clothing, and other supplies into Saskatchewan; the Roman Catholics managed sixty-two cars, the Presbyterians ten, and the Lutherans eight. The total of 249 cars was beyond all expectations and these supplies were augmented generously by a flood of hampers into the province from friends and relatives across the country.

While the voluntary drive was being launched, the Saskatchewan government set up the Saskatchewan Relief Commission to take charge of making grants to municipalities, providing loans for seed grain, binder twine, feed, fodder, and repairs. It organized the multitude of volunteer agencies, which dispensed the donated supplies, into a province-wide Saskatchewan Voluntary Rural Relief Committee. It was perhaps the most important decision taken in Saskatchewan, for out of it came a system for maintaining the people that was without equal in Canada.

It was well that this was so, for during the next five years distribution of relief to the south country of Saskatchewan became the province's major industry. In one area, 890 out of a population of 895 were on relief. In the community of Minton, the disaster was so complete that even the chickens had to be supplied with relief food. There was nothing edible left for them to scratch.

It was a Chinese cook in a restaurant in Fillmore who described it best, in 1934, when he said in fractured English:

'No wheat, no pasture, no garden. Nothing of everything all over.'

The governments came inexorably to the conclusion that settlement of much of southern Saskatchewan had been a mistake. Fully half the land was sub-marginal and another quarter was barely marginal. The good years had been too few and the ravages of drouth too awesome to face any other course but to return the sub-marginal land to grass.

The Dominion government provided the money and the province of Saskatchewan tackled the immediate problem. It opened huge winter pastures in the parklands, and cattle and horses by the thousands were shipped into them from southern Saskatchewan. Farmers from the south moved into the north to bail straw for emergency winter feed. In Ottawa, the Bennett government began work on one of the most constructive pieces of legislation it ever passed—the Prairie Farms Rehabilitation Act of 1935. This gave *de facto* recognition to the existence of a national emergency that was neither a temporary condition nor one that would be corrected by improvement in world conditions. Using the experimental farms as a nucleus, it launched a program to construct water-catching dugouts on 50,000 farms, convert 2,000,000 acres of sub-marginal land into community pastures, and change the face of the West with forestation, reclamation, and irrigation.

I was a spectator at the birth of P.F.R.A., and it was an experience with memories to last a lifetime. It began with a routine assignment, in July 1936, to cover a provincial election meeting in Souris in western Manitoba. A shortage of *Free Press* cars developed, and as Bob Scott had a story to do on the grain crop we combined forces in one car. He was to go with me as far as Souris, and I would go on with him to Regina to help with the driving, and catch a train home from there.

From Winnipeg to Souris would ordinarily have been a four-hour drive over a gravelled highway, but as Scott wanted to look at a sunflower-growing experiment at Morden we took the long way around. We barely made it to Souris in time for the meeting. The blistering 100-degree heat of mid-afternoon and periodic encounters with grasshoppers gave us a boiling radiator, and we had to stop periodically to clear it off and let it cool down. The gravel roads were heavy with dust, and approaching traffic could be seen a mile away by the dust cloud. For most of the afternoon we alternated between smothering in the car when we closed the windows to keep out the dust and grasshoppers, or choking to death when we opened the windows to let in some air. We stopped every few miles while Scott got out, looked at the crop, and read the evidence of changing weather in the pattern of the growing grain. The long siege of 100-degree temperature around Winnipeg had turned the fields prematurely brown; yet here and there we would encounter large patches of almost unbelievable lushness where summer thunderstorms had fallen during the heat wave. And that was the story of all Manitoba that summer. The rains that broke the heat-wave gave the late grain a second chance and Manitoba was able to harvest a fair half-crop.

The political meeting was a routine affair. Before we took off in the direction of Oxbow, Saskatchewan, the next morning, we found a garage with an air hose and blew the dust and barbecued grasshoppers out of the radiator. Then we scrounged some window-screen to tie in front of the radiator in case we encountered more 'hoppers. Finally, we bought a five-gallon can that we filled with water and kept on the back seat. We followed the C.P.R. line down the Souris River Valley to Hartney and Lauder and Napinka, and wherever the road crossed it the river was bone-dry.

As we headed south-west that morning, we soon saw ahead the formation of dust clouds from the Manitoba Dust Bowl. Within minutes after rounding a curve in the road west of Napinka we were in the middle of a dust blizzard. The sun disappeared into a dull amber haze. The sharp dust particles ricocheted off the windshield. Straight ahead, visibility was reduced to a few feet, yet somehow or other the air for a couple of feet above the road remained clear. I could see the gravel road just ahead of the car, but nothing else. I eased the car over to the extreme right of the road, and we drifted along at about ten miles an hour. Then, we were out of it. We had come to a field on the south side of the road on which there was a fair stand of grain. The blowing soil stopped, almost as if on command. But as we crossed an intersection and left the field of growing grain, the dust started up again. For the next few miles, that was the pattern: dust—no dust; dust—no dust.

Approaching Melita we reached what Scott had come to see—a

ploughed field that wasn't blowing. Far off in one corner, some equipment was working and we headed down a sideroad towards it. This was where the government's counter-offensive began, where they started to beat back the dust bowl. We got out of the car and went to talk to the men running the tractor and discs.

The government man had a tractor with an attachment behind that was being used to dig a series of ridges a foot deep up and down the field, cross-ways to the west wind. They described the process as 'listing' and they said it had been used successfully in Oklahoma and Kansas. The wind, that day, was more from the south than the west. The dust was blowing heavily into the worked-over field from the adjoining land, but over the treated area the blowing stopped. As we resumed our journey, Scott was enthusiastic about what he had seen, though he had many reservations that he talked about as we fought the dust from Melita to Pierson and into Saskatchewan.

In less than half a day, I had had my fill of black blizzards. There was escape occasionally from the dust as the nature of the terrain changed, but there was no escape from the heat and no escape either from the desolation around us. Even the Russian thistle, which covered the abandoned fields like a worn-out carpet, was stunted and brown with dust. Here and there, half-starved horses and cattle hung over fences, or huddled in the shade of barns and sheds trying to escape from the flies that tormented them. We drove through village after village without a sign of life, past empty farm after empty farm. The fences along the road were drifted high with the blowing dust and the weeds of seven years' drouth. This year's crop of Russian thistle would not go tumbling before the wind for another six weeks, but traces of the weed from the year before still protruded through the drifted silt at the fence-posts. Here and there, the fence was completely covered, indicating drifted soil at least three feet deep.

As we drove west into the blowing dust again, we stopped occasionally, hoping that the wind would die down. The universal driving habit in western Canada was to go barrelling down the middle of the road. The roads that were not plain dirt were covered with crushed gravel, and as the traffic quickly threw the gravel from the centre of the roads to the sides constant grading was needed to keep the gravel in place. In the depression, the municipalities gave up the struggle. After the roads dried up in the spring, the gravel was scraped over to the side and left in mile-long piles until the next heavy rain. After the rain, the graders dried up the roads and smoothed them out by the simple process of moving the gravel across to the other side, where it was left until the next rain. Prairie highways were always bordered by loose gravel, which motorists quickly learned to avoid. To hit the gravel at moderate speed would up-end a car, and loose gravel was one of the prime causes of automobile accidents. With everybody driving in the centre of the road to avoid loose gravel, head-on collisions also were common.

We missed such disasters by mere whiskers several times, as oncoming trucks loomed up suddenly out of the blowing dust. After each close shave, we stopped and waited for the air to clear. The only green to be seen anywhere in the country was in the north-south road allowances. The drifted soil along the fence lines acted as a snow-fence in winter and had drifted the snow onto the road to augment the moisture supply, slow the melting, and retard evaporation. Simply by noting this fact, we had stumbled into the august company of experts that was combing the west for ways to stop the dust storms. The listing we had seen was, in a way, a product of observation of the effects of fence-line drifting. So was the massive program of tree-planting that occupied western Canada for the next two decades. Man in his ignorance had unleashed the destructive forces of nature, and nature, in turn, had silently pointed the way to bring these forces back under control.

The car put an end to our speculations. The radiator started to steam. The window screen was shaken free of a thick coating of bugs. We recharged the radiator with water from our can and headed west again. The wind had veered to the west and we were driving straight into it. We had gone perhaps ten miles when the radiator boiled again. Once more we stepped out of our Turkish bath into the blast furnace and refilled the radiator. We decided, as it was being clogged by the blowing dust coming at us head on, that we should turn north on the first road we came to, away from the wind, in the hope of getting to a town with a garage with an air hose.

The name of the town we reached is lost to memory, but there were a hundred like it in southern Saskatchewan in 1936—a town with a couple of grain elevators, two or three mud streets, two or three dozen houses, a main street of half-abandoned stores, and the friendliest garage operator in western Canada. It was, at first glance, a ghost town, for not even a curious dog wandered over to sniff at us when we stopped in front of a small blacksmith-shop and garage. The doors stood open, the ten-gallon glass chamber atop the gas-pump was a quarter full, but there was nobody around the garage either.

'We'll just sit here and somebody will turn up when they spot *Free Press* on the side of the car,' Bob said. 'They always do, and it's usually Bill Marter's local correspondent.'

Marter was the editor of the *Free Press Prairie Farmer* and he had correspondents in every hamlet in western Canada. They were usually wives of postmasters or station agents. Few of them ever earned more than $8 or $10 a year, but being the *Free Press* correspondent was a small-town status thing and there was always fierce competition for the job.

Instead of the correspondent, a small boy drifted by and asked if we were looking for Alex. I said that if Alex was the garageman, we were looking for him, so he ran off to fetch him.

We explained our problem to Alex and he took charge at once. He didn't have any air pressure, he explained, because his power plant had gone out last spring and he hadn't been able to get it fixed. He supplied the town's street lights with power, but nobody paid taxes any more, so the town couldn't pay its electric bill. Neither could a couple of merchants who also bought power from him. If they couldn't pay him, he couldn't get the generator fixed.

The thing to do about the radiator, he said, was to get a whisk broom and poke it into the cores and loosen the dust and to throw away that screen. It was no good in dust. The trouble was, he didn't have a whisk broom or the price of one, so Bob advanced him a quarter and he went off to the store. For the next forty-five minutes, he tediously jabbed the whisk into the radiator and he got it clean in the end.

The radiator clean, we backed out to the gas pump to refill the gas tank and change the oil. He started to pump the gas from the underground tank into the measuring glass and stopped half-way.

'Tell you what I better do,' he said. 'I better slip home and get me a clean rag to strain this gas for you. I'm getting pretty close to the bottom of the tank and the pump is liable to slurp up some dirt.'

We agreed that was a good idea, and I couldn't help asking why he had let his supply get so low.

'T'ain't me,' he said. 'It's the oil company. When I finish selling what's in my tank, I'll be out of the gas business, 'til the fall anyway. They put me on C.O.D. a couple of years ago, and, unless I can do a bit better on my collectin' this fall than I did last year, maybe I'll be out of the gas business for good. But like everybody says, you can't get blood out of a stone.'

He went off half whistling something that sounded like 'The

Prisoner's Song' and returned with a swatch of woollen cloth that he fitted carefully over the end of the hose before inserting it into the tank. When the tank was full, he took off the rag and examined it carefully.

'Well, what do you know,' he exclaimed, 'we didn't need it after all! Not a speck of dirt on it. Must have more gas down there than I thought.'

We were about to drive off when I remembered our water can and I asked him if we could get it filled some place in town. That one he had to consider carefully, after which he asked:

'Let's see how much you got in the tin?' There was still a gallon or so in the bottom.

'Tell you what,' he said, 'suppose I spare you half a can. That will do you in case she steams up again before you get to Carlyle. You can get it filled there 'cause some of the farmers up the road are hauling water from up around Carlyle. My well ain't quite dry yet, but it's the only one in town and we are saving it for drinking.'

The gas, oil, grease, and a new fan-belt we needed came to around $7, and while Alex was pondering what to charge for cleaning out the radiator, Scott handed him a ten-dollar bill and told him to keep the change. Scott was putting the car in gear to take off when Alex had an after-thought.

'Mister,' he said, 'I've got to ask you a special favour, if you don't mind. I sure do appreciate you paying me so much for cleaning out your radiator. It was right generous of you, and you'll never know how much I appreciate it. But do you happen to have two fives or some ones instead of the ten? It's awfully hard to spend anything out of a ten-dollar bill around here these days.'

As we headed north, we ran into an additional source of discomfort. The cloud of dust we trailed after us began to seep into the car. Perhaps the wind direction had something to do with it because when we reached Highway 13, east of Carlyle, the seepage stopped. But there was no improvement in the heat. Our clothes stuck to us, and the seat of the car was damp with sweat. I could feel blisters developing on my feet from the concentrated heat of the floor-boards. We drank copiously from our big water can, but the water was so warm it increased instead of quenching our thirst. What we both wanted most was a drink of cold water or, as Bob Scott suggested, a drink of nice cold buttermilk. We decided that we would drive into the next farmhouse we came to and see what we could get.

The first place we tried was a group of buildings set in a grove of trees off to the right of the highway somewhere west of Forget. We went down a side-road and headed for the farm, which turned out to be a first-class conversation piece. It was a typical Saskatchewan farmstead with its small unpainted house, a combination horse barn and cattle barn, a miscellaneous collection of sheds, and a small chicken-house and blown-over privy. Everything was empty, and had been for a long time, except the house.

The house was completely furnished, as we discovered when we tried the door and found it unlocked. There were thousands like it in Saskatchewan—twenty feet by twenty-five, a shed roofed with the kitchen across the back, and the front end divided into two bedrooms. There was an ancient Canada's Pride range in the kitchen and a Quebec heater in one bedroom. The kitchen also contained an early-model Hoosier cabinet, a large square oak table with half a dozen chairs. One of the bedrooms contained two large beds with the mattresses still on them and a set of springs was standing against the wall. The windows were stuffed around the edges with newspaper strips to keep out the dust. Nevertheless, everything in the house was covered with dust, the floor was gritty under foot, and there was a long drift of dirt a couple of inches high across the kitchen floor that had blown in through a crack under the door. It was much hotter inside than outside and full of flies, so we got out quickly. Midway between the house and the barn stood a cast-iron pump, but the mechanism had rusted and the handle could not be moved. We passed a couple of unlikely looking farms without going in and then drove into another yard that also turned out to be empty.

We began to wonder whether the country was in fact as empty of people as it seemed to be from the road. Then we turned into a place that looked deserted, but was occupied by a young woman with two school-age boys. The woman came to the kitchen door when she heard the sound of our car and then, when she spotted *Free Press* on the side, she came out to us.

We explained that we stopped in to ask for a drink of water. Her smile indicated her undisguised pleasure at having visitors coming to call. Her name, she said, was Ellen Simpson, and as we shook hands she led us around to a verandah on the east side of the house. After dusting off a couple of chairs with her apron, she returned to the kitchen and then hurried back with the water in a glass jug and two glasses on a small metal tray that was a souvenir from the Regina Fair. Her two boys, who had been staring at us from the doorway of the barn when we drove into the yard, came out to examine the car and to sneak glances in our direction. They turned out to be Billy, who was nine, and Bobby, who was six. We were probably the first visitors they had seen in weeks—in months, even.

Mrs. Simpson was a typical young farm wife—clean and rough-handed, capable-looking and self-reliant, with a tanned face more handsome than pretty. She was probably thirty, and she sat on the verandah and told us about Joe, who had gone north a week before to bale straw for winter feed. The crops were a failure again, and it was going to be terrible when winter came. Everybody who had any livestock had gone north.

It was lucky in a way, she said, that they had been forced to sell most of their cattle and horses two years before, because now they would need less feed. Anyway, there was a limit on the number they were allowed to keep over winter—two horses and a cow. The rest had to be sent to the government pastures in Manitoba for the winter, because only relief feed for three head was supplied. It was all right sending cattle, she said, they'd go to eating any place feed was put in front of them. But not horses. They had sent six horses in 1934, she thought it was, and the horses were so homesick for so long that they were nothing but skin and bones in the spring when they came home. They had sold them and now only had one team left. By lending and borrowing horses back and forth with neighbours, they had got their crop in. But it wouldn't be worth cutting, so Joe had gone north with the hay gang.

We asked her about the abandoned place we had seen first, and she supposed those people had gone north, at least the father probably had. There had been quite a bit of doubling up of families the last couple of years, which could explain where the family had gone.

'Most of the people in the towns along here are old farmers,' she said. 'It's nicer for them to be in town, close to church and things. Well, when one of them dies off, a daughter might take her kids in and stay with her Mom or Dad while her husband's away. If they don't have any stock, there's no reason why they shouldn't double up for the winter. Saves fuel, for one thing.'

Her explanation made sense, but I was curious about walking away from a farm and leaving a house wide open.

'Well, why not, for goodness sake?' she replied. 'Who'd steal anything around here? And, anyway, what is there that anybody has left now that's worth stealing? Besides, somebody might be passing through, like a family pulling out, who needs shelter for the night. What's wrong with them using the house if it ain't inconveniencing anybody? I know we never think of locking our place. Matter of fact, we'd sure have a time trying to remember where we put the key last time we had it.'

She talked and talked, as if she had been storing up conversation for a month and was trying to get the bin empty before the next batch had to be stored. It was a little cooler on her verandah than it was on the road, and we were out of the dust, so we were in no hurry to leave. When we did get up to go, she became almost alarmed.

'Oh no, you can't go now.' She was almost in tears. 'You must stay for dinner. There's no place between here and Regina for you to get a decent meal, and you must be hungry. Oh, please stay! I've wanted for so long to have somebody for a meal. And we'll have it right here on the verandah where it's cooler. Please, please stay.'

We stayed, but it was very much against Bob Scott's better judgment. In most things Scott was tolerant and agreeable, but one point he was prepared to argue. He blamed most of the agrarian unrest in the west on the food served to the prairie farmers. Farm boys, he claimed, left home to escape their mother's cooking. Farm meals were invariably ample, he said, but were as indigestible as they were inedible. On our journey he had talked about the importance of choosing eating-places with great care, and about not being trapped into accepting offers of meals from friendly farmers. I deferred to his experience.

There can be no doubt that there was enough to eat for everybody in the Dust Bowl. The basic subsistence level was established and maintained by the early operation of the Saskatchewan Relief Commission. Whoever needed food, got food. Supplies of fruit and vegetables that were donated and shipped in were distributed as fairly as possible at local depots. Additional needs were supplied on approval of the local municipal councillors. Even as the depression deepened, drouth-area farmers only drew on relief supplies to augment food supplies they grew for themselves. The dry weather was good for turkey-raising, and not only did turkeys provide easy-keeping winter food, they brought in some cash income at Christmas. Most farms expanded their chicken flocks and chicken feed was recognized by the Relief Commission as something to which the farmers were entitled. As long as the feed and water held out, a cow could be kept, so there was usually milk available for the children to drink and butter for the bread and potatoes. In many areas, game birds increased rapidly. The birds could find water the animals could not. The grain that wasn't worth cutting provided winter food for pheasants and prairie chicken. In the Parkland, deer and rabbits were plentiful.

There was food for the tables, but the impossible farm facilities almost guaranteed that the cooking would flirt with disaster. Over most of the drouth areas, by 1936, half the cookstoves were hopelessly antiquated. The grates were burned out; the oven-tops were corroded to paper thinness; pots, pans, and kettles were burned out. The preparation of any sort of fancy dish was out of the question, as temperamental ovens diverted cooking to the top of the stoves.

There was seldom much of a problem with roasting pork, but home-grown roast beef on the farm was worth a lot of effort to avoid. In many cases, two or three farmers would get together and share in a steer that was slaughtered in the fall. There was seldom any way the carcass could be hung so that the meat would age properly. When it was killed in late November it was cut up at once and allowed to freeze immediately. No culinary wizardry in the farm cook's repertoire could produce anything except a tough roast from such meat. On the other hand, there was nothing wrong with the boiled dinners, which were the most popular solution to the tough-meat problem; nothing wrong, that is, except the cooking. On the beat-up kitchen ranges and with the great variation in the quality of fuel, something simply had to go wrong with meals. Where there had been bush or trees growing before the drouth hit, fuel for cooking was no problem. It was simply gathered, cut, and split. On the bald-headed prairie, where nothing grew, the summer fuel was 'buffalo chips'.

Despite Scott's forebodings, our dinner that day was both nicely cooked and served. It was then well into the afternoon, and we began to suspect that she had eaten her own noon meal, whether 'lunch' or 'dinner', and that she had cooked especially for us. Or perhaps she cooked an early supper. Anyway, while we were preparing to wash up at the bench at the back door, the boys took the kitchen table around to the verandah and Mrs. Simpson got out her best tablecloth. There were two tin wash-basins hanging on hooks on the outside wall, and I took a pail from under the bench and went looking for water. The three rain-barrels were all dry. Then I spotted the pump and was heading for it when Billy ran up and took the pail.

'I'll get you some water,' he said, and ran over to a homemade water-wagon that stood near the barn. 'Our well's been dry for a long time. My Dad gets the water from the lake. We sure have to watch we don't run out of water before my Dad gets back. That's why we don't give much to the horses. We gotta give part of theirs to the cow, because if you don't water the cow she can't give milk very good.'

He drew a quarter of a pail and carried it back to the bench. Bob Scott and I stripped off our shirts and went at it. When we were finished, Bob carried the water that was left in his basin over to the garden and threw it on the carrots. I simply emptied my basin on the ground. Bobby, who had been watching, rushed into the kitchen.

'Mommie,' he shouted in a hoarse whisper, 'Mommie, the man threw the water away! He just threw it away!'

His mother shushed him. 'It's all right, Bobby, don't worry about it. Mr. Scott just didn't know about saving water.'

Water disposal came back into the conversation at dinner. Since their well had gone dry, Joe had hauled water from the lake eight or ten miles away. Like other thousands of water-poor people in Saskatchewan and Alberta, they had reduced water conservation to a fine art.

'It's a real gyp,' said Billy, 'because Bobby always gets to get the first bath 'cause he is the smallest. Then I get to bath and then Mom and then Dad. But Bobby always gets the clean water and I never get the first bath.'

'What you should have done,' our hostess explained with a laugh, 'was to empty your basins into that barrel by the back door. That's my clothes water. Perhaps you won't believe it, but the dirt quickly settles to the bottom of the barrel and the water on top is quite clean although some of the soap still stays in the water. A funny thing I've noticed—I get my clothes a lot cleaner with less work and less water since we had to start saving wash-up water. After I'm through with my wash, the water goes on the garden. If it had not been for the wash water, there'd have been no garden this year. It's hard to believe such a little bit of water could make such a big difference.

'Oh, and another thing,' she went on. 'There was an article in your paper about cooking-water. I used to empty all the dishwater and cooking-water into the slop pail, and we'd feed it to the pigs. The pigs loved it. Then I read where there is great food value in the cooking-water, that we'd be better off to drink the water and throw away the potatoes. Well, we tried drinking the vegetable water, but none of us really developed a liking for it. Anyway, Joe said if there was a lot of food value in the water, we'd get it eventually from the pork and the chickens.'

'The most fun,' said Billy, 'was last year when it rained, remember, and the water barrels all got full. My Dad pushed the wagon over near the big barrel and Bobby and I jumped into the barrel.

Boy, it was keen! We'd jump in and get wet and come out and put soap on and jump in! Boy! My Dad said if it rains again this summer, we can do it again. We sure hope it rains, don't we, Bobby?'

Their mother laughed most enthusiastically of all, blushing as she did so.

'After the boys were in bed,' she said, 'Joe and I just happened to look at each other and we got the same idea at the same instant. We grabbed the towels and got undressed and before we knew it, we were jumping in and out of that rain barrel like a couple of kids. We often wondered what the neighbours would've thought if they had driven into our yard that night!'

When our hostess brought the coffee she said casually, 'This is real coffee. You can always tell when we've had a little windfall of some kind 'cause real coffee's the first thing we buy.'

Up until that moment, I had never known there was anything else but 'real' coffee. But Bob Scott did, for he had sampled Saskatchewan barley coffee many times, and they exchanged ideas about how to turn dry barley into a coffee substitute. The first step was to roast the barley seeds in a pan. Some people covered the pan and some did not. Some would leave it in the warming oven for a couple of weeks. Others would try to bring it as close as possible to the burning-point without actually burning it. After roasting, it was run through the coffee grinder or the feed grinder and boiled.

'But we've never been any good making barley coffee,' our hostess said. 'It tastes awful, really. You're better off to dry out the coffee grounds and use them over again with about a spoonful of new coffee added.'

Scott suggested that part of the problem might be the water. In ordinary times, Saskatchewan water was hard enough to float battleships, he said, and he'd noticed in recent years that it was getting worse in the towns, so it was bound to be worse on the farms. It was enough to spoil any coffee, he said, and the vegetables cooked in it, too.

We must have sat talking with Mrs. Simpson for a good hour after lunch before we ran out of conversation. This was about as typical a farm family as would be found in south-eastern Saskatchewan. They had acquired the farm almost a dozen years before as newly-weds, with down-payment money borrowed from both parents. A string of three good crops had set them on their feet, and they had acquired an adjoining quarter-section in 1928. Like everybody else, they were starting to convert from horses to tractors in 1929, when the drouth began. They still had the two tractors they bought in 1929, a grain truck that was new in 1930, a couple of binders, and a threshing machine they had bought second-hand and looked as if it would last forever.

And they owed—Mrs. Simpson had no idea how much. At first, she said, they had worried themselves sick over their debts. They owed the bank, and they owed on the mortgage, and for machinery, and for taxes, and then for seed loans. They hadn't paid any interest on their debts in years, let alone made payments on principal. But she fell into the phrase that had become as common to the Dust Bowl as '*mañana*' was to Mexico—'You can't get blood out of a stone.' It was quite clear that the Simpsons had stopped worrying about their debts a long time ago.

There was a perfect word for our hostess and her two sons, and it probably applied to her absent husband as well. The word was 'irrepressible'. And that was the word for most of the farmers we talked to, though there weren't as many as chirpy as Mrs. Simpson. I asked her why they hadn't joined the trek to the north in 1934, when a quarter of the farmers in the Dust Bowl further west had moved out. Her answer came quickly, as proof that it was a familiar subject. They were among friends they had known for most of their lives, and there were ties to families and friends that kept them from breaking the circle. There was a touch of gold-miner psychology to it as well—a reluctance to stop digging for fear the next shovelful would uncover the mother lode. They had sweated out the bad times for so long, things just couldn't go on like this forever. When they got down in the dumps, they had only to remember the crops they had grown during those first years.

Life went on for farmers on relief in Saskatchewan as it did for the unemployed on relief in Regina, Winnipeg, and Edmonton. There was a dance someplace every week, Mrs. Simpson said, and even the poorest couple seemed able to dig up the fifty cents admission price. The fact that half the people who went to the dances couldn't dance didn't matter. The going and coming was special fun, particularly in the winter, when they filled the wagon-boxes with straw and turned the journey into a neighbourly tally-ho and sang all the way to the dance and back. Then there were showers and wedding parties and christening parties for the women, and curling and bonspiels for the men, though lack of water for ice-making had cut down on the curling.

It was surprising what nice weddings they were having, with so little to start with, she reflected. The wedding dresses and bridesmaids' dresses were lent back and forth and nobody thought anything about it. And why not? she asked. What good was a wedding dress after a wedding, except to wear to another wedding? You sure had to hand it to these kids, she said, so many of them getting married, even when they didn't have to, and starting out with nothing and no prospects either.

By the time we got back onto the road, it was late afternoon. Scott decided he had seen enough of south-east Saskatchewan, and we decided to head for Regina by following the C.P.R. north-west from Stoughton. Nature stepped in and changed our plans. Just before we got to Stoughton, we were hit by the thickest clouds of grasshoppers either of us had ever seen. They blew out of the south and west in numbers beyond computation. The swarm was upon us so suddenly that our windshield was solidly encrusted with splattered insects in a matter of seconds. We pulled over and stopped. Scott, who was experienced in such things, said so dense a swarm would pass over and the thing to do was wait until it did. It would descend some place, eat everything in sight, and take off again.

He was right, of course, but our car was a ghastly mess. The crashing grasshoppers had given it a sickly, stinking green coating. The windshield wipers only created a gooey smear, so we rummaged around in the trunk for something we could use as a scraper. There was nothing. We searched the ditches for a couple of hundred yards. Then I recalled that I had a Rolls razor in my bag. This was a razor with a sword-shaped blade that came in a patented case with a hone and a strap. I turned the blade into a scraper and it worked perfectly.

We almost had the windshield clean when a farmer came by in a truck and stopped to see if he could help. He had a wide putty knife, which he put to work for us. After the grasshopper grease was off, we washed the windows with water from our can and took off once more. The grasshopper smell in the car, on top of the heat and the dust we had already inhaled, was too much and I became bilious. We decided to detour to Weyburn and drive to Regina the next day.

In Weyburn we made a deal with the son of a garageman to clean the grasshoppers off our car for a dollar. It took him almost two hours and a gallon of coal-oil. We hung around the garage for an hour, talking to farmers who drifted in and out, and then invited a couple to join us for a glass of beer. We spent the evening converting lukewarm beer into perspiration as we eased in and out of a dozen conversations.

Any one of the farmers we talked to could be cited as typical. They differed only in the details of their lives, for their outlook was the same. All their responses had become reconditioned by a new way of life, in almost exactly the same way that our responses to life on relief had been reconditioned in Winnipeg. They, too, lived in a near-moneyless, egalitarian society with new sets of values. Integrity, for example, became something measured by a man's reactions to his neighbours and not to his financial obligations, back taxes, and relief loans he would never be able to repay.

There was, of course, some money still being circulated. The country elevator operators were still being paid, though some of the elevators were shut. The bank managers and station agents and section foremen were also being paid regularly. The schools were being kept open by government grants and while the teachers might be forced to live on $30 or $40 a month, and part of that postponed, their pay went into circulation. Even in the worst of the area, some crops were grown each year. Thus a point that had once shipped out a million bushels of wheat might ship only 60,000 bushels, but that 60,000 bushels would circulate $20,000 in the community. When the crop failed to a point where the grain was too short to cut, cattle were turned into wheat-fields. A prime steer might bring only $20 at a packing plant, but that price also meant that calves could be bought for almost nothing. A subsistence farmer might add $5 to the worth of an animal where he had once added $50. But five animals would produce $25 and, on the buying side, $25 could go a long way in 1936.

It wasn't worth anybody's while to raise anything for sale in those years, if the returns were judged by normal standards that had applied in the 1920s. But it is the nature of any farmer to want to be raising something. So where they could they raised calves and pigs and chickens and turkeys. If they got free feed from government relief stocks, had no overhead, paid no taxes, any income derived was all in spendable dollars.

As the years passed, the memory of any other kind of economy dimmed for the people in the south country, and for some there was almost contentment in their new way of life. So there was laughter to be heard in the beer parlours, and around the dinner table, and in front of the radio. If my own memory of the grasshoppers and dust and hot winds of 1936 gradually dimmed, the cheerfulness of the people who had stuck it out in the Dust Bowl at a point in time when everything reached its absolute worst never has.

From here, they said, there is no way to go but up. They were wrong. The year that was to come would make 1936 seem a bumper-crop year by comparison. What the south had gone through for seven years, northern Saskatchewan would discover in one blistering, frightful summer when nothing grew anywhere in the whole Palliser Triangle. And yet, in the midst of 'nothing of everything', the people still had joy in their spirit. In mid July 1937, when all hope for any kind of crop had gone, the town of Assiniboia staged a free community band-concert in the middle of the main street, and invited the whole of Saskatchewan to come to a street dance.

CHAPTER XVI

THREE MEN OF
OFF-BEAT CONVICTION

The prairie depression produced no men of greatness, and certainly no great men worked any vast changes upon the times. Nevertheless, the Thirties were wonderful years for the spawning of off-pattern characters who added flavour to the times. They turned up in politics, in law, in medicine, and in all the ordinary walks of life. Mostly they were men of towering convictions, and it never mattered whether their beliefs made sense or not. Perhaps this was because, in that era, no one could be sure who was crazy and who was sane. The respectable inspirations, when tested by the depression, turned out to be mainly moonshine, while some of the wildest notions of the crackpots were eventually written into the laws of the land. No latter-day electorate could have taken the Bible Bill Aberhart of 1935 seriously. No modern secretary would have tolerated any of Bald-headed Bobby Moore's tantrums, any more than a transit tycoon would have given him a thirty-passenger bus to get rid of him. Davy Rait, the free-loading English mendicant, could not now get into the *Free Press* newsroom, let alone establish squatters rights to sleep in a hard-backed chair by the library door.

And Paul Ausborn. He, with Bobby Moore and Davy Rait, made up the triumvirate of the depression I like best to remember. They had nothing in common, but each in his own off-pattern way was an example of the sort of character who roamed Winnipeg in the depression and gave spice and zip to the times.

Paul Ausborn was a man who heard voices, a sea captain who had sailed the Baltic for the Kaiser in the First World War. After the war,

235

he sold his ship and bought an apartment block in Kiel and served the Weimar Republic in a small way by teaching navigation to German youth. It was while teaching navigation in 1926 that the voices told him that Adolf Hitler was coming to power in Germany and would lead the world to war. If Ausborn wanted to save his family from the horrors of war, the voices said, he must flee as far from Germany as possible. He sold his property and fled—to a farm at Foxwarren, Manitoba.

Ausborn farmed at Foxwarren from 1928 until he made a chance visit to Winnipeg in 1933. He was appalled to discover the unawareness of Canadians to the menace of Hitler, who by then had come to power in Germany. The voices called him to take up the struggle against Nazism, or Canada, too, would be destroyed. He sold his farm and with $3,000 moved into Winnipeg in January 1934 to fight the German Reich for the hearts of the German Canadians.

Through his old connections with the Social Democrats in exile, Ausborn obtained a large collection of pictures of the atrocities being committed by the Nazis in Germany. He rented a store on Logan Avenue to show his gallery of infamy to Winnipeg. Nazi sympathizers wrecked his exhibit. He started over and put another exhibition together. At the same time, he scoured the German-Canadian community for supporters and could find only a handful. When the Communists discovered he was going their way, they rushed in to try to take him over, but nobody ever took over Paul Ausborn.

Unhappily, Ausborn was overwhelmed again and again by the force that the Nazis were exerting on the German population of western Canada, and by the lack of interest in his work on the part of other Canadians. He was beaten up by Bundists, and harried by city policemen who saw nothing wrong in Hitler, because the only people Hitler was bothering were Jews and Communists.

As an indication of Ausborn's physical courage, he and two young friends once invaded a huge pro-Nazi picnic and distributed 6,000 anti-Nazi pamphlets and miraculously escaped unharmed. But in his efforts to rouse the city to the menace of Nazism, he lost every battle, every skirmish even. Nazi agents, on the other hand, infiltrated the university, the schools, the churches, and every other part of the German community. Ausborn was ostracized by the Germans, most of his family deserted him, and with his money gone he was reduced to living on relief.

The *Free Press* was one of the agencies he cultivated and, as I was the labour reporter, Ausborn became one of my early problems. His enthusiasm was boundless and his drive never slackened. When he heard Thomas Mann had escaped to New York, he formulated plans to bring Mann to Winnipeg, under the auspices of the University of Manitoba, to address an anti-Nazi rally. That proposal was scuttled by the pro-Nazis in the University German Department, but Ausborn barely stopped to catch his breath. Einstein was also in the United States. If he could get Einstein to come to Winnipeg to speak, would we support him with publicity? He rushed off to see M. J. Finkelstein to enlist the help of the Jewish Congress.

Ausborn never seemed to waste time sleeping or eating. He had located a friendly printer, and when he wasn't writing exhortatory prose for pamphlets he was out delivering literature, holding meetings, flitting endlessly about like a confused gad-fly in search of a place to bite. He had established a spy network inside the German-Canadian Bund and was forever turning up with exposés of prominent local Germans, which he wanted the *Free Press* to publish. When I explained why the libel laws made that impossible, he would storm off in anger and we might not see him again for a month.

One day early in 1937 he came in to see me in a state of near-collapse. He had received word of the death of an old friend at the hands of the Nazis, and announced he was going to enlist in the International Brigade and fight in Spain. Maybe, he said, he would find peace in Spain. At fifty he was too old to fight, so he drove an ambulance on the Madrid front that summer. He came home to Winnipeg in the fall to give the organizing of another anti-Nazi front a whirl. His Spanish interlude made him completely *non grata* with the city police, but most of us on the *Free Press* had read *Mein Kampf* by then and were taking both Ausborn and Hitler seriously. But until the very outbreak of the war, anti-Nazism was a lost cause in Winnipeg and the boisterous rejection of appeasement by the *Free Press* won it few plaudits.

For a few months after the war started, Ausborn's stock rose. The city police stopped shoving him around for distributing leaflets, and began asking for his help in identifying internable pro-Nazi Germans. They ran smack into the original stubborn German. He had fought Nazism with every weapon he could find, but being a police spy was not for him. Chief of Police George Smith and Assistant Commissioner Meade of the R.C.M.P. even joined forces to try to enlist Ausborn into the counter-espionage service. They got him on a bad day. The blundering Winnipeg police 'Red Squad', which had taken to running down Nazis, had just lugged off two of Ausborn's most loyal supporters for internment. The police had mistaken their typically German cap-touching greeting for a Nazi salute!

What Ausborn wanted most of all was to get a war job, any kind of war job. Not being a naturalized Canadian citizen, he required police clearance. The R.C.M.P. refused to clear him. It was be a spy or nothing. The editorial staff of the *Free Press* made Paul Ausborn a federal case and set out to unhorse the Mounties. Victor Sifton had become Master-General of Ordnance in Ottawa, and he agreed to talk to the Department of Justice. He did so, but months passed and nothing happened, nothing whatever. I went to see Arthur Macnamara, by then Federal Deputy-Minister of Labour and boss of the National Selective Service. He sent explicit instructions to his Winnipeg office to find a war job for Paul Ausborn. But the R.C.M.P. saw to it that no war job was ever found for him, although his enemies, the Bundists, gained highly paid havens in war plants. The best we were ever able to do for Paul Ausborn was find him a job running a steam boiler in an orphans' home. Fortunately, he didn't need an R.C.M.P. clearance for that.

Towards the end of the war, he heard voices again.

'The *Kommunismus*, Mr. Gray,' he said, 'we must be careful we do not let the *Kommunismus* take Germany or we must fight the whole war all over again.'

If Paul Ausborn was the greatest character Winnipeg produced in the depression, and I think he was, Davy Rait was the slightest, and somewhere in between belonged Bobby Moore. R. Maxwell Moore had come out from England before the depression to promote the Birch Manor Farm Settlement Scheme in the bush country east of Winnipeg in the vicinity of Shoal Lake. It was the sort of thing an English land company might have been expected to be conned into—the exploitation of heavily-timbered land in an area that would use up two or three generations of settlers before it became profitable farm land, if then. With the depression, the English sponsors withdrew from the project leaving Bald-headed Bobby stranded with it.

I encountered Moore first at the Woodyard as a one-man riot in search of a place to happen. An aria of high-pitched curses floated out through the superintendent's office one day, followed by a blur of a figure trailing a briefcase as he departed spewing indignation and threatening vengeance on the relief staff. Thereafter, wherever I went in Winnipeg for fifteen years, Bobby Moore seemed to be there. He was a professional meeting-attender, and he never came just to watch. He always had something to say.

Unhappily for Bobby, he invariably became flustered half-way through his speeches. Then he would glance around like a panicky calf looking for a way out of a chute, mumble his thanks to the chairman, and toss what was left of his text on the nearest table or chair. Yet he always went to great trouble preparing his presentations. He had established rights of access to the *Free Press* and *Tribune* typewriters, together with all the paper he needed to prepare his material in six, eight, and ten copies.

He was trying to organize a government-sponsored back-to-the-land scheme with his land as the base of operation. Winnipeg, he argued, was full of farmers on relief who would be better off on farms. So let the various governments co-operate with him and set up houses for the people on his land, subsidize them to get started, and then make it possible for them to pay for the land. Unfortunately for Bobby, the governments already had their back-to-the-land movement, and it was going badly. Bobby didn't have a saleable deal, but that never discouraged him from trying to sell it. The Birch Manor project was his whole life.

In the winter, he combined the attendance at annual meetings of the Anglican Church with drum-beating for Birch Manor. He had a feud going with rectors' wardens—all of them—for he seemed to have spread his adherence to all the Anglican churches in town. He would sit quietly near the front of the hall until there was a perceptible lull in proceedings. Then leaping to his feet, he would dump the contents of his briefcase on the seat beside him and lash out at the warden for not looking after the interest of the rector. With hardly a pause, he would launch into the reading of his appeal for the support by the church of his great Birch Manor project. Half-way through, he would run out of breath, stammer incoherently, and distribute what copies he had to the nearest parishioners. Then he would vanish into the night.

Bald-headed Bobby knew everybody in Winnipeg, and everybody in the public eye knew him. City councils, legislative committees, royal commissions, and conventions were all fair targets for Bobby. In between, he harassed the local tycoonery for financial support. Though Bobby's demands were modest they were insistent, and the trouble involved in evicting Bobby empty-handed far outweighed the size of the donation needed to get rid of him. After the tycoons and their secretaries had gone through his mill a couple of times, they usually arranged a truce of sorts, so that the barons saved time and trouble by putting Bobby on a regular retainer of $5 or so every three or four months. Naturally, his list of patrons included all the political as well as the business *padroni* of Winnipeg. I once attended a press conference in Premier Bracken's office when the door burst open and a flustered Bobby spilled into the room.

'My God,' he said incredulously, 'the silly bitch was telling the truth! Said you were busy, and I see you are. Sorry, John, I'll see you next week. Cheerio, sorry.' He was gone. Mr. Bracken never turned a hair for he was long accustomed to Bald-headed Bobby. Though Bobby normally spoke in the muted accent of a cultivated English gentleman, he became a sputtering spewer of gutter oaths when crossed. He had every secretary in Winnipeg terrorized, and he was calling around often enough to keep them reminded of his identity.

In making his appointed rounds, he was tireless for a man in his fifties. Bobby was always in a hurry, and he spent more time riding streetcars and buses than most motormen. He had obtained a permanent transit-system pass many years before from the president of the Winnipeg Electric Company, but too many of the calls he made were a long way from the bus stops. One day, Ed Anderson, the president, allowed Moore to talk him out of the use of an obsolete thirty-passenger bus that had been retired from service. The bus drank gasoline in huge gobs and it was not long until Bobby was back on his feet.

'Whatever became of your busy, Bobby?' I asked him one day.

He let out a roar of laughter.

'My God, you should've been there,' he laughed. 'I ran out of gas in front of the post-office. So I left it there, while I attended to some business. When I returned, a bobby is standing there trying to make out a summons because it's parked in front of a hydrant. He couldn't figure out how to make out the summons because there were no licence plates on the bus! I rush up and tap him on the shoulder. He turns around and I shove the keys in his fist. "Here you are my good man," I say, "it's all yours—drive it in good health!" Then I beat it down Garry Street. My God, you should've seen the stupid look on the bastard's face when I popped those keys into his hand.'

Mostly, Winnipeg suffered Bobby gladly. It was well that it did, for it was Bald-headed Bobby Moore who saved the city from bloodshed on the night of June 30, 1935, when the single unemployed seized the Princess Street soup-kitchen. The word had come into the *Free Press* office that the provincial government was sending down the Mounties to clear out the building. Howard Wolfe, the city editor, and Abbie Coo, the news editor, were discussing the probabilities when Bobby horned into the discussion.

'Bill Major,' he shouted, 'is a plain damn fool! Damn it all, he can't do this. Where is he? I'll talk to him.' He telephoned the Attorney-General, and talked him out of sending in the Mounties and did it with logic that was unassailable.

'Bill,' he pleaded, 'for the love of God, I know that soup-kitchen!

You don't have to evict those stupid buggers. They'll evict themselves before morning. You can't stand the stink of that place when it's empty, and if you give those bastards another hour they'll be coming out screaming for air. But if you send in the Mounties, Bill, somebody is going to get killed. I guarantee that!'

There was a lot more. In the end it was Bald-headed Bobby Moore who saved Winnipeg from the sort of fate that befell Regina less than twenty-four hours later.

Davy Rait was the epitome of the complete bum, of every rich man's idea of what the shiftless unemployed were like. Instead of going begging for succour, he waited for succour to find him, and complained if it was late. Rait established squatter's rights in the *Free Press* newsroom in 1924, and slept there nightly until he was lugged away forceably to an old-folks home in 1938.

Davy Rait had one enduring passion—avoiding work in any form. On the basis of fourteen days of exceedingly casual labour upon his arrival in Winnipeg in 1924, he managed to spend the rest of his life in total idleness. He had turned up in the *Free Press* sports department, looking like a toy-sized belted earl, and had talked his way into writing a horse-racing column. The horse races had only recently come to Winnipeg, and Rait had enough of the size and shape of a jockey to lend credence to his story that he had ridden in England and had written racing news for English papers. His manners were elegant, his bearing was as regal as his stature permitted. His accent featured the same broad 'a' and clipped phrase that Bald-headed Bobby affected. While he peppered his conversation with allusions to the English upper crust of the racing world, he kept the story of his own life hidden in secrecy. He was somewhere between sixty and seventy years of age in 1924.

From all accounts, Davy Rait wrote a readable racing column. Unhappily he picked few winners, and like all horse-players ended the season flat broke. Moreover, he knew nothing else: when the racing season ended, so did his column. He simply sat down, literally, in the *Free Press* sports department to await the return of the horses the following year.

His first year as a sports-department squatter was the hardest. The fact that he slept sitting erect in a chair attracted only passing notice. The sports department was partitioned off from the rest of the newsroom, and it usually filled up early in the evening with sports personalities, bootleggers, and men-about-town looking for a place to drink. Passed-out drunks were often encountered during the night, and for a long time Rait was assumed to be one of them. He used the visiting sportsmen as the springboard for his scrounging career. Sooner or later, a drinking visitor would get hungry and suggest going out to eat. Rait would be first on his feet to accept the invitation, and while the sportsmen might wonder how he got into the act nobody ever suggested he buy his own meal.

There was, however, the problem of the other meals, and Rait cleverly turned the *Free Press* staff into a collective patsy. In the composing room and newsroom, there were about eighty employees. If he could 'borrow' as little as twenty-five cents from each one once a month, he could solve his eating problem. That became his life's work.

Like everything else he did, Davy Rait played the role of the mendicant in the grand manner. He was the personification of embarrassment as he explained that his cheque had been delayed, and asked would it be possible to help him out with a loan of twenty-five cents until it came through. No cheque ever arrived and no loan was ever repaid, but he had a steady income once he had his system operating. When the donation was forthcoming, Davy accepted it with the grace of a country squire accepting a peasant's tithe.

The *Free Press* newsroom, in those days, covered 3,000 square feet of the dirtiest, dustiest, draftiest, and most unkempt floor space in western Canada. The rough, scarred oak floor was scrubbed spring and fall. There were rumours of a janitor service, but the day-side always assumed that the janitors worked at night and the night-siders, never having seen a janitor either, assumed they worked days.

In summer fresh air was supplied by drafts that blew in like gales around the window frames. By late autumn most of the more open crevices were stuffed with paper, and as winter passed the air became danker and danker. It was this, I think, that drove Davy out of the sports department, because the atmosphere in there carried the additional flavour of stale beer, stale cigar-smoke, and a trace of the odour of arnica that lingers after prize-fighters have left. Eventually he located an ideal spot for his sleeping—in a corner near the library door. It was relatively quiet and there was a ventilating shaft somewhere in the vicinity. After midnight, traffic into the library practically ceased.

For the next ten years, Davy Rait slept in his chair by the library door. He roamed aimlessly around the newsroom until midnight, when only the late-shift editors were left. Then he would pick up a large wire wastebasket, fill it with crumpled newspapers, and carry it to his corner. There he would take off his shoes and bury his feet up to his knees in the crumpled paper. He would sleep undisturbed until the day-side reporters began to arrive the next morning. Then he would come to life slowly, meander into the washroom for his ablutions, and disappear for the day into some unknown Winnipeg backwash.

Davy's assessment scheme was, however, doomed to ultimate failure. Collections dropped off, his clothes got shabbier and shabbier, he lost weight and became a mere wraith of a man, and one day in 1929 he fainted in the office. When his reporter-friends discovered that he hadn't eaten for several days they rallied around for a while, and Davy's hand-out was put on an organized basis.

A dozen reporters, desk men, and sports writers agreed to underwrite Davy for $3.50 a week. This would give him a minimum of twenty cents for breakfast and a thirty-cent dinner. If he could scrounge a quarter here and there from the uncommitted members of the staff, he would be able to lunch occasionally.

The organized hand-outs lasted until the first *Free Press* paycut at the onset of the depression. Until he discovered the soup-kitchen, Rait undoubtedly had a thin time of it for several months. But the soup-kitchen gave him the best years of his life in Winnipeg. He got two meals a day, every day. With the aid of some minor forgery on the part of a *Free Press* reporter, who masqueraded as Rait's landlord, he conned the authorities out of $1.25 a week from room rent, which kept him in tobacco. Thus it was that he joined the small army of social termites, wastrels, hustlers, morons, and derelicts who, for the first time in their useless lives, stumbled over a system of social security none of them had ever expected to find.

In the end, security destroyed Davy Rait, though the process was exceedingly slow. He was no longer beholden to *Free Press* reporters for hand-outs, though he still sought them as before, and his manner became more abrupt. He gradually came to take a proprietary interest in the place and used to wander around tidying things up and acting as a receptionist who directed visitors to proper desks. When I first went to work for the *Free Press*, I assumed he was on the staff, and contributed a dozen quarters to him before I discovered his real status. That happened when I blundered onto a practical joke the sports writers were playing on Scott Young, a new office boy.

The *Free Press* at that time was being run by E. H. Macklin, an

Irish banshee who loved whisky, printers, and profanity, and hated editors, reporters, and preachers. He was no bigger than Davy Rait, and both sported little white beards. Macklin's sulphuric vocabulary was known all over Manitoba, and *Free Press* reporters kept out of his way.

Early in his career on the *Free Press*, Scott Young inquired about the old man sleeping by the library door.

'That's Mr. Macklin,' Clem Shields warned him, 'so for God's sake don't let that door slam when you go in or out. If you do and he wakes up, run and don't look back! And don't come back for your pay because he'll see you don't get any!'

Thereafter the awed new-comer tiptoed past the sleeping Rait, until disaster struck one night. Out of the library, ten paces behind Young, lumbered John W. Dafoe, the editor-in-chief. Young held the door ajar for Mr. Dafoe and hurried on. The old man, preoccupied as usual with an international crisis, paid no attention to the door. It closed with a loud bang behind him, and Davy Rait awoke with a scream. He stood up in his wastebasket and shouted abuse at Dafoe's back until the editor was out of sight, while the awe-struck Young ducked behind a counter. So convinced was Young by this exhibition of the 'Macklin terror' that for weeks thereafter he removed his shoes before slipping past the sleeping Rait.

The end came for Davy Rait when Victor Sifton, who had become publisher, crossed his path. Sifton had noticed Davy asleep periodically and assumed he was a reporter sleeping off a hangover. He made some inquiries that produced little more than fizz for answers. Eventually he raised the question of Rait's identity with George Ferguson, the managing editor.

'Oh,' said Ferguson dismissing the subject, 'that's only Davy Rait.' Sifton was still puzzled.

'Yes, so everybody tells me,' he said, 'but *who* is Davy Rait?'

That threw Ferguson.

'By God, Victor, you've got me there! All I know is that he was here when I came ten years ago.'

'But what does he do? Does he work here?'

Sifton listened to Ferguson's explanation with utter disbelief. Surely people didn't just walk into the *Free Press* office and take up residence! Who gave him permission to sleep there? How did he live? Where did he take a bath? The baffled publisher retired to puzzle out these questions in the quiet of his room.

Davy Rait had to go, Sifton was certain of that. But where and how? You couldn't just toss him out on the street after all these years. For weeks the best minds on the *Free Press* wrestled with the problem of Davy Rait. They decided the solution was to get him an old-age pension. Everybody agreed, except Davy.

'What,' he demanded, swelling himself up like an indignant Chihuahua. 'A Rait accept charity? A Rait become the ward of the state? Never. Sir, your proposal is an insult and an outrage.'

Ferguson carried Davy's reply back to Sifton's executive council. By this time Rait had become a very frail old man, and Sifton, unaware that Rait was getting single relief, worried about the damage to the *Free Press* image if Davy should die of hunger on the premises. Rumours might start that *Free Press* reporters were literally starving to death. So, while the directors worried about what to do with Davy, they arranged to supply him with a weekly meal-ticket at the Greasy Spoon across the street. Rait, who now had more food than he could consume, sold the meal tickets at a cut rate to reporters. He preferred the soup-kitchen.

As more months passed, Rait became more difficult. We discovered one day that he had developed a pack-rat mania. He had taken possession of three unused cupboards. One he filled with piles of sandwiches wrapped in brown paper that he obtained daily at the soup-kitchen but never ate. In another were dozens of paste-pots, pairs of scissors, balls of string, and engravings without number, the mysterious disappearance of all of which over the past year had generated bitter bouts of name-calling between reporters, editors, and composing-room foremen. In the third cupboard he kept his winter coat and unwearable old clothes.

Arrangements were made with the Sisters of Charity in St. Boniface to take care of Davy Rait at the expense of the *Free Press*. There only remained the problem of getting Rait across the river and into the home. Two reporters and a photographer were assigned to get the job done. When persuasion failed, he was carried—kicking, biting, and screaming—from the newsroom down the elevator and into the garage.

Once in the car, he subsided completely, begged a cigarette, and asked where he was being taken. He accepted his fate stoically. At the Sisters of Charity Home for the Aged he was bathed, nightgowned, and put to bed. Trouble was anticipated over the bedding-down of Davy Rait, and it was fully expected that he would go berserk at the first touch of sheets to his flesh in years. Everybody was pleasantly surprised when he subsided peacefully, thanked everybody politely, and invited his kidnappers to come back and visit him occasionally.

Two days later the Mother Superior telephoned the managing editor of the *Free Press* to complain that the Sisters of Charity had been swindled. Far from loathing beds, as she had been told, Mr. Rait had a positive passion for bed. He refused to budge out of his bed on any consideration. Though perfectly capable of taking care of himself, he insisted upon keeping the staff running after him. If they didn't run, his screams disrupted the ward and annoyed all the other residents. He was demanding special food. If he didn't get it, he was liable to fling a tray at the matron. One matron, more determined than the rest, had undertaken to get Davy out of bed and dressed. She was nursing a badly bitten arm. Would Mr. Ferguson kindly send someone to take this dreadful little man away?

Mr. Ferguson certainly would not. He reminded the Mother Superior that a bargain had been struck and he expected the Mother Superior to be a woman of her word.

She was, and Davy ended his days on a note of triumph.

'Wonderful place, delightful service,' he told one of the boys who visited him periodically. 'Couldn't ask for anything better, really, after they got used to my ways. And do you know this: I'm the only guest in the place who is permitted to smoke in bed.'

He never budged from his bed until he died.

Ausborn, Moore, and Rait. They had only one thing in common—conviction combined with an undeviating purpose in life. It was conviction that gave life whatever meaning it had for them. And it was conviction, during the depression, that made Winnipeg a place unique among Canadian cities. It was to be found everywhere, in Chinatown in the struggle between the Chinese Freemasons and the Kuomintang, in the North End in the struggle between Ukrainian Nationalists and Ukrainian Communists, in the South End in the melancholy controversy between pro-Franco and anti-Franco Catholics. Marshall Gauvin lashed out against all religions, dictators, and politicians, equally. John Dafoe thundered against appeasement and Mayor Ralph Webb thundered against the Red menace. The League Against War and Fascism thundered against Ralph Webb, and L. St. George Stubbs thundered against everybody. Winnipeg, in the depression, was the happy hunting-ground for any man with a cause, and it was in particular a friendly environment for the espousers of lost causes, like Paul Ausborn, Bobby Moore, and Davy Rait.

CHAPTER XVII

THE PROPHET AND THE
MONEY-CHANGERS

In most discussions of the regions of Canada, Manitoba, Saskatchewan, and Alberta are usually lumped together into the three
prairie provinces, as they are in this book. The curious truth is that
they have very little in common, and even the use of the word
'prairie' is a misnomer. The dictionary defines 'prairie' as 'a meadow
destitute of trees and covered with long grass'. Very little of western
Canada fits into that definition, for what is not bush, forest,
foothills, and lakes is more likely to be arid short-grass country. Nor
is there much in the way of common bonds of tradition, ethnic
grouping, or commercial enterprise.

Cattle-raising in Manitoba has little in common with ranching
in Alberta. The problems of wheat-growing in Manitoba were seldom the same as those in Saskatchewan or Alberta. It was no accident that the three wheat pools each grew in a different direction
from a common seed of an idea. In 1933 when the radical idealists
chose Regina as the birthplace of the Co-operative Commonwealth
Federation, the title came right out of the soil. Saskatchewan has
always been Canada's egalitarian province, the province in which
no one ever got rich as scores got rich in Manitoba and in Alberta. It
was indeed a commonwealth, and nothing suited it better than the
co-operative way of life it so largely achieved. The co-operatives
gave the people of Saskatchewan the only real alternative to extinction. It was co-operate, or give up and get out; they co-operated and
survived.

The region was riven with economic and geographic divisions, and the people themselves were more mismatched. Cosmopolitan Winnipeg had nothing in common with homogeneous Calgary, and the melting-pot of southern Manitoba was a world removed from Nordically pure southern Alberta. The Jews, Ukrainians, Poles, and Icelanders, who gave Winnipeg its flavour, were largely unknown along the Edmonton-Calgary-Lethbridge axis. Winnipeg had begun to break away from the frontier at the turn of the century. Calgary in the Dirty Thirties was still a market-town writ large, with its oiled-gravel streets, cattle-baron folk heroes, insularity and predilections for fundamentalist Christianity and conservative politics. Winnipeg was a city of dissent, where anybody with a revolutionary idea could get a hearing and attract a following, and so it had been since the days of Louis Riel.

The difference between the two may be illustrated by recalling just two of the outstanding local characters of the era. Winnipeg sheltered and nurtured Marshall J. Gauvin, Canada's only professional atheist, while Calgary produced William Aberhart, the country's foremost apostle of fundamentalist Christianity. Winnipeg could no more have produced Aberhart than Calgary could have tolerated Gauvin. Winnipeg's intellectual climate was as wrong for Aberhart as Calgary's was wrong for Gauvin. Both Gauvin and Aberhart were great preachers, though Gauvin would have boggled at the term. Gauvin was brought to Winnipeg in the 1920s by the One Big Union as a sort of one-man extension university for adult education. When his course of lectures was completed, he settled down in Winnipeg, founded the Rationalist Society, and became its lecturer and driving force.

Gauvin was born controversialist and he laid about him in all directions—at Christian Science, spiritualism, Christian modernism, Roman Catholicism, Hitlerism, and Fascism. Yet it would be an exaggeration to say that Gauvin kept Winnipeg in ferment.

Winnipeg had always been a city in ferment with the ideas wayfaring strangers dropped off, from the single tax to British Israelism. In so cosmopolitan a community, everybody belonged to some minority, and the differences in both thought-processes and conviction made Winnipeg's minorities volubly aggressive.

Yet it was not in boisterous, radical Winnipeg, but in orthodox, arch-conservative Calgary, where the wildest collection of economic ideas of the era changed the political complexion of western Canada. When William Aberhart married evangelical Christianity to Social Credit economics, he created a union that was perfect for Alberta. It was as essential for any new Alberta leader to be a 'man of God' as it was for him to be able to speak English. The early English remittance men may not have been overly devout, but the Germans and Scandinavians indubitably were; the Americans who came in from the Middle West brought along a deeply ingrained Methodism, and the Mormons, who trekked in by the thousands, were impelled by the hottest fires of religious conviction. Calgary was a port of call for all the American revivalists of the 1920s, and such notables as Aimee Semple McPherson, C. S. Price, William Branham, and Charles Fuller regularly filled the arena for week-long evangelical crusades. Another itinerant revivalist, L. E. Maxwell, was God-directed to Alberta all the way from Missouri to set up the Prairie Bible Institute for the mass production of missionaries. Anybody with a fundamentalist Christian gospel to preach could round up a congregation in Alberta.

William Aberhart topped them all. Three years after he launched his radio sermons in 1925, 300,000 Albertans were regularly listening to his interpretations of biblical prophecy. So popular did he become that his air-time was doubled and redoubled until, in 1935, he was on the radio for five hours every Sunday. The rest of the Sunday airspace was so occupied by radio preachers that Alberta, for the day, became one vast evangelical encampment. William Aberhart thus had both following and stature in Alberta long before Social Credit was invented. When he suddenly veered from biblical prophecy to monetary reform, the people of Alberta were ready for him and the economic environment was perfect.

Alberta was the last-settled of the provinces, and most of the mistakes made in Saskatchewan were repeated and exaggerated in Alberta. The same sort of arid, shortgrass country that was homesteaded in Saskatchewan was homesteaded in Alberta. In Alberta's case, the folly of trying to farm the dry belt was hammered home earlier, so that the exodus began long before the depression. The eastern border country of Alberta, which the land-settlement policies of the Dominion government and the railways had combined to ruin, provided a preview in 1917 of the disaster that would hit Saskatchewan in 1937. It cost the Alberta government $20 million to clean up the mess and, by 1927, 6,000 farms in eastern Alberta had been abandoned.

In Manitoba, two generations of farmers were able to get settled on their farms before the depression hit. They were caught, of course, in the mechanical revolution, but were better equipped financially to cope with the cost of converting from horses to tractors than the farmers of Alberta. Because the frontier was so much closer in Alberta, many settlers were only starting to get their heads above water when the big rush into machinery began. But the times were good outside the dry belt, and between 1926 and 1931 Alberta farmers bought 12,000 tractors, 6,000 trucks, and 2,000 combines. A great deal of it they bought on freely granted credit.

'Don't worry about it. Pay for it when the crop is off,' was the siren cry. 'If that ain't convenient, take a year or two.'

Credit for everything was free and easy. Most towns harboured at least one mortgage arranger who earned a commission finding borrowers. The chartered banks were eager to lend money, particularly to farmers who wanted to buy livestock. The banks believed it was a wise investment for farmers to buy yearling steers to run in the stubble and grow fat on the grain lost by the new combines. It was eminently sound and sensible advice in 1930, but those who took it went broke by 1933. For the ranchers, similar disasters were fashioned by the purveyors of sound advice. The cows they bought in 1930 with borrowed money for $75 produced fine calves, which were raised and sold in 1933, 1934, and 1935. The steers brought $15 or less when they went to market—barely enough to keep pace with the accumulating interest, with nothing left over for repayment of the principal. When the cow herd itself was liquidated, it took a very small nibble from the original indebtedness.

Interest became a word to conjure with in Alberta. Of all the farmers in Canada, those in Alberta could least afford high interest rates. Alberta was out in the Canadian left-field, where all the economic forces worked together for the worst. Alberta farmers paid the highest freight rates to get their cattle and wheat to market.[*] Hence they got less for everything they produced than anybody else, and they paid more for everything they bought. In addition to

[*] The Crow's Nest Pass freight rates provide a statutory ceiling on the charges that may be levied for moving grain and certain other commodities. But this is not a flat rate applying all over western Canada. Freight rates vary, under the ceiling, according to mileage. Thus it costs Alberta farmers about ten cents more a bushel for freight for their wheat than it does Manitoba farmers. With wheat at $1.75 a bushel this is not important. But when wheat was selling for forty-five cents a bushel in storage at Fort William it was an intolerable burden. Livestock quotations on the market pages today show that Calgary prices are usually $2 per hundred below Winnipeg, while Winnipeg is $2.50 to $3.50 under Toronto. There will be day-to-day changes reflecting special market conditions, but over the long term these differentials will apply.

During the depths of the depression, it was possible for Manitoba farmers to truck their cattle to market and get a small return. In Alberta there were literally hundreds of cases where the cattle brought less than the trucking or freight charges against them.

the economic disadvantages, Alberta's climate became perversely hazardous. The terrible winter of 1933 all but destroyed the southern cattle-industry. The grain farmers in 1932–3 fared little better. After two short crops, they were in default on their bank loans, machinery loans, and mortgages, in addition to their livestock loans. Yet, as they began to take off their crops in 1932, things did look a little better. Alberta had a good crop that year. Even counting the Dust Bowl, it averaged twenty bushels to the acre. But, long before they could get it sold, the price of wheat fell to the lowest point in history. On December 16, 1932, the price of cash wheat on the Winnipeg Exchange touched thirty-eight cents a bushel for No. 1 Northern. For the farmers of Alberta, that meant a top price of twenty and one-half cents at the elevator. But as the crop graded well below No. 1 Northern, even that price was subject to a discount of four or five cents. In the remote, high-freight-rate areas, wheat that day completely lost its value.

It is true that this was the historic low, that the average price obtained by the farmers for their 1932 crop was higher. Yet over a wide area of Alberta the actual cash income of the farmers amounted to only a few pennies a bushel for their crop. Joe Nolte of the Stettler area hauled fifty-four bushels into the elevator that winter and got a cash grain-ticket of $2.95 for the load. He took the ticket to the editor of the Stettler *Independent* to record the event for posterity, for, as he pointed out, after deducting threshing expenses he had a net cash return of one cent per bushel. His story was topped by another farmer who harvested thirty-three bushels to the acre and took it to market when the price of No. 1 Northern was twenty-eight and a half cents at the elevator. That autumn had been cold and wet and much of the grain was tough and smutty. This caused the second farmer's wheat to be discounted eighteen cents a bushel. Threshing and twine cost seven cents; hauling, three cents a bushel. Thus a bumper crop returned its grower *one-half cent* per bushel.

Farmers have lived with crop failures since the time of Joseph in Egypt. They know that if their crop fails this year, it will grow next year. If there is a succession of failures, they can always pack up and move on to better land. But the utter collapse in the price structure combined with poor crops was so unprecedented that there was nothing in Canadian experience to provide understanding or comfort. The disappearance of crop value was not something that was taken care of by the next good crop. The price went down and it stayed down regardless of crop or demand.

The social *malaise* of Alberta was part of the price the people paid for the economic hallucinations of its financial wizards in the years that followed the crash. The destruction of the price structure of Canadian agriculture was the inevitable result of binding Canada to the gold standard after the British devalued the pound sterling by forty-five per cent in 1932. Australia and other grain-exporting countries followed the British devaluation. Canadian wheat could only be sold by allowing the price to drop to a point where it was competitive with grain from other countries in terms of British money.

The lives of the Alberta producers were further complicated by the total lack of understanding on the part of the lending institutions. They assumed, because Alberta had raised a good crop of wheat, that the farmers of Alberta would pay their debts, and should be forced to pay them if they hesitated. Yet it was demonstrably true that the only way in which the farmers could survive with fifteen-cent wheat and three-cent beef was to default on their debts.

In 1933, the farm debt of the province exceeded $300 million, which required an annual interest payment of a minimum of $24 million. It would have taken almost the whole of the 160-million-bushel wheat crop produced in 1932 to cover the interest charges alone. But even default was not enough. Poor crops plus the collapse of prices had brought *de facto* bankruptcy to many Alberta farmers. What was needed was some agency that could scale down the increasing back debt to a point where the producers could see some hope of paying it. Provincial Debt Adjustment Acts only protected certain debtors from mortgage foreclosure, but none had any provision to reduce liabilities.

To blame the moneylenders entirely for their ruinous policies would be manifestly unjust. They were only doing what all the resident experts were saying had to be done. The Honourable E. N. Rhodes, in his budget speech of 1932, set the tone for the nation and gave the financial community a rallying cry. Said Mr. Rhodes:

'The preservation of the national credit is a prerequisite of the return of prosperity.'

The federal corporation tax was raised to eleven per cent and the sales tax to six per cent to preserve the national credit. At this point, Mr. C. Fraser Elliott, Federal Commissioner of Taxation, warned that taxation was reaching the level of diminishing returns.

Unhappily for the integrity-protectors and credit-preservers, the demand for some kind of debt-reduction legislation became clamorously insistent. The thunder from the farms alarmed the financial interests, but instead of trying to understand the situation they became hypnotized by their own propaganda. Out onto the firing-lines went spokesmen for the Canadian Bankers' Association and the Dominion Mortgage and Loan Association to beat the drum for sanctity of contract and financial integrity. Variously derogated as 'spokesmen for Canada's fifty big-shots', 'bankers' toadies', and 'lackies of the financial interests', they supplied Aberhart with straw-men for as long as he lived.

The tactics of the financial institutions would have been disastrous, even if they had had a sound case. Their case was hopeless. Alberta was the place where usury was invented, a benighted land seemingly beyond the protection of the Canada Bank Act. The law placed a legal ceiling of seven per cent on bank interest, but few Alberta chartered-bank managers lent money at that rate. The nominal rate was eight per cent, but it could be higher and it was usually compounded every three months, in advance. Farm-machinery dealers might occasionally charge only eight per cent for the first year. If the loan ran over into the second or third year, the rate might well go to ten per cent. Farm mortgages seldom carried less than eight per cent, occasionally ran to nine or ten per cent.

With the collapse of prices, city businessmen and country merchants alike joined the farmers in the debt squeeze. The effect of ruinous farm prices on the economy of Alberta was almost as shattering as the drouth was on that of Saskatchewan. The implement dealers did almost no business. In Alberta, fewer than 100 trucks and combines together were annually added to machinery inventory, whereas in the previous five years, the annual market had exceeded 1,000 of each machine. By 1936, Alberta farmers owned 3,500 fewer cars than they had in 1931.

The collapse of business in some of its other branches was just as complete. The construction industry disappeared. In Edmonton, building permits in 1934 were less than ten per cent of what they had been in 1930. In all the cities of Alberta, house-building came to a dead stop, despite the fact that a growing population had created severe housing congestion. There was, moreover, a great need for a complete rehousing of the rural population, of whom more than half lived in three-roomed shacks or worse. Even in Calgary and Edmonton, a quarter of the houses in 1931 contained three rooms or less. Production in the province's vital coal-mining industry declined by a third. Lumber production dropped seventy-five per cent and fisheries by seventy per cent.

With the gradual disappearance of farm purchasing power, the small towns that lived off the farm trade stagnated. A process of dis-investment began to take place. Autos were converted into Bennett Buggies, which, in the beginning, were simply Model T Fords with horses attached. The horses were hitched to the front axle, the reins were passed in through the windshield, and the farmer drove the horses with one hand and steered with the other. Later on, the car chassis was converted into a wagon, and a tongue was permanently attached.

Country blacksmiths did a brisk business keeping farm machinery operating, but only rarely did their customers find cash to pay for the job. Usually payment was made with chickens, eggs, sacks of potatoes, or sides of pork. Spending on household amenities ceased, buildings fell into disrepair, clothing wore out and was not replaced. It wasn't possible, even in the good crop districts, for anybody serving agriculture to make a living, and folk in the country towns as well as the farmers themselves waited with unconcealed eagerness for the relief trains that came through with surplus fish and fruit from British Columbia.

Stepping up efforts to collect debts in such an environment was completely futile; but it happened. In 1933 early frosts destroyed the crop over a wide area. When the news got back to one Ontario mortgage company, it immediately put an extra squeeze on the frozen-out farmers. It rushed out a letter to all its debtors, demanding they immediately promise in writing to apply half the crop they would produce the following year against back interest. If they failed to sign the undertaking, legal action would be taken over the 1933 interest default.

The way in which farm debt grew was continually being spelled out so that all who ran could read. It came out in detail at the hearings of the Debt Adjustment Boards, which were able to delay foreclosures in 1932 and 1933. It was further documented in the proceedings of the Farmers' Creditors Arrangement Act after 1934. Every member of Parliament from Alberta had a pocketful of hard cases to recite. Everybody knew of cases where a mortgage company refused to make any concession to a hard-pressed farmer, foreclosed the mortgage, and then resold the farm for a fraction of what its customer had owed.

In such an environment, the enlightened attitude of the Canadian Pacific Railway stood out like a gigantic gas flare. It not only followed a policy of non-foreclosure, but on two occasions cancelled all interest charges in years of crop failure.

After the collapse of farm prices, the market for farms dried up and there was an easing off in foreclosures. But there was no softening in the general attitude towards interest rates or back interest. Even in 1936, after Aberhart was in power and preparing legislation to drastically reduce farm debt, none of the loan companies had a single constructive proposal to make. Instead, they warned pointedly that governments which interfered with the sanctity of contracts might well impair their own credit. The whole future of farm credit in the West, they said, depended upon the maintenance of integrity of the borrowers at all costs.

And yet, in the trouble they were having with the moneylenders, the farmers of Alberta had one of the best minds in the world of finance on their side. He was J. M. Keynes. In his famous *Treatise on Monetary Reform*, he rocked the financial interests back on their heels with these words:

> Nothing can preserve the integrity of contract between individuals, except a discretionary authority in the state to revise

what has become intolerable. The powers of uninterrupted usury are too great. If the accretions of vested interests were to grow without mitigation for many generations, half the population would be no better than slaves to the other half. Conservative bankers regard it as more consonant with their cloth to . . . shift public discussion of financial topics off the logical on to the alleged 'moral' plane, which means a realm of thought where vested interests can be triumphant over the common good without further debate. But it makes them untrustworthy guides in a perilous age of transition.

For a guide out of the depression, however, the people of Alberta turned not to Keynes but to the Bible and William Aberhart. The Bible, of course, is replete with texts upon economic themes, and Aberhart could put his tongue to the most appropriate for any occasion. He was able to carry conviction, because for five years the people of Alberta had been trying all manner of bootstrap dodges to work themselves out of the depression. If the coin of the realm had disappeared, they tried out alternatives. Many communities worked out systems of dispensing relief in return for work on roads and relief vouchers largely replaced currency as they did in Manitoba and Saskatchewan.

In Alberta everything revolved around one central conundrum: 'We can grow all the food we can eat. We have all the resources with which to build a good society. We have lumber for homes, the need for homes, and the men who can build homes. We have coal the country needs, the men to mine it, and the railways to move it. We need new schools and hospitals, and we have the men and material to build them and the men and women who are eager to staff all our institutions. But people go hungry and nobody works and society falls apart. Why?'

The new leaders of the C.C.F. in Manitoba and Saskatchewan searched for their answers in Keynes, the Webbs, Cole, Chase, Laski, and the British Socialists. In Alberta the search got to Major Douglas, via William Aberhart, and it ended there. Aberhart was a Johnny-come-lately to Social Credit in 1932, but after he chewed on and digested the idea he gathered up all the loose ends of the existing Social Credit organizations, welded them into a cohesive whole, and put together the greatest political machine the province had ever seen. He was able to do so because he settled upon the one thing everyone in Alberta understood—the money famine. Nobody in Alberta had enough money, and it was the lack of money that brought stagnation. Albertans did not have to wait for a new social order or to change the whole economic system before they could start to live again. They needed only money.

The provincial election of 1935 was much more a religious crusade than an election campaign. As such, it stirred the bitterest of hatreds—set brother against brother, neighbour against neighbour, turned reason and tolerance into vices and made virtues of unreason and intolerance. In the reportage of that election campaign, much was made of the circus aspects of the Aberhart crusade. His 'Man from Mars' radio skits, in which he reduced the stuffed-shirt pronunciamentos of 'the fifty big-shots' to gibbering idiocy, were retreaded for live election audiences. He planted hecklers in the audience to provide a change of pace, staged skits acted out by young people's groups, dressed up a caricature of his United Farmers of Alberta opponents, and brought down the house when a heckler identified himself:

'My name is Dunn, Mr. Kant B. Dunn.'

Aberhart was a master showman, and the evangelical zeal that had made him a household idol gave him another advantage. His followers regarded any criticism of his economic theories as blasphemous attacks on Aberhart's character, and his opponents were identified with the forces of Satan. After listening to his radio sermons for years, the people of Alberta were eager to believe him when he turned to economics.

To a debt-ridden population, being forever chivvied about by creditors, Aberhart's advocacy of 'debt-free money' was a ten-strike. When he demonstrated how credit was created with a stroke of a fountain pen, the people, who had travelled for miles to his meetings, understood perfectly. Had they not seen the job done, exactly as he demonstrated it, by bankers and mortgage companies? When he referred to his Social Credit dividends as priming for the economic pump, all his rural listeners understood precisely how Social Credit would work because they knew how you got a pump to work.

When Aberhart's Mr. Kant B. Dunn charged that Social Credit would destroy the value of money as it had done in Germany, Mr. Aberhart switched metaphors, to the circulation of blood in the human body. The circulation of money was the lifeblood of the economic system. To restrict circulation of money could destroy the system, as restriction of the circulation of blood could destroy the body. But, keep very little blood moving and it could accomplish miracles. The heart, as he argued, uses only a few quarts of blood, but it pumps a million quarts a year through the system. And so it would be with his Social Credit dividend of $25 a month. Give the economy a transfusion of $10 million a month, and create ten or twenty times as much purchasing power! It was heady and convincing stuff.

Aberhart was at his best in resorting to allegory, and he heavily favoured such parables as the one about the counterfeit dollar bill. He used it in changing versions in 1935 and was still getting great mileage with it four years later, when he brought his campaign into Manitoba. It concerned a man who found a dollar bill on the street of Hanna one day and promptly spent it for groceries; the grocer bought some eggs from a farmer with it; the farmer paid the blacksmith, who spent it for a shirt. Mr. Aberhart chased the dollar all over town, out into the country and back, over the next town, up to the city. Wherever it went, it got business going again to everybody's profit. Only when the banker discovered it was counterfeit was it retired from circulation. If a single counterfeit dollar could accomplish so much, why would Social Credit not be able to do infinitely more?

Perhaps Aberhart's strongest point of all was the way he was able to turn the whole issue back to the people themselves, as he had been turning the issue of salvation back to them for their own personal decisions over the years. He would build up to an emotional climax and then let fly with his fast curve-ball:

'But if you have not suffered enough, it is your God-given right to suffer some more!'

Then he would urge them to close their minds to the profaners of Social Credit, as they would to profaners of Christianity, to study Social Credit, and then to become part of his great crusade. No recital of Aberhart's platform performance can ever do justice to the man. He had a genius for projecting conviction, for getting inside the hearts of those who came to jeer, so that they stayed to cheer. Yet off the platform he could be an arrogant boor, as I discovered when I tried to interview him.

Aberhart was consumed by hatred of newspapers and their reporters. He believed we were all lackeys of the vested interests and would write any lies we were told to write, that we sought information from him only to distort his views in print, and were congenital liars and transparent dissemblers. In my reading of the Social Credit literature, it seemed there was a resemblance between Aberhart's 'just price system' and Benito Mussolini's original blueprint for his corporate state. I boned up on both subjects in the hope that Aberhart would provide the kind of answers that would make a good interview. It was a complete flop. Though both Solon Low and Lucien Maynard, who were along, were friendly and co-operative, Aberhart was biting, discourteous, and captious, and what began as an interview ended in a shouting match. I left the interview almost despising the man, but that night I was captivated by his *tour de force* at the Marlborough Hotel rally. Raconteur, spell-binder, rabble-rouser, evangelist, pleader, entertainer. He was the best, and by far the best, modern Canada produced.

In the 1935 election, however, few of the political experts who covered the campaign could believe that either Aberhart or his party were real. Not the least unbelievable aspect was his leading a party in a provincial election and not being a candidate himself. The people turned out by the thousands for the Aberhart show and the Social Credit rallies. But would they turn out in like numbers at the polls? In their buttonholing and poll-taking, the diviners of trends found surprisingly few Albertans who would admit publicly they were going to vote for Aberhart. These people, it turned out, formed part of the legion of electors who had quite literally followed Aberhart's advice—they made up their minds and avoided getting into arguments with anyone who might change them.

On election day, the voters stormed to the polls in the greatest numbers in Alberta history, destroyed the United Farmers of Alberta as a political force, almost destroyed both the Liberals and Conservatives, and elected fifty-six Social Credit members in a legislature of sixty-three. Not one of the Social Creditors had ever sat in a legislature before! Within a matter of months, the people went back to the polls in the federal election, turned out one of the ablest groups of members any province ever sent to the House of Commons, the U.F.A. 'Ginger Group', and replaced it with a covey of doctrinaire nonentities. In neither election was there any other issue but money and credit.

The people of Alberta never did get the $25-a-month dividend Aberhart promised them. But they got something more enduring, and more valuable. Aberhart gave them hope when he challenged and destroyed the notion that there was nothing anybody in Canada could do to solve the problems of the depression. He was Alberta's antidote to apathy and defeatism. By insisting on trying to do something—anything—he broke the spell of the do-nothing school of political sorcerers. The refusal of the financial institutions to compromise on interest rates or accumulated debt he met head on. He cut the interest payments on Alberta bonds in half. He enacted legislation to cancel all arrears in mortgage interest that had accumulated since 1930. When this legislation was declared *ultra vires*, he enacted valid legislation to establish boards that could postpone enforcement of payment. The creditors learned that in Alberta postponement could become synonymous with cancellation.

Aberhart's long offensive on the usury front at least focused national attention more sharply on the subjects of currency, interest, and credit. The uproar in Alberta was partly responsible for establishing the Rowell-Sirois Commission to poke under the rocks of Canadian Confederation, while the federal Liberal government began inching towards the management of the currency supply. The despised funny-money men of Alberta never did achieve Social Credit, but within a decade they saw their wild-eyed ideas seized upon, modified, refined, and adopted by a country at war. Even their 'just price system' found its counterpart in the Wartime Prices and Trade Board. Nobody has ever been able to explain to Albertans what the essential difference is between a Social Credit dividend of $25 a month for everybody and a family-allowance dividend of $6 a month for each child—except the obvious difference in money.

They would have died rather than admit it, but the financial Merlins of the Ottawa East Block, by the production miracles they wrought in war-time, demonstrated that there was something to the old Aberhart slogan—'Anything which is physically possible is financially possible.' But the great impact of the Social Creditors, and the U.F.A. monetary reformers who antedated them, was in the field of monetary policy. The fiscal brain-trusters who scorned Keynes in 1935 embraced him passionately in 1941. Even while Aberhart was coming to power, some prestigeous outsiders were training their sights on the hard-money policy that helped bring Alberta to the edge of ruin. A. R. Upgren, with H. C. Grant, Jacob Viner, and Alvin Hansen collaborating, showed that Canadian adherence to the gold standard cost the wheat producers of western Canada $47 million a year, or more than all the taxes all the munici- palities in Manitoba, Saskatchewan, and Alberta could collect. What it cost in anguish and humiliation for the producers of Alberta was beyond the measurement of even the ablest economists.

CHAPTER XVIII

WHY NOTHING LIKE THIS
WILL EVER HAPPEN AGAIN

The era of the 1930s was born in disaster, lived in a turmoil, and expired in a whimper. Never before did Canada stand smaller in the eyes of Canadians at home or beholders abroad. Nothing within or without the country provided Canada with a sense of national purpose. Hitler in Czechoslovakia and Japan in Manchuria were none of our business, and the alleviation of unemployment was conceded to be beyond our ability. From 1933 onward, employment expanded slowly, but barely fast enough to keep pace with the growth of population and far from rapidly enough to absorb 1,200,000 workers and farmers and their dependents who were still on direct relief in 1937. At the time of the Munich crisis in September 1938, there were still more than 5,000 families on relief in Winnipeg. That was an improvement, to be sure, compared with Christmas week of 1933, when there were 8,000 families and 700 single women. Things were a little better, too, in the Alberta cities, but nothing was any better in Saskatchewan.

And yet, for many people in western Canada, the 1930s were the best years of their lives. Moreover, for all the people of the prairie regions, even those on relief, there were some good things that helped to remove some of the sting from economic privation. The best thing of all was friendship, for people had time then to be friends. A retired farmer in Alberta explained it this way:

'Before the depression, the people who lived on the north half of our section had never been in our yard, or we in theirs. We had known them for ten years. We would see them in town, meet them at church once in a while, see each other in the fields; but we were so all-fired busy all the time we just never did get to visit. The bad years brought us together, we started helping each other, then visiting back and forth, and after a while we had a friendship going that lasted for the rest of our lives.'

The people all across the West discovered there was no essential relationship between income and enjoyment of life. Even in the poorest rural communities, the Saturday-night dances drew large crowds all fall and winter. In the Parklands, there was endless experimenting with chokecherry wine, and making home-brew could never be completely suppressed. Yet, few people needed liquor to enjoy a party. There was probably never as sober a time in western Canada as in the depression years. Convictions for drunkenness in Manitoba dropped from 1,830 in 1929 to 730 in 1933, in Saskatchewan the drop was from 790 to 286, and in Alberta it was from 1,810 to 589. Bootlegging and the like dropped by sixty per cent.

Liquor, as a problem, however, hardly existed. In the *mores* of the times, liquor had a part only in the lives of the upper reaches of the executive class. They may have kept liquor on hand in their homes; none of the rest of us did. For most of us, a glass of beer or two on payday and an occasional beer on a hot evening accounted for our consumption. There were the dedicated drinkers, of course, whose intake helped swell the regional averages. Yet in none of the three provinces did the consumption of alcoholic beverages in 1935 exceed $5 per capita.

The key to the good life in the 1930s was the price of everything. The best rib-roasts cost nine or twelve cents a pound, depending on whether the year was 1932 or 1935. The blouses and skirts girls wore to work could be bought for fifty cents to $2.00. Men's woollen underwear was often on sale for $1.19, good shoes were available at

$4.50, overshoes for ninety-five cents, and men's dress shirts of good quality could be bought for a dollar.

When I went to work for the *Free Press* for $20 a week, I was taking home more pay than most retail clerks in Winnipeg. The highest paid reporter on the *Free Press* staff, in 1935, earned under $40 a week, and the senior news editors were paid little more. Yet a family of three, such as ours, could get by comfortably on $20 or $25 a week. Rents were depressed, and clothing prices were simply unbelievable. Our three-roomed suite cost us $15 a month, and later we were able to pick and choose among five-room bungalows renting for $25 a month. Few of us ever paid more than $21.50 for a two-pants suit, or more than $20 for a warm and wearable overcoat. On $25 a week, Kay and I saved enough money in a year to take Pat on a bus trip to New York. After paying for our bus tickets, we had $60 to spend on food and hotels. It was enough to last a week in New York.

There was almost no improvement in prairie wage rates until the Second World War. After the invasion of the C.I.O. in 1937, wage rates rose in the East with hard-won union contracts, but nothing comparable happened in the West. Nevertheless our wages generally were ample for our needs, because many of the things that were later to become necessities were luxuries we never needed. One was a telephone. Only two of the reporters on the *Free Press* had telephones, and the company paid half their bills, so that they would be on call if there was a big news-break. Only one reporter owned a car in 1937. Cars were not something everybody had to have. They were things people hoped to be able to afford some day, after they had saved up enough to buy one. The young business and professional men in the city were very much in the same position as newspaper reporters and mechanics.

One of the great boons of the depression, which could not be appreciated until it was gone, was the fact that most people could keep most of the money they made. The federal taxation exemption of $2,000 for married people took most of the populace out of the clutches of the tax-gatherers. Only the established members of the professions earned more than $4,000 a year, and few jobs in government service or industry paid that much. Bank managers of important branches might earn $3,000, but few other bank employees got close to $2,000.

The unlimited supply of cheap labour and cheap materials made the depression a happy hunting-ground for home-builders. To demonstrate what was possible under the Dominion Housing Act, the City of Winnipeg built a two-storey, three-bedroom house on Burnell Street for $4,000, including the price of the lot. Thousands of people trooped through the house, and its construction set off a minor housing-boom. Of this there could be not the slightest doubt; people who were able to build new houses under the first Dominion Housing Act got better value for their housing dollars than has ever been possible since. Many of the pick-and-shovel excavators and hammer-and-saw mechanics who got their start in the late thirties became the rich contractors for the next generation, which could afford to pay a lot more and get a lot less.

This, however, was a Manitoba phenomenon. Nothing similar happened in Saskatchewan and Alberta. Canada was well into the war before there was any noticeable recovery in Saskatchewan, where half the population was still on relief in 1938. In Alberta the mortgage companies stopped lending completely, and the banks almost stopped, after Aberhart launched his holy war on the financial interests. It was long after the war ended that the first National Housing Act mortgage was granted in Alberta.

Yet the most important development of the depression was not something that could be seen or measured, because it was taking place beneath the surface in the hearts of the people of western

Canada. It was the universal conviction that what we had was not good enough. Our thirst for security, for some form of insurance against the climatic and economic storms that were destroying us, gradually found expression in all the political parties, and in the churches, professional societies, service clubs, and universities as well. The term 'fringe benefit' crept into the language, and even non-union employers began to flirt with pension plans and welfare schemes. Our fiscal wizards became Keynesians-in-a-hurry and the greatest free-trader of them all, John W. Dafoe, put his signature to the *Rowell-Sirois Report*, a document that would have sent the ghost of Adam Smith hurtling into orbit.

Yet the conversion of John Dafoe was hardly more spectacular than that of R. B. Bennett, who went into office as a multi-millionaire Tory-of-the-Tories and emerged a crusader for social reform. It was R. B. Bennett, corporate lawyer, bank director, mortgage-company director, who fathered the Farmers' Creditors Arrangement Act, which was to wipe out more than $200 million in farm debts to banks and mortgage companies. And it was the business leaders in hundreds of Canadian communities who joined the Reconstruction Party in 1935 to try to reorganize our chaotic economy. Throughout the West the need for such reforms as minimum wages, unemployment insurance, hospital insurance, and crop insurance became so taken for granted that we stopped arguing about them. We destroyed R. B. Bennett, repudiated his New Deal, and then quietly and slowly and perversely enacted everything he proposed into the laws of the land.

The seeds that were to destroy the economic system of the 1930s were germinating as the 1920s ended, and in no place was the process as apparent as in agriculture. The agricultural depression in western Canada was a many-sided thing, and many factors accentuated particular aspects of it in some places, and modified other aspects in other places. A less reactionary national monetary policy could have prevented great hardships over the areas that had reasonable crops. But even the most enlightened monetary policy could have done little for the Dust Bowl farmers who, in the end, began to suspect that the rains had vanished forever. An enlightened social-security program might have helped thaw the economy around the edges, but it could not have touched the core of the problem that was created by the Dust Bowl in combination with the collapse of food prices.

The drouth itself could be blamed on nature, but the Dust Bowl was as much man-made as the collapse of prices. Millions of acres were broken to the plow that never should have been broken at all. It was land for grazing and was good for nothing else. The thin dry topsoil began to blow in 1931, and it blew, summer and winter, until 1938. Only after the wind had done its worst, and had blown many thousands of settlers off the land, did the governments take action. In 1935 the Bennett government set up the Prairie Farm Rehabilitation Administration to deal with wind erosion and drouth as a permanent emergency.

Task forces were sent out from the Lethbridge and Swift Current Experimental Farms in 1936 to direct emergency cultivation to halt the blowing soil. Networks of deeply ridged fields were put together, and when the hollows between the ridges filled up, the fields were gone over again and again. Where weeds had taken over and helped to break the power of the wind, crested wheat grass was seeded into the Russian thistle and stinkweed. It was done with more hope than confidence; but it worked out, for the showers did germinate the seed and in the end the soil blowing was stopped, and for good. New techniques developed at Swift Current made it possible to grow wheat without soil erosion, and new grass mixtures doubled and quadrupled the cattle-carrying capacity of the ranges.

The problem of how to turn the Palliser Triangle into a productive cattle-raising and wheat-growing empire has been solved.

Almost three million acres of land in western Saskatchewan and Alberta were taken out of cultivation and restored to grass, then fenced and cross-fenced and converted into community pastures for the farmers in the area. In the course of time, rivers were dammed, huge new irrigation schemes were developed, and the whole face of the West was changed for the better. The land that blew in the Dirty Thirties will never blow again as long as it remains in grass, or is cultivated by wind-proofing methods. And a great deal of what was done was possible because, over the years on thousands of farms, the farmers themselves had come to realize there was something wrong with the way they were farming.

Long before Edward Faulkner wrote *Plowman's Folly*, the people on the land were becoming disenchanted with the mould board plough and the finely cultivated fields that were so vulnerable to wind and water erosion. As early as 1919, a system of strip-farming had been invented by Leonard and Arle Koole, who wheat-farmed on the arid plains north of Lethbridge. Instead of plowing their fields in mile-long furrows from east to west, they divided their land into long narrow strips running north and south. They left alternate strips of stubble from the old crop until the new crop was well enough advanced to prevent the high winds from getting the long sweeps required to lift the topsoil from the cultivated strips. It was to strip-farming that the farmers of south-western Saskatchewan turned first in an effort to contain the blowing soil.

By the onset of the drouth, the scientists at Swift Current and Lethbridge had answers for most of the scientific problems associated with dry-land farming. What was needed was tillage equipment capable of cultivating the soil the way it had to be cultivated. The equivalent of two years' precipitation was required to grow a crop of wheat in the Palliser Triangle. Therefore, half the land had to be summer-fallowed each year. The summer-fallow had to be cultivated to kill the weeds that robbed it of moisture, and it had to be cultivated so as to leave all the stubble and dead weeds on the surface of the ground.

The search for such equipment became the obsession of the drouth-stricken farmers from Pincher Creek to Boissevain. They dug out huge frames from old steam-plows and attached homemade duck feet to them. They worked out methods of attaching two and three cultivator blades to heavy support-bars and endlessly tinkered with standard tillage equipment. Summer after summer, Saskatchewan farmers took their crude sketches of half ideas to Dr. Evan Hardy and H. A. Lewis at the University of Saskatchewan, and to the soil scientists at the Experimental Farms. But it was not until 1934 that C. S. Noble, who farmed north of Lethbridge, came up with the idea that, more than any other, was to help save the West. A simple, heavy steel sub-soil knife that cut the weeds off at the roots without disturbing the trash on the surface, the Noble blade changed the face of the Great Plains and revolutionized dry-land farming around the world. With the wheat combine and the cotton harvester, it was one of the three most important agricultural machinery developments of the twentieth century.

Despite the radical improvements in farm practices that have been achieved since the conquest of the Dust Bowl, wind and water erosion will always be a problem in the West. There will be crop failures, and unemployment, and economic dislocation. But these will all be problems that can now be managed and lived with, an impossibility during the depression. The hard-money fiscal system, the root-hog-or-die social system, and the boom-and-bust wheat-marketing system have all joined the mould-board plough in the limbo of prairie history. All came together at one time to produce the Dirty

Thirties, and the chance of their ever returning together is no longer worth considering. If our experience teaches us anything, it teaches us that; even though few of us who survived the ordeal can help looking back over our shoulders now and then—and perhaps shuddering a little as we look.

INDEX

Aberhart, William, 235; antidote to apathy, 266; and bankers, 258; conversion to Social Credit, 109–10; and the counterfeit dollar, 264–65; debt-free money, 264; election of 1935, 263; equating Christianity to Social Credit, 265; foremost fundamentalist, 252; and newspaper reporters, 265; radio preacher, 109, 253; *see also* Social Credit

Accounting and Office Management Company, 162–66

Alberta: appeal to Ottawa for aid, 142; attitude of money lenders toward, 261; barter trading, 260; compared with Manitoba and Saskatchewan, 251–54; Debt Adjustment Act, 258; easy credit, 254; effect of drouth on ranches, 139–40; effect of price collapse on economy, 260; errors of settlement, 254; ethnic strains, 252; farm debt and interest burden, 257–58; geographic handicaps, 255–56; interest rates, 259; 'preservation of national credit', 258; price collapse of 1933, 255–57; prices-debts-interest depression, 1; school teachers support Social Credit, 110–11; treatment of unemployed, 107; weather, 139–140ff

Aliens, deportation of, 167

American craft unionism, 176

American Mercury, 151–52, 154, 156

Anglo-Saxons, 168

Ansley, Earle, 110

Anti-Semitism, 161; *see also* Jews

Anti-Slave-Camp Conference, *see* On-to-Ottawa Trek

Apathy of unemployed, 36, 111

Armstrong, George, 35, 176

Assiniboia, Sask., 234

Ausborn, Paul, 235–40

Babies on relief, 30, 95

Bankruptcies in Winnipeg, 7

Barley coffee, 229

Bell, George, 129–30

Bennett, Rt. Hon. R. B., 103, 114; crusade for social reform, 273; elected, 7; relief camp strikes, 199; vindication by history, 273

Bennett buggies, 137, 260

Binder, Harry, 193, 203, 206

Birch Manor Settlement Scheme, 239

Blackmore, John, 110

Boiler-room swindlers, 125–26

Bone-harvest at Oxbow, Sask., 146

Boondoggles, 49–59 *passim*

Boons of the depression, 45, 267, 270

Bootstrap enterprises, 169

Bracken, Hon. John, 26, 203, 204, 241

Brokerage scandals, 15, 115–16, 120

Brown, Bishop William M., 99

Brown, R. A., 129–32

Calgary: C.P.R. shops closed, 109; Chinese on relief, 181; collapse of cattle prices, 109; fundamentalism and conservatism, 253; housing, 259; oil promotions, 4, 129–30; relief system, 22; single unemployed, 181; Sunshine Society, 182; weather, 139–140ff; women, 182

Calgary *Albertan,* 130

Calgary *Herald,* 181

Canada: Bank Act, 259; consequences of

279

Introducing the
Western Canadian Classics

Fifth House Publishers is pleased to present the Western Canadian Classics series, designed to keep the best western Canadian history, biography, and other works available in attractive and affordable editions. The popular and best-selling books are selected for their quality, enduring appeal, and importance to an understanding of our past.

Look for these Western Canadian Classics by James H. Gray at your favourite bookstore.

Booze: When Whisky Ruled the West, $14.95 pb.

Men Against the Desert: A Great Canadian Success Story, $14.95 pb.

Red Lights on the Prairies: An Unconventional Social History, $14.95 pb.

(Prices subject to change)

Back cover photograph: Destitute and desperate, Abram and Elizabeth Fehr and their seven children were photographed in 1934, in Edmonton's Market Square, in what has become one of the most famous and telling images of the Great Depression. GLENBOW ARCHIVES ND-3-6742